TRAINING EVALUATION HANDBOOK

TRAINING EVALUATION HANDBOOK

Tony Newby

Amsterdam • Johannesburg • London
San Diego • Sydney • Toronto

© A.C. Newby 1992

All rights reserved. No part of this publication may be reproduced, stored in a retrieval system, or transmitted in any form by any means—electronic, mechanical, photocopying, recording, or otherwise—without the permission of Gower Publishing Company Limited.

Published in the U.K. by
Gower Publishing Company Limited
Gower House, Croft House,
Aldershot, Hants GU11 3HR, England

Published in the U.S.A. by
Pfeiffer & Company
8517 Production Avenue
San Diego, California 92121-2280

CIP catalogue records for this book are available from the British Library and the U.S. Library of Congress.

ISBN 0-88390-350-4

Printed in the United States of America

Contents

List of figures ix

List of tables xii

Preface xiii

PART I THE ROLE OF EVALUATION

1 Introduction   3
2 The strategic context   9
   What is not a training need?   13
   Conclusion   19
3 A framework for evaluation   22
   Concepts   22
   Evaluation context, emphasis, criteria and techniques   24
   Techniques overview   26
   The benefits of evaluation   33
   Neglect of evaluation   34
4 Getting it right first time   37
   The marketing approach to training needs   37
   Determining priorities   39
   Setting learning objectives   39
   Content design   42
   Implementation of training   43
   The training infrastructure   44
   Manager-trainer partnership – what goes wrong?   44
   Evaluation   45
   Creating the organizational framework for evaluation   46
   From vicious circle to benign circle   48
   Starting to evaluate   49

Learning evaluation skills 50
Appraisal systems 52
Conclusion 52

PART II EVALUATION TECHNIQUES

5 Designing the evaluation project 57
Is evaluation really necessary? 57
Where to begin? 58
How much evaluation do you need? 58
The politics of evaluation 59
Starting to design an evaluation project 60
Planning the evaluation project 60
Choosing evaluation techniques 70
Analysing the data 72
Descriptive statistics 75
The evaluation report 75
6 The questionnaire 78
When to use questionnaires 78
What do you want to know? 81
Drafting the questionnaire 82
Piloting the questionnaire 89
Full-scale implementation 90
Analysis of data and reporting the findings 91
Specimen questions 92
7 The interview 96
What kinds of information do you require? 97
Drafting the interview schedule 97
Piloting the draft schedule 101
Full-scale implementation 106
Data analysis and reporting your findings 109
8 Critical incident review 120
Implementing critical incident analysis 120
Conclusion 127
9 Repertory grid 128
Using repertory grid 129
10 Action planning 137
Using the action planning technique 137
Action planning and evaluation 140
11 Reactionnaires 143
Commitment and cooperation 144

The limitations of reactionnaires	145
For what are reactionnaires useful?	145
The design of reactionnaires	147
Question design: some common problems	151
Administration of reactionnaires	159
Analysing the data	161
Conclusion	163
12 Written tests	**166**
Types of test	167
Test construction: an overview	167
Recall/supply items	170
Recognition items	174
13 Practical tests	**180**
Design of practical tests	183
Examples of test items	187
14 Behaviour analysis	**195**
When to use behaviour analysis	195
What is being assessed?	196
What is involved in behaviour observation?	196
Designing the observation instrument	199
15 Cost-benefit analysis	**217**
Costing methods	218
Costable inputs and priceable outputs of training systems	222
The cost identification matrix	226
Cash-flow budgets	226
Cost-benefit and cost-effectiveness analysis	229
Appendix I: Scientific method and evaluation	**237**
Control groups	237
Sampling	240
Appendix II: Statistical issues in testing	**245**
Scoring tests: raw scores, criterion referencing, norm referencing	245
Comparing groups	246
Comparing frequencies	250
The guessing correction	252
Reliability	253
Validity	256
Item analysis	258

CONTENTS

PART III CASE STUDIES

Introduction to Part III	263
16 Personal development of computer engineers	265
Evaluation – the key questions	265
Selective summary of findings and implications	267
General conclusions	270
17 Training trainers	271
Evaluation – the key questions	271
Conclusions and commentary	273
18 Job procedures	275
Evaluation – the key questions	275
Selective summary of findings and implications	278
General conclusions	279
19 Customer service	281
Evaluation – the key questions	281
Examples of test questions and answers	282
General conclusions	286
20 New entrants	287
Evaluation – the key questions	287
Summary of findings	288
21 Outdoor development for managers	291
Evaluation – the key questions	291
Selective summary of findings and implications	292
General conclusions	294
22 The manager's role in training	296
Evaluation – the key questions	296
Selective summary of findings and implications	297
General conclusions	299
23 Six mini-cases	300
Practical testing	300
Reactionnaire	300
Questionnaire	301
Test reliability	302
Cost-benefit analysis	302
Critical incident diary	303
Index	305

List of figures

1.1	Reviewing the true costs of training	6
1.2	Identifying where lack of competence may exact bottom-line penalties	7
1.3	Common training situations	8
2.1	Training goals and organizational purposes	11
2.2	Review of the diagnostic activity within an organization	14
2.3	The competence/motivation loop	18
2.4	Training activity probe	20
3.1	Simplified model of the training cycle	24
3.2	The systematic cycle in training	25
4.1	The manager-training partnership: getting it right	45
4.2	The systematic cycle in training	47
4.3	The vicious circle and the benign circle	48
4.4	Corporate commitment to training	51
4.5	Introducing evaluation into an organization	52
5.1	Planning the introduction of evaluation into an organization	61
5.2	Evaluation projects – design issues	62
5.3	Planning the evaluation project	63
5.4	Simple frequency analysis (I)	73
5.5	Simple frequency analysis (II)	73
5.6	Simple frequency analysis (III)	74
5.7	More complex analysis (combining II and III)	74
5.8	Summary of descriptive statistics	76
6.1	Specimen covering letter for a questionnaire	90
7.1	Specimen interview schedule questions: to ex-participants	102
7.2	Specimen interview schedule questions: to nominating managers	102
7.3	Hearing what you don't want to hear	103
7.4	Interview practice	105
7.5	Data matrix	110
7.6	Ratings of course presentation	111
7.7	Analysis of nominal scale to illustrate the mode	112
7.8	Evaluation report summary statement	119

LIST OF FIGURES

8.1	Critical incident interview schedule	122
8.2	Critical incident questionnaire	123
8.3	Critical incident diary form	124
8.4	Appraisal interview: form for analysis of job tasks/training topics	125
9.1	Repgrid form	130
10.1	Personal action planning form	141
10.2	Follow-up schedule	142
11.1	Personal learning objectives	148
11.2	General information	149
11.3	Sessional short reactionnaire	150
11.4	Sessional longer reactionnaire	151
11.5	Distance learning reactionnaire	152
11.6	Detailed end of event reactionnaire	153
11.7	Short end of event reactionnaire	154
11.8	Assessment of personal course objectives	155
11.9	Assessment of formal course objectives	155
11.10	Future activities	156
11.11	Covering letter for a reactionnaire	161
11.12	Summary of responses to a scaled question	162
11.13	Graph showing pattern of responses	162
11.14	Histogram showing pattern of responses	163
11.15	Responses to open questions: categorization and summary	164
12.1	Short-answer items	171
12.2	Tabulated short-answer item	172
12.3	Range of valid answers to a short-answer item	173
12.4	Completion item	174
12.5	Multiple-choice items	176
12.6	Matching items: names and words	178
12.7	Matching items: picture and words	178
13.1	Recall/identification item	187
13.2	Procedure item	188
13.3	Training objectives to be tested	189
13.4	Monitoring of preparatory work	190
13.5	Monitoring of sales call	191
14.1	Checklist for a listening skills exercise	200
14.2	Checklist for analysis of new sales staff	201
14.3	Analysis of individual frequency of contributions	202
14.4	Matrix showing who speaks to whom and how frequently	202
14.5	Differential contribution rates over time	203
14.6	Blank master page of behavioural descriptions	205
14.7	Training objectives of session	207
14.8	Assessment checklist	208
14.9	Individual feedback summary form	215

LIST OF FIGURES

15.1	A five-day supervisory skills programme: break-even analysis	221
15.2	The cost identification matrix	227
15.3	Conventional training programme with steady throughput	228
15.4	Conventional training programme with high short-term throughput	229
15.5	CBT programme with high initial development costs	230
AI.1	Control group designs	239
AII.1	Norm-referenced scores	247
AII.2	Criterion-referenced scores	248
AII.3	Gain ratios calculation form	251
AII.4	Facility values	258
16.1	Interview schedule – participants	266
16.2	Interview schedule – managers	267
17.1	Training trainers interview schedule	273
18.1	Interview schedule – supervisors, till operators, cash office staff	277
18.2	Interview schedule – store managers, departmental managers	278
20.1	New entrant questionnaire	289
21.1	Outdoor development interview schedule	293
22.1	Manager's interview schedule	298

List of tables

3.1	Criteria for judging the worth of training	27
3.2	Criteria of worth in evaluation	28
3.3	Evaluation techniques	29
5.1	Component elements of evaluation and techniques	69
5.2	Types of training subject and evaluation technique	71
6.1	Comparison of strengths of questionnaire and interview	79
6.2	Limitations of questionnaire and interview	80
13.1	Extract from master list of behavioural descriptions	192
14.1	Behavioural descriptions	204
14.2	Behavioural descriptions	209
15.1	Development times for different training methods	231
15.2	Performance records: some examples	233
AI.1	Sample size and population size	242
AI.2	Sample sizes	243
AI.3	Evaluation techniques and sample sizes	244
AII.1	Gain ratios	250
AII.2	Split-half method	254
AII.3	Examples of planning matrix	257
AII.4	Index of discrimination	259
17.1	Behaviour checklist	272

Preface

I began to write about evaluation of training in the late 1970s, driven mainly by a dissatisfaction with what was then available to guide the professional trainer on how to assess training effectiveness. That drive was reinforced by finding myself from time to time on the receiving end of ill-conceived 'training' activities that, when the hype and mysticism were stripped out of the course descriptions, proved to be purposeless.

In the mid-1970s, I was fortunate to be part of an upsurge in serious vocational training in the housing field. This expansion in quality and quantity of training was accompanied by research – notably from Marion Brion's team at the City University, London – in which I played a very modest part but which influenced my own thinking greatly in respect of the need to achieve and measure effectiveness in training. Subsequently, a career move took me to the Department of Occupational Psychology at Birkbeck College, University of London, and the stimulus of the active research culture promoted by Professor Peter Herriott, Dr Peter Bramley and others. There I was able to work on in-company evaluation issues and to move into the consultancy work that, over the years, has ensured that my writings on evaluation remain firmly rooted in the reality of day-to-day practice of training in organizations.

One of the more depressing features of research is that computer-based searches of training literature throw up literally tens of thousands of source references with some mention of 'evaluation'. Very few sources, however, go beyond making statements of the kind 'evaluation is a good thing that trainers ought to do'. Fewer still make any effort to demonstrate how evaluation can be put into practice. Too many, on the other hand, indulge in the academic game of concept-splitting whilst avoiding the practical questions to which trainers need workable answers.

The research work and my growing spread of consultancies in both private and public sectors helped refine and extend the practical techniques of evaluation and in time brought me to the point where I felt that there might be a market for a 'how to' guide for trainers on the subject of evaluation techniques. In 1985, therefore, I published and marketed an eight-volume soft-back guide called *TEAM* (the Training Evaluation Audit Method) which to my surprise and pleasure was put to use by hundreds of UK companies and which sold in modest numbers in sixteen countries worldwide.

PREFACE

Since then, my experience has continued to develop and some new factors have become prominent in my thinking on the subject. I have become increasingly conscious of the way that evaluation studies reveal again and again the same range of avoidable problems. These are typically problems to do with the match or mismatch of strategic purpose at an organizational level with learning purposes at the level of training activities.

I have come to see the element of 'strategy' as the essential correlate of 'evaluation', each being equal in importance and inherently necessary to the other. Evaluation, properly conducted, will inevitably highlight flaws in corporate training strategy (and thus can act as a catalyst to improvement). A relevant strategy for training will, conversely, make the task of evaluation easier and should directly result in fewer negative evaluation findings.

This new volume sets out to update the original guide to evaluation techniques and to add substantial new sections on training strategy and its integration with evaluation. There is also much new material on the practicalities of putting together an evaluation project, culled from the experiences of hundreds of evaluation projects with which I have been involved during the last decade.

The aim, throughout, has been to provide the professional trainer, the personnel specialist and the line manager who holds training responsibilities with a useful, readable guide that spells out step-by-step how to make training strategy and training evaluation work for the benefit of the reader's organization.

Tony Newby
March 1992

Part I
THE ROLE OF EVALUATION

1 Introduction

This book is written for people working in organizations who need to make investment decisions about the merits and demerits of activities which are variously labelled as 'training', 'development', 'change programmes', 'attitude change', 'communications exercise', and the like. All these activities have in common a stated intention (sometimes cynically stated) to cause changes which benefit the employing organization and, sometimes, the individual employee.

As well as conventional 'courses', we are concerned with such learning activities as follow:

- Kerbside conferences and other coaching opportunities.
- Training elements within regular staff meetings.
- Distance learning.
- Corporate communications events.
- Problem-solving teams.
- Computer-based training (CBT).
- Interactive video.
- Action learning.

Indeed, virtually any activity intended to improve people's capability to perform a work task is included. All these activities will be grouped under the heading 'training'.

'Learning for learning's sake' may have its justifications but, outside of academia, where a rationale for 'pure learning' can be sustained, those justifications do not extend to helping either commercial or public sector organizations to operate more effectively or efficiently. It is an axiom of this book that strategy and evaluation are concepts that make sense only within a context of purposeful activity. Purposeful activity is not, of course, the exclusive preserve of commerce and industry.

The purposes of this book can be clearly stated:

1. To describe the links between training strategy and training evaluation.
2. To enable readers to develop a soundly-based strategy for training in their organizations.
3. To enable readers to develop a strategy for systematic evaluation of training activities.

THE ROLE OF EVALUATION

4. To provide detailed guidance on the design of evaluation instruments.
5. To inform readers through illustrative case studies of evaluation in practice.

In keeping with the practical orientation of this book, you are invited to develop a personal action plan to make use of the ideas it describes. Personal action-planning instruments are included at appropriate points in the text. In addition, you are invited to photocopy the page headed 'Ideas Diary' and to use this both as a bookmark and as a running list of key points that you would like to try out in the future. In this way, your Ideas Diary sheets will build up into a detailed plan for implementing strategic and evaluation concepts.

This book is intended to improve the quality of training that is provided within organizations. It is therefore a useful preliminary question to ask whether training *matters*, in general and to each reader. In the past there has been a tendency to 'put up with things' (specifically, low standards) in training which suggests that little was expected and therefore training was not perceived to matter. Periodic outbreaks of training 'fads' reinforce the idea that it is not serious, that – at best – 'training will do no harm'. However, there are two, more systematic ways to form a judgement about whether or not training matters.

The first is to make an accurate calculation of what training currently costs the organization: how much is training depleting the gross profit (GP) line – and what estimate can you make of how much it is adding back? Would GP be higher or lower if all training ceased?

Training incurs direct costs: the money, time and expertise required to design and run training events; the pay and overheads of course members. In addition, there are the indirect costs of training premises and administration. Training also incurs opportunity costs. There are opportunity costs for the organization as a whole – money spent on training might be spent instead on new equipment; operatives could be producing goods rather than sitting in a training room. And there are opportunity costs within the training budget itself – the money spent on, say, a senior manager attending a prestigious business school course might leave no money for on-job training of clerical grades. Using Figure 1.1 you will be able to calculate costs presently being incurred.

The second method of calculation is to identify all those areas where performance deficiencies are costing money, and where suitable training might be expected to improve performance levels. Figure 1.2 provides a framework for completing this task.

A more anecdotal way of answering the question 'Does training matter?' is to reflect upon a number of very common training situations: Figure 1.3 provides some examples. A likely response to these situations will be that some suggest training ought to be significant, others that it is a waste of time. The alternative conclusion is that in each case a proper assessment of purpose, of learning effectiveness and of value for money is needed. A more subtle training cost to monitor is that incurred by poorly designed, badly directed training. This is the cost of learning irrelevant or incorrect skills, and of partial learning.

INTRODUCTION

Ideas Diary

THE ROLE OF EVALUATION

If you want to compile an accurate picture of the amount that is being spent on training, complete the 'price list' below.

£

1. Fixed capital

   - Building and training rooms.
   - Fixtures and fittings – chairs, tables, wall-boards, carpets.
   - Fixed services (e.g. aerial sockets, wired CCTV and computer links).
   - Equipment – audio-visual equipment, typewriters, word-processors, demonstration machinery, tools.
   - Provision of a training resource centre and/or library.
   - Motor vehicles.

2. Working capital

   - Consumable supplies (e.g. stationery).
   - Maintenance of equipment and premises (routine maintenance plus breakages).
   - Materials used during training (e.g. in metalwork, catering, assembly tasks).

3. Administrative and personnel costs of the training function

   - Cost of employment for the training manager and administrative and clerical staff.
   - Apportioned costs of rates, rent, heating, lighting, cleaning, etc. for training rooms or premises.
   - Salaries (etc.) of instructors/trainers when not engaged in development of training programmes or in giving instruction.

4. Cost of providing instructors/tutors
   This cost is that incurred in training trainers whether they are line managers, experienced workers, or externally recruited training officers. This cost includes the following:

   - Fees for external 'training of trainers' courses.
   - Marginal costs of attendance at existing internal courses.
   - Recruitment and selection costs.
   - Refresher and developmental training for established trainers.
   - Salaries and salary overheads, plus expenses during the training of trainers.

5. Cost of training development

   - Salaries (etc.) of trainers whilst carrying out analyses of training needs, development of objectives and content for training activities, and evaluation of programmes.
   - Fees to consultants for similar purposes.
   - Expenses incurred in producing visual aids, printing of course materials, etc.
   - Computer time changes (for development of CBT).

6. Cost of giving instruction

   - Cost of trainers' employment
   - Travel and accommodation expenses.
   - Membership fees for professional associations.
   - Subscriptions to training journals.
   - Fees for external consultants.
   - Licence fees for use of copyright materials.
   - Guest speakers' expenses and fees or (if internal) a proportion of salary.
   - External course fees and expenses.

INTRODUCTION

		£
7.	Costs arising from participants' attendance at training events • Apportionment of salary or wages and employee overheads during attendance on course. • Travel and accommodation costs. • Cost of temporary replacement staff. • Costs (where quantifiable) of lost 'output' due to attendance on course.	

Figure 1.1   Reviewing the true costs of training

	Problem present (tick)	Best guess at cost (£ p.a.)	Cost in comparable organization	What it should cost (£ p.a.)
Operational pentalies Accidents Customer complaints Equipment downtime Equipment utilization Quality control failures Delivery delays Missed targets Lost sales Wastage and breakage Backlog of orders Market share Etc.				
Personnel penalties Absenteeism Grievances Turnover Promotable staff Training time Recruitment errors Etc.				
Financial penalties Overtime payments Failure to meet targets Rising overheads Excess inventory Costs per sale Penalty clause payments Credit control losses Etc.				

Figure 1.2   Identifying where lack of competence may exact bottom-line penalties

7

THE ROLE OF EVALUATION

- Area managers keep talking about the need to 'motivate' their salespeople, but the real problem seems to be that they do not know how to close a sale.

- Training course descriptions are written in sociological gobbledegook — and you can't challenge them because almost anything might be interpreted to be a result of the training provided.

- There is a training course which your people are always keen to attend, but you are not at all sure what good it is doing.

- There's so many courses and training packages on offer today, how can you sort out the good from the bad?

- 'I wonder how other people occupy their minds while they're sitting through films like this?'

- Salespeople come back from a training event bubbling with ideas and enthusiasm, and a week later it has all vanished.

- There's only 20 or 30 seconds contact between sales staff and customers: what can training do to make the most of that contact time — and how will you know if it's had any effect?

- You want certain key staff to negotiate better on big contracts but the 'product' that your training department provides just doesn't match your expectations.

- 'This piece of equipment is the very latest in training technology. Therefore, you should ...'

- The financial director phones you: 'I know everyone enjoys these sales conferences you run, but I need something more specific to take to the Board to justify future spend. They still believe in training, but they need some hard evidence of what good it's doing.'

Figure 1.3 Common training situations

A working definition of good training is that it is an investment that yields identifiable pay offs in the form of better job performance. The answer to the question 'Does training matter?' is 'Yes, if it is good training.' And it is the notion of good training as the means to improved job performance that provides the link between corporate strategy and training strategy explored in the next chapter.

2 The strategic context

For both managers and trainers within organizations, there are two central concerns about all forms of training. These concerns are relevant whether the emphasis is on the shop-floor or clerical level, on management development, or on board-level learning about new trends and concepts. These two concerns are effectiveness and value.

'Has it made a difference?', 'Was it worth it?', and 'Is there a better alternative?' are the three questions which underpin the strategy for, and evaluation of every initiative designed to enhance the knowledge or skills of people at work. Strategy is concerned with ensuring that the purpose and delivery of training activities is correct. Evaluation involves making judgements about the correctness of that strategy (including the means adopted), and particularly about the outcomes or specific benefits that the strategy delivers.

Strategy and evaluation are complementary and inseparable. There has long been a tendency to see evaluation as a toolbox of techniques – questionnaire, interview, etc. – for the assessment of training in isolation from its context. Much of what passes for evaluation can be summed up in the weary question, 'What did you think of that course?' However, evaluation carried through in a systematic way, with serious intent, not only provides an excellent feedback and quality control mechanism, but also *necessarily* raises questions about the role of training, the activities of managers, and the corporate mission. This aspect of the evaluation process also makes it a useful vehicle in its own right for setting change in motion. This element of strategy will be discussed later.

Central to the concept of strategy is the idea of purpose. It is the contribution that training makes towards the achievement of an organization's purposes that provides the justification for investment of resources of time, people and money in that training. Cameron[1] suggests a four-category framework for understanding organizational purposes. All organizations, except universities, fit into this framework. The four categories are as follows:

1. **Goal-directed organizations** which pursue specific targets (turnover, profit, market share, and so on) and measure their own effectiveness by whether those targets are met or exceeded.

2. **Resource-acquiring organizations** which depend upon their ability continually to replenish key input resources. Examples include mineral resources for an extractive company, skilled programmers for a software house, or investment funds for a unit trust.
3. Organizations which characterize their own effectiveness primarily in terms of **internal functioning**, such as good internal communications, high levels of staff participation in decision processes, positive orientation towards quality issues, or low levels of internal conflict.
4. **Constituent-satisfying organizations** which exist primarily to serve the needs of a particular group (or groups) of people, for example, advice bureaux, workers' cooperatives, governmental organizations. Commercial organizations, too, may be responsive to their particular constituents – shareholders, consumer groups, employees.

Cameron's framework suggests that any specific organization will be predominantly directed by one of these purposes, although secondary purposes may also be a significant influence. From the perspective of training strategy, it is essential to pinpoint which purposes dominate in a given situation. In particular, it may be the case that officially stated corporate purposes receive only lip-service; it is also common to find a difference of dominant purpose between higher and lower levels in an organizational hierarchy. Senior management tend to concentrate on a goal-directed view of effectiveness; at supervisory level, internal functioning – in the form of smoothly-working teams, or inter-sectional harmony – often is the operational measure of effectiveness.

Corporate strategic purpose is the bedrock on which rests something as remote and detailed as a single learning objective within a particular training event. For example, in training salespeople to increase their effectiveness with customers by improving their listening skills, one learning objective might be '... will use reflective summaries to demonstrate understanding of customer needs'. It should be possible to show how that – and any other – learning objective contributes towards the achievement of some defined corporate purpose. As an aside, the connection must also work in the other direction. Defined corporate purposes – mission statements – only start to make a difference to work performance when they have been translated into detailed task requirements for individuals (the on-job equivalents of learning objectives).

When organizational purposes and training objectives are in harmony, training is a powerful contributor to organizational success. When the connection is lacking, training is a luxurious overhead which can reasonably be presumed unnecessary.

Use Figure 2.1 to review corporate purposes in your own organization and to review the extent to which training is contributing to those purposes.

A cynical view of the corporate mission statement argues that it is closer to being an obituary than a manifesto. The risks are twofold: that mission statements become bland generalities – 'motherhood' statements that change nothing and motivate no one – and that they become obsolete. All organizations today operate in a fast-

> 1. What is the dominant form of organizational purpose? (Goal-direction/resource-acquisition/internal-process/constituent-satisfaction)
>
> 2. Are there significant differences between organizational purposes at, say, senior level and at, say, sectional level?
>
> 3. How is training responding to those differences?
>
> 4. What are the current top three priorities for the organization?
>   a)
>   b)
>   c)
>
> 5. For each current priority, list what contribution training is making and then what contribution you would like training to make.
>
> | Organizational priority | Training is contributing | Training ideally should be contributing |
> |---|---|---|
> | a) | | |
> | b) | | |
> | c | | |

Figure 2.1 Training goals and organizational purposes

changing environment, and their definition of corporate purpose must respond: it has never been easier for a company to be prepared to fight the last war but one.

Insurance against blandness comes from a policy of actively pushing the translation of mission goals into workplace behaviours, at all levels. That alone goes a long way towards ensuring the relevance of training activities. Protection against obsolescence requires that corporate purpose is tested regularly against external reality, that the market drives the mission statement. Then, the mission statement – translated into workplace performance standards – can drive the organization to respond appropriately.

Most change is a fairly slow evolution in response to economic and social changes, though occasionally the pressure is urgent, following merger, or due to collapse of an important market sector. Similarly, most change is reactive – a process of adjustment to events – but sometimes it is deliberately engineered to pre-empt commercial disaster. Complacency about market position or poor quality of customer service may demand a shake-up; recruitment and retention problems may require a change in managerial culture and style.

Unfortunately, it can be difficult to ensure that the ambitions for change in an organization are matched by appropriate means. Too often, the more grandiose the objectives for change, the more superficial the methods adopted. On the one hand, policy-makers may expect radical change to occur within patterns of organizational behaviour that have developed over decades, and expect it from brief, under-researched, and unreinforced 'training' events. Ready-made solutions are no solutions. On the other hand, trainers (especially external suppliers) collude with this unrealistic expectation, for the very human reason that there is much money to be made. 'Snake oil training' and 'blessing the crowds with a hosepipe' are two popular judgements from those on the receiving end.

In Chapter 4, the methods for achieving well-designed training will be outlined. The starting point, however, is in clear corporate purposes and a 'marketing' (as distinct from a 'selling') approach to training needs. In selling mode, the training function in an organization will have a repertoire of training activities which are presented (usually in the form of a 'courses brochure') to line management customers. It is implicit in this approach that these ready-made training events are in some way the fulfilment of the customer's requirements. Energy mainly goes into persuading the customer to commit to the proposed activity. And, as frequently happens with pressurized sales, there is a spate of last-minute cancellations. Course delegates are often unaware of the reasons for their attendance and 'happy sheet' ratings (questionnaires given to trainees at the end of the course) are not matched by changes in job performance. In time, people become very resistant to attending such courses. The funding of training comes into question. The more enterprising departments declare their independence from in-house training and buy in their own external suppliers. Ultimately, central training may be abolished.

The marketing approach starts from a very different position, an analysis of what the customer wants. It is driven by needs – and there are only two ways in which training needs can arise:

1. A person is currently under-performing due to a knowledge or skills deficiency: this is a *remedial* need to do existing things better.
2. It is anticipated that a person will need to perform tasks in the near future, for which that person lacks the required knowledge or technique: this is a *developmental* need to learn new skills.

The essence of the marketing approach in training, as elsewhere, is to identify the gap between what exists and what is wanted. When a training activity is designed in response to such a need, several positive results follow:

- Training content relates to job realities rather than abstracted principles.
- People undergoing training are much more likely to see the activity as useful and relevant – and therefore learn more readily.
- On-job performance improves.
- Measurement of improved performance becomes more feasible.

Use Figure 2.2 to review the level of diagnostic activity in your own organization.

At the heart of productive training is the process of *diagnosis*: discovering by enquiry in the workplace just what it is that people need in order to become more effective in their jobs. An emphasis on observed work behaviour avoids several of the traps that invite ineffective training. Diagnosis starts with such questions as 'What are people doing (or not doing) that needs to be changed?', or, 'What would you, the manager, like to *see* people doing differently after they have been trained?' This sidesteps the trap of stating training needs in terms of the personality traits of an idealized occupant of the job: anything more than minor personality change is difficult to achieve, takes a long time, and lies outside the remit of training. 'Smith finds it difficult to get useful information out of prospects' is a much more useful diagnosis, on which practical training measures can be based, than any of the following statements:

'Smith needs to be a more outgoing person.'
'Smith is a bit short of motivation.'
'Smith needs a sales refresher course.'
'Smith has a negative attitude to customers.'

A behavioural approach also avoids the trap of talking about 'awareness' as a training goal. 'Awareness' is a weasel word which should immediately put any buyer of training services on guard. It suggests training in the 'nice to know' rather than 'need to know' category; it also implies that no practical consequences should be expected – awareness rarely translates into behaviour without specific encouragement; and above all it is a warning sign that there probably has not been a correctly targeted diagnostic stage in the training design. All too often, 'awareness' events are run when either trainer or client is not clear what it is that they are trying to make happen. Once that desired result is specified, the training can be used to develop knowledge and skills, rather than a vague awareness.

The diagnostic function also guards against a number of common but spurious justifications of training.

WHAT IS NOT A TRAINING NEED?

R & R

Training is sometimes provided as a perk of the job – a sort of rest, reward and recreation approach. The clearest indications of this are when discussion of training events centres upon the comfort of the hotels or the status that attaches to attending courses at a particular institution. Institutional ties are a particular giveaway. A common reflection of the R & R attitude is the question posed by managers to people returning from training activities: 'Did you have a good time?' This is not to argue that training ought not to be interesting and enjoyable, but to warn against the means becoming the end.

THE ROLE OF EVALUATION

1. Does *anybody* review training needs on a regular basis?

2. Which, if any, of the following diagnostic techniques are used regularly?

	By trainers	By managers
Performance appraisal discussion		
Career development review		
Critical incident method		
Behaviour observation		
Repertory grid		
Task checklists		
Analysis of performance data		
Internal consultant inquiries		
External consultant inquiries		
Firefighting		

3. Do you feel there is over-dependence on certain methods? Where might it be useful to introduce other diagnostic techniques?

4. Think about the whole range of training activities in the organization. List each activity under the heading (below) that most nearly describes it.

   a) Rest and recreation

   b) Solution in search of a problem

   c) Flavour of the month

   d) Making sure the budget is spent

   e) Part of pay, conditions, or industrial relations

   f) Acts of faith ('it won't hurt, it might help')

g) A motivating experience

h) Something the boss has insisted on

i) Meets a clearly defined, job-related skill or knowledge deficiency

Figure 2.2 Review of the diagnostic activity within an organization

'HAVE SOLUTION, WILL TRAVEL'

Trainers become very attached to particular programmes which they have developed and enjoy running. This is a positive bonus, so long as the need which the programme meets is a real need. However, over time the need may disappear, but the training course continues with a momentum of its own. At that stage, trainers are operating in a selling, not a marketing mode and training resources are not being efficiently allocated.

Ready-made solutions are particularly rife in the public-course market. There, the basic problem of matching product to need is made even more acute by the conflicting interests inherent in a course group drawn from different organizations and different levels of experience.

FADS

'Flavour of the month' training has quite a long history. It is understandable that organizations want to know about new ideas and methods, although a reluctance to question the invisibility of the Emperor's New Clothes has sometimes been puzzling. Fads occur in training content and in training technology. The best insurance against heavily hyped trivia remains a sharply focused diagnosis of training needs, followed by a review of what would be the most cost-effective method to meet those needs.

'HAVE MONEY, WILL SPEND'

When a trainer with money to spend meets a supplier with solutions on offer, the result may be mutual happiness but it is unlikely to do much for bottom-line performance. In recent years fewer training budgets have had the necessary 'slack' for this kind of cheque-book training, but it is still possible to find organizations where training expenditure occurs without any systematic scrutiny. In one instance, a company that required a detailed investment appraisal of any spending on capital equipment over

THE ROLE OF EVALUATION

£5 000 regularly spent around £20 000 – on the basis of the flimsiest of analysis – to send a manager on a business school course.

'IT'S PART OF THE EMPLOYMENT PACKAGE'

The prospect of further training can be an attractive part of the recruitment package for all levels of employee. The principle is a sound one. Where it can go wrong is in the execution.

Where training is provided *primarily* because it is part of the employment package, the purposes of training are likely to be distorted. A similar pattern can be observed in organizations that adopt an unqualified philosophy of 'we believe in personal development'. The effect in both cases may be training for training's sake, without regard to organizational priorities. Sometimes, the training that is selected will be of considerable interest and use to the participants – outside of their work context – but of little or no relevance to their jobs.

The key principle to hang on to, where training is provided as part of the employment package or in response to an organizational philosophy of 'personal development', is that such training should still meet job-related needs.

COUNTRY CLUB TRAINING

This approach to training is typified by the comment: 'It won't do any harm.' Implicit in that statement is the thought: 'But I don't expect it to make any difference.'

This situation is often found where managers have little interest in or understanding of training, and see their role as limited to making nominations for courses. This state of affairs is compounded by trainers who sell a menu of courses based on little or no diagnosis of needs.

Low expectations of training are matched by poor quality of training provision, in a downward spiral of indifference and ineffectiveness. No amount of tinkering will improve a hopeless situation. The only way to cut this Gordian knot is to close down the training function and restart it with new personnel who are committed to a professionally run, organizationally relevant training service.

MOTIVATION AND PERSONALITY

It is common for training needs to be confused with desired personality traits such as 'having a good attitude' or being 'well-motivated'. Whether you like it or not, the fact is that training is not a process that can achieve substantial changes in personality. Training can change the knowledge and skills that people employ in day-to-day behaviour at work but personality change is the realm of the psychiatrist.

> 'Area Managers keep talking about the need to 'motivate' their salespeople, but when you go out with one to visit a customer, the problem seems to be that they do not know how to close a sale properly.'

THE STRATEGIC CONTEXT

What has happened here is that instead of diagnosing the actual performance deficiency – the failure to close a sale effectively – the manager has decided that the problem lies in the *attitude* the salesperson brings to the job, that is, their lack of 'motivation'.

'Motivation' may sometimes be a valid target for training activity, but only in a narrowly defined sense. Managers often talk about the need to motivate their staff. Sometimes this is regarded as a matter of exhorting people to greater efforts, sometimes as a matter of leading by example. On other occasions it is seen as a matter of developing the right sort of climate in an organization, or the right package of incentives. All of these strategies have a role to play, in the right time and place, but none of them is in fact a *training* strategy. They are valid and useful tools of *management* and managers themselves sometimes need to be trained to use them effectively. This, however, is a quite different task from asking trainers to develop training activities that will motivate employees to better performance: this is asking trainers to do the managers' job.

Only one element of motivation can be treated as a topic for staff training: that element is *job-competence*. Whether or not someone feels motivated to do something depends to a large extent on whether or not he or she feels capable of doing it successfully. Hence, training which increases a person's ability successfully to perform job-related tasks will also increase that person's motivation to attempt those tasks. This is illustrated in Figure 2.3.

The central idea in the competence/motivation loop is that people are more willing to do things when they feel competent to do them. By providing training which increases skill competence, the individual is enabled to do the job better. By doing things more competently, the individual is rewarded not only by material results (e.g. higher sales) but also by an increase in self-esteem and confidence. This provides the motivation to do even better in future, and encourages further use of the appropriate skills. The more skills are used the greater the reinforcing (or motivating) effects of success. Beyond a certain level of competence, the individual may be able to bypass formal training and continue to increase competence by practice alone (Loop B).

Within the competence/motivation loop, training certainly may lead to better motivated employees, but that motivation is a by-product of training concerned with *specific skill development*.

SOLUTIONISM

Analysis of training needs is a constructive way of involving line managers in the training process. Managers are more likely to lend support to training for which they have helped to diagnose the need. However, one note of caution needs to be sounded about management involvement: the problem of 'solutionism'.

Managers are not professional trainers. Unless they are shown how needs analysis should be conducted, managers may engage in 'solutionism', that is, if a manager is asked about training needs the reply will usually be in terms of a *proposed solution*

THE ROLE OF EVALUATION

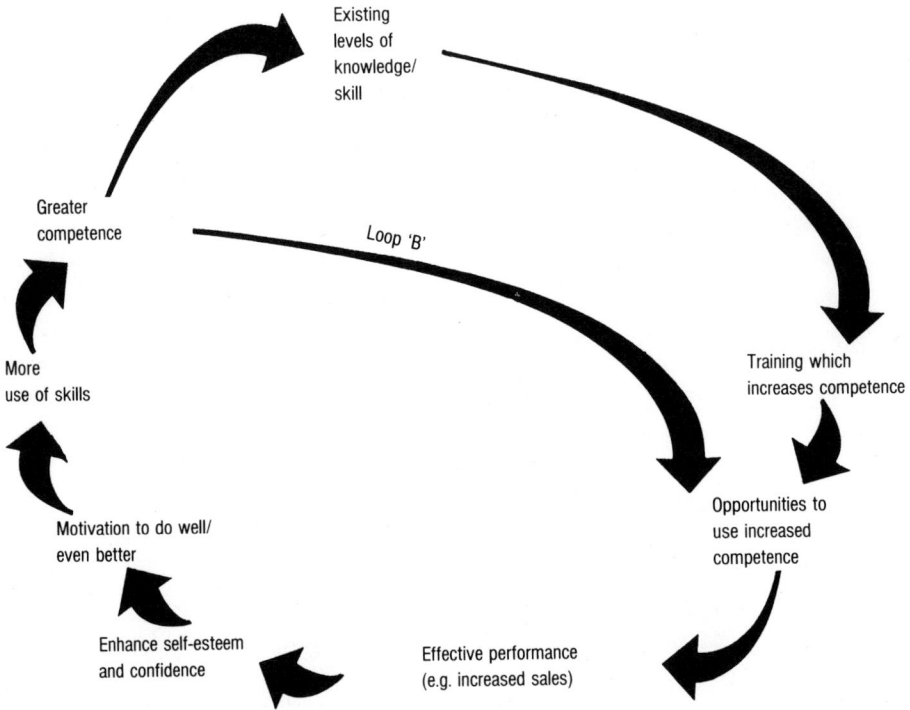

Figure 2.3 The competence/motivation loop

rather than a *diagnosed problem*. For example, 'I think they all need some refresher training.' Or, 'What they need is a course in interpersonal skills', rather than 'They have difficulty in dealing with customer complaints face-to-face.' Effective needs analysis encourages the manager to work with the trainer to identify existing trouble-spots or potential future problems. This is a very different matter to prescribing ready-labelled solutions.

Solutionism often crops up during staff appraisals. An effective appraisal includes a two-way discussion of performance strengths and weaknesses, with possible alternative strategies for action being considered. Too often, this degenerates into a quick look through course brochures and a nomination for 'one you haven't done yet'. The need for improvement is lost sight of behind the course title.

'THE MD SAYS SO'

This is a special case of solutionism. What makes it special is the organizational power and position of the person who originates the idea. In short, the training department cannot say 'no'. That said, there is still a lot of room for manoeuvre. If the MD or the chairman decrees that there must be, say, comunications skills training for all employees, then the training strategist can quite legitimately conduct an analysis of the actual 'communications skill' problems that exist in the organization. There are bound to be some and relevant training can then be designed to meet those needs.

The worst response is to abdicate all responsibility, indulge in cheque-book training, and then blame the MD for having the idea in the first place. Nobody wins.

ENFORCED NEEDS: WHEN IS COMPULSORY TRAINING JUSTIFIED?

Compulsory training is most acceptable and effective when it is combined with a somewhat modified marketing approach. In other words, the training is based upon a thorough needs analysis, but does not rely on voluntary participation.

Training may be made compulsory for a number of reasons, the most legitimate of which are as follows:

1. Safety requirements.
2. As a possible way to remove the need for dismissal on grounds of lack of competence.
3. Where training exists at a low level of effectiveness and low esteem but efforts are being made to change this situation in ways which the 'consumers' will not appreciate until they experience them.
4. Where there is a low level of key skills across the whole organization (or within particular functions or occupational groups) and it is necessary to bring everyone up to a minimum level of competence.
5. Where ongoing training has been specified in the contract of employment.

However, it is always preferable to have voluntary and committed participants in a learning activity than to have reluctant conscripts. The adage about leading a horse to water applies with some force to training.

Use Figure 2.4 to analyse any particular training activity in your organization. It will help clarify the diagnostic basis of the training (or lack of it), enable you to identify the behavioural outcomes of the training, and start the process of thinking about the ways in which you can begin to answer the three core evaluation questions:

'Has it made a difference?'
'Was it worth it?'
'Is there a better way?'

CONCLUSION

In this chapter, we have emphasised the close relationship between corporate strategy, successful training and evaluation. Corporate purpose needs to be tested regularly against external reality, so that the mission statement – graduated down in the form of work performance standards – can drive the organization (and its training activities) to respond appropriately. The common threads running through strategy, training and

THE ROLE OF EVALUATION

1. Training activity to be surveyed?

2. What current or anticipated job performance need does this meet?

3. What justification was originally presented for this training?

4. What would you expect to see someone doing differently after the training?

5. What, if any, evidence is there that the training has made a difference to job performance?

6. In your judgement, are the identified changes in performance such that they justify the time and money invested in the training?

Figure 2.4 Training activity probe

evaluation are the importance of clear purposes (which provide both targets and criteria of achievement), identifying results, and assessing value.

An emphasis on strategy ensures that the design and delivery of training activities matches real needs. Evaluation is concerned with judgements about the correctness of that strategy (including the means adopted) and particularly upon the outcomes that the strategy delivers. Efficient training design is grounded in a market-driven diagnostic process that responds to strategic concerns and which, performed well, allows the evaluation process simply to certify the quality of training outputs rather than to prescribe remedial measures.

Chapter 3 outlines the conceptual framework for evaluation and Chapter 4 discusses in some detail how the elements of strategy, design and evaluation can be pulled together to enable the Human Resource Development (HRD) professional to 'get it right first time'. The design and development of an evaluation project for a specific application (such as a particular training course) will be examined in Chapter 5.

NOTE

1. Cameron, K. (1980), 'Critical Questions in Assessing Organizational Effectiveness', *Organizational Dynamics*, Autumn, pp. 66–80.

3 A framework for evaluation

This chapter outlines the conceptual framework that underlies the evaluation techniques described in this book. The intention is to simplify the web of confusing and sometimes contradictory terminology that surrounds the subject, in order to help training practitioners to use evaluation as a routine tool.

CONCEPTS

EVALUATION

The training strategist needs to answer the following questions:

1. Is training achieving the results that it was set up to achieve?
2. Are the actual results worth having?
3. Were the results achieved by the most cost-effective methods?

These are all measures of the worth of training and it is the process by which 'worth' is determined that constitutes our definition of evaluation.

WORTH

There is a common assumption that worth only means monetary worth. This leads to the unnecessarily narrow view that evaluation is concerned only with assigning monetary values to the costs and benefits associated with a particular piece of training. This 'bottom-line' worth of training is certainly important, especially for organizational credibility, but there are many other valid and useful criteria of worth to which the training strategist may pay attention in particular circumstances. These criteria are developed further in a later section of this chapter (see p. 28).

SCIENTIFIC EVALUATION

It is misleading to speak of a science of evaluation because this implies formulae or mechanisms that result in judgements of absolute validity. Of course we should apply evaluation techniques in as objective, rigorous and scientific a manner as circumstances allow. It is better to collect information systematically than arbitrarily. But there is no absolute, objective, or universally-applicable standard against which a training activity can be evaluated because ultimately the criteria of evaluation are determined by what the evaluator deems appropriate for a particular situation. Furthermore, limits upon methodological rigour are frequently imposed by organizational constraints. Like politics, evaluation is a practical activity, and both are aptly described as arts of the possible.

Does this mean that evaluation is hopelessly subjective, unable to offer any meaningful discriminations between 'good' and 'bad' practice in training? I would argue not. In the first place, subjectivity has two common meanings. One implies bias, unreliability, individual opinion, and lack of objectivity. At its most obvious, this is the subjectivity of the trainer who judges the success of a programme by whether he or she 'feels mustard' at the end of the event. End of course euphoria, whether caused by satisfaction or relief, is never an index of what learning has been achieved, nor of how much of the new knowledge or skills will be put to use when course members return to their jobs. Evaluation by gut feeling has had a long run in spite of (or perhaps because of) its unreliability as an indicator of learning. It is time that kind of subjective evaluation was laid to rest.

The second meaning of subjectivity is concerned with the process of conscious thinking which is inherent in making judgements of worth. This is the 'conscious and reflective experience of the subject'. Such subjective experience can be lifted above the individual anecdotal level in several ways. Individual judgements can be grounded in specific concrete examples, for example 'You said that the course helped you with staff communications. Can you describe some instances where you've achieved different results because of what you learned?' Individual judgements can be tested by making them public, for scrutiny and for comparison of responses, for example '85 per cent of respondents said that . . .'.

In addition to subjects' self-assessments and the judgements that may be made by their managers or peers, there are also directly observable data on which to base evaluation, for example identifiable changes in the way that people do a job; measurable shifts on relevant indices of performance; cost-savings and value-enhancements.

In summary, there are both measurable performance data and cross-validation techniques by which the 'objectivity' of self-report and similar 'subjective' evaluations can be increased.

CRITERION OR NORM-REFERENCED MEASUREMENT

Criterion-referenced measures use as a yardstick a pre-defined standard of performance which will usually be part of the specified training objective. This is the usual approach for assessing training because we want to know whether or not trained persons are now competent to do something. Criterion referencing is used throughout this book.

THE ROLE OF EVALUATION

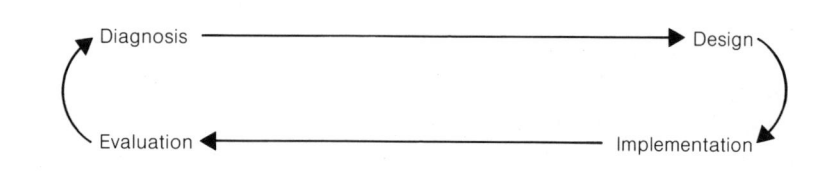

```
        Diagnosis ───────────────────────► Design
       ▲                                          ╲
       │                                           │
       ╲                                          ▼
        Evaluation ◄─────────────────── Implementation
```

Figure 3.1 Simplified model of the training cycle

In contrast, norm-referenced measures compare each individual to other people in the assessed group. It is thus a competitive measure and one that does not guarantee competence, since the individual may perform very well relative to a group of mediocre ability. The norm-referenced approach has, of course, a long tradition of use in the educational world.

EVALUATION AND VALIDATION

The definition of evaluation as the assessment of the *worth of training* is intended to cut through the tangle of different terminologies employed by writers on the subject over the last twenty years. It is too easy to get locked into medieval disputations about which 'box' a particular evaluation process should fit into, especially when the boundaries are anything but hard and fast. I take the view that it is much more fruitful to take the broadest definition of 'evaluation' to encompass all the processes of evaluation and validation which make for so much confusion in the literature, and to concentrate energy instead upon the pragmatics of employing evaluation for meaningful organizational purposes.

THE SYSTEMATIC CYCLE OF TRAINING

It is helpful to think of training as a cyclical process in which evaluation is as natural and essential a part as is identification of training needs (see Figure 3.1). Indeed, unless there is evaluation to 'close the loop', there can be no cycle – merely a straight-line sequence from determining what a training activity should be, through to implementing it. In such a sequence, there is no feedback mechanism to correct errors and fine-tune content or process. Figure 3.2 provides a visual representation of the training cycle and the evaluation feedback loops.

EVALUATION CONTEXT, EMPHASIS, CRITERIA AND TECHNIQUES

Evaluation is concerned with judgements of worth. Different people have legitimate interests in evaluation data and will employ different criteria of worth to select that data. These evaluation criteria should be *relevant*. This means that the measure of knowledge or skills gain which is employed in the training task is a good predictor of

A FRAMEWORK FOR EVALUATION

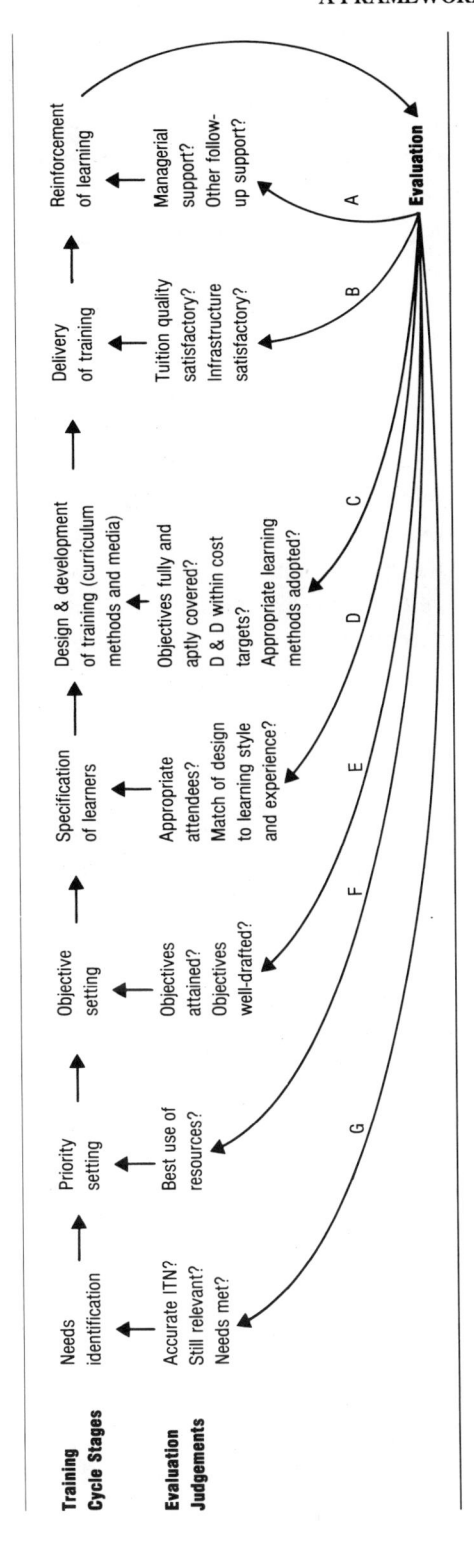

Training Cycle Stages	Needs identification	Priority setting	Objective setting	Specification of learners	Design & development of training (curriculum methods and media)	Delivery of training	Reinforcement of learning
Evaluation Judgements	Accurate ITN? Still relevant? Needs met?	Best use of resources?	Objectives attained? Objectives well-drafted?	Appropriate attendees? Match of design to learning style and experience?	Objectives fully and aptly covered? D & D within cost targets? Appropriate learning methods adopted?	Tuition quality satisfactory? Infrastructure satisfactory?	Managerial support? Other follow-up support?

Arrows A–G connect **Evaluation** back to each stage.

Figure 3.2 The systematic cycle in training

THE ROLE OF EVALUATION

how the assessed person will use that learning in real work situations. The criteria should also be *reliable* and provide a consistent measure when used by different evaluators, and when applied to an individual's performance on different occasions. It is often important to provide training for evaluators who employ a particular type of criterion, especially in the context of behaviour observation, so as to ensure consistency (Chapter 14 discusses such training in detail). The criteria that may be employed are summarized in Table 3.1.

Judgements of worth can be made within any one of four main contexts of evaluation:

1. Assessments of worth within the training event, such as 'How much has been learned?' or 'Have the chosen methods worked well?'
2. Assessments made in the workplace after the training event, such as 'What new skills can the trainee demonstrate?' or 'What is helping or hindering job-applications of skills learned?'
3. Assessments of the value of training in terms of indices of performance, which include *operational indices* (e.g. wastage rates, quality); *financial indices* (e.g. increased output from given resources); and *personnel indices* (e.g. improved time-keeping)
4. Assessments of worth on criteria not directly related to work performance, based upon social, moral, political, or philosophical criteria (applied, for example, to an equal opportunities programme).

Within each of these four contexts of evaluation, there are several possible aspects of the learning process on which the evaluator may choose the particular focus of the study. In Context 2 – evaluation in the workplace following the training activity – the evaluator may wish to assess (for example) the use made of that learning when back on the job, or whether the learning goals covered by the training do still correspond to real organizational needs. The four contexts, the related focuses of evaluation interest, and the appropriate criteria of worth are summarized in Table 3.2.

In summary, the four broad areas or contexts for evaluation each divide into several focuses which form the main emphasis of evaluation interest. Each focus is linked to a criterion of worth and to one or more techniques of evaluation, such as questionnaire or behaviour observation. Table 3.3 summarizes the linkages between context, and focus and evaluation techniques.

TECHNIQUES OVERVIEW

Part II of this book describes in detail how you can use each of the main evaluation techniques to assess the worth of training. What follows here is a brief overview of those techniques.

A FRAMEWORK FOR EVALUATION

Table 3.1 Criteria for judging the worth of training

Criterion	Judgement most appropriately made by:	Principal audiences for those judgements
Enjoyment/interest	Learners	Trainers
		Managers
Amount of change in knowledge or behaviour	Trainers	Trainers
	Leaners	Learners
	Managers	Managers
Effectiveness of learning methods and/or training decision	Trainers	Trainers
	Researchers	Academics
Relevance of training to the job	Learners	Trainers
	Line Managers	Learners
		Managers
Use made of learning in work tasks	Learners	Trainers
	Line Managers	Learners
		Managers
Personal development/growth	Leaners	Trainers
		Learners
Performance indices (operational/financial/personnel measures)	Line Managers	Managers
		Trainers
Cost-benefit comparisons	Trainers	Managers
		Trainers
'Fit' between training policy and organizational strategy	Trainers	Managers
	Line Managers	Trainers
Social/moral/public relations benefits of training	Senior management	Government
	Politicians	Public
	Trainers	Interest groups
Availability of trained manpower	Politicians	Employers
	Government policy advisers	Trade Unions
		Government
'Fit' between training policy and national economic strategy	Politicians	Government
	Government policy advisers	Professional bodies
	Professional bodies	Employers
	Interest groups	
Changes in organizational climate	Researchers	Managers
Changes in socio-economic indicators	Researchers	Government
	Government policy advisers	Interest groups
		Public
Changes in employment patterns	Personnel managers (in-company)	Managers
		Government
	Government policy advisers (national trends)	Public
		Professional bodies
		Interest groups

QUESTIONNAIRE

A questionnaire is a printed document comprising a number of questions and (typically) prepared alternative answers. It is distributed to respondents, by post or by hand, for each individual to complete in private and then to mail back to a central collating point responsible for analysing the data.

THE ROLE OF EVALUATION

Table 3.2 Criteria of worth in evaluation

Context	Focus of evaluation	Criterion of worth
1. Evaluation within the training event, focused on the learner or the trainer.	a) Judgements about the quality of the trainees' experience during training	Enjoyment/interest
	b) Feedback to trainees concerning their learning achievement	Amount of change in knowledge or behaviour
	c) Measures of change during training	Amount of change in knowledge or behaviour
	d) Feedback to trainers concerning learning methods and training design	Effectiveness of designs and methods
	e) Assessment of terminal competence	Level of knowledge or behavioural performance
2. Evaluation in the workplace, post-training, focused on the learner and on the work environment.	a) Matching the learning goals to the needs originally specified	Relevance of training to the job
	b) Use of learning or changes in work task behaviours	Effectiveness of designs and methods
	d) Factors affecting the use made of learning in the workplace	Effectiveness of designs and methods
	e) Individual learning and development	Personal development or growth; career development
3. Evaluation in the context of the organization as a whole, focused upon measures of effective performance.	a) Changes in organizational performance	Change in operational, financial and manpower indices
	b) Trainee implementation of individual action plans or projects	Use made of learning in work tasks; change in performance indices
	c) Cost-effectiveness of training	Cost-benefit comparisons
	d) Congruence of training and organizational mission strategies	'Fit' between policies
4. Evaluation focused upon social, cultural, political or ethical values drawn from the environment within which the organization operates.	a) Contribution of training to national prosperity	Availability of trained manpower; 'Fit' between training policy and national strategy
	b) Social costs and benefits	Cost-benefit comparisons of social effects of training
	c) Ethical, philosophical, or political rationales for training	Attitude change; changes in organizational climate; changes in socio-economic indicators; changes in employment patterns (e.g. 'equal opportunities' effects)

Questionnaire is the method to choose when large numbers of people need to be surveyed and when the questions that you want to ask will readily allow a closed format, yes/no or multiple-choice response. A questionnaire allows you to ask more (though simpler) questions than, say, an interview, but typically produces low rates of returned documents, whereas interview usually approaches a response rate of 100%.

Table 3.3 Evaluation techniques

Context and focus of evaluation	Appropriate techniques*
1. Within the training event	
a) Judgements about the quality of the trainees' experience during training.	SESSIONAL REACTIONNAIRES; EVENT REACTIONNAIRES; group discussion; individual comment
b) Feedback to trainees concerning their learning achievement.	WRITTEN TESTS: BEHAVIOUR OBSERVATION: REPERTORY GRID: ATTITUDE SCALES: PRACTICAL TESTS; video/audio recording; programmed learning; computer-based training
c) Measures of change during training.	Pre/post use of WRITTEN TESTS, BEHAVIOUR OBSERVATION PRACTICAL TESTS: REPERTORY GRID; attitude scales
d) Feedback to trainers concerning learning methods.	SESSIONAL REACTIONS FORMS: TESTS OF LEARNING GAIN (FROM 1.a) or 1.c)); EVALUATION INTERVIEW
e) Assessment of terminal competence.	OBJECTIVE TESTS; BEHAVIOUR OBSERVATION; PRACTICAL TEST; ESSAY; oral examination
2. Back at the job	
a) Matching the learning goals to the needs originally specified.	QUESTIONNAIRE; performance appraisal reviews; EVALUATION INTERVIEWS
b) Use of learning or changes to work task behaviours.	ACTION PLANNING; BEHAVIOUR OBSERVATION; CRITICAL INCIDENT ANALYSIS; EVALUATION INTERVIEWS; QUESTIONNAIRES; appraisal performance review; self-appraisal; pre/post sampling of work activities, work quality, and/or work quantity; participant observation
c) Feedback to trainers on learning methods and training strategy.	Data from 1.d) combined with EVALUATION INTERVIEW; COMPARATIVE ANALYSIS OF COST-EFFECTIVENESS OF ALTERNATIVES; QUESTIONNAIRES
d) Factors affecting the use made of learning in the workplace.	Data from 2.b) combined with EVALUATION INTERVIEW
e) Individual learning and development.	EVALUATION INTERVIEW; REPERTORY GRID; self-analysis; personality inventories
3. Organizational effectiveness	
a) Changes in organizational performance.	ANALYSES OF PERFORMANCE INDICES – operational measures (e.g. output quality or quantity, wastage or spoilage, sales volume, equipment downtime, accident rates, expressed customer satisfaction, reduced complaints); financial measures (e.g. unit costs, return on investment); manpower measures (e.g. turnover, absenteeism, organizational climate)
b) Trainee implementation of individual action plans or projects.	REVIEWS (INDIVIDUAL OR GROUP-BASED) OF PROGRESS IN IMPLEMENTING PLANS OR PROJECTS (this may usefully be combined with evaluation activity 2.d))
c) Cost-effectiveness of training.	COSTING; COST-BENEFIT ANALYSIS; COST-EFFECTIVENESS ANALYSIS
d) Congruence of training and organizational mission/strategies.	INTERVIEW; content analysis of formal and operative policies
4. Social, cultural (etc.) values	
a) Contribution of training to national prosperity.	COST-BENEFIT ANALYSIS
b) Social costs and benefits.	COST-BENEFIT ANALYSIS, values analysis
c) Ethical, philosophical, or political rationales for training.	Surveys of organizational climate; statistical indicators of socio-economic change; human resource accounting

Note: *Techniques covered in Part II of this book are shown in capitals.

INTERVIEW

The evaluation interview is usually a one-to-one session between a trained interviewer and a respondent. Duration may range from a few minutes only, up to one hour. Between 30 to 40 minutes is a good rule-of-thumb maximum length for interviewers who do not want to outstay their welcome or strain the attention span of their respondents.

Interview is the prime choice where understanding of respondents' thought processes is required, where explanation of actions and decisions is needed, or where the kinds of answer cannot be accurately anticipated, so that the interview is in the nature of a 'fishing expedition' to identify responses that can subsequently be incorporated into a questionnaire.

The interview normally follows a pre-drafted schedule of (mainly) open-ended questions, often with improvization of ad hoc follow-up questions to pursue particular points of interest. Responses may be recorded in writing by the interviewer or tape-recorded for subsequent analysis. Both the interview and the subsequent analysis of data are very time-consuming and the technique will therefore usually be restricted to small samples of the target population.

CRITICAL INCIDENT REVIEW

This technique is useful where evaluation data need to be obtained either from supervisory management, concerning subordinates, or where trained persons are asked to provide self-reported data on the use they have made of training inputs. The strength of the technique is that it offers a way to put behavioural substance onto the bones of well-intentioned but vacuous statements such as 'That was a really terrific course' or 'That training really changed my life'.

The critical incident method is a way to collect direct observations of workplace behaviour in situations that are significant ('critical') in performance of the job role. The respondent will complete a (typically) daily diary of 'critical' incidents, for subsequent analysis by the evaluator. The period of time required for effective sampling will vary with the nature of the job. Data are examined for evidence of connections between learning objectives (and training content) and observable job activity.

REPERTORY GRID

Repertory grid offers a method for identifying behavioural correlates of individual attitudes on a particular subject. It is a complicated and time-consuming technique to employ, although it can give interesting results not readily available by other means. Where repertory grid is used as an element of the training process, typically self-diagnostic, it is the logical method to employ for subsequent assessment of learning gain and changes in perception.

However, this method does not provide a measure of actual changes in how people work, only in how they see a given subject now compared to previously. Although attitude change *may* lead to behaviour change, the connection is not automatic. It is generally preferable to use behaviour analysis techniques to evaluate what actual change has occurred after people have been trained, rather than to rely on the inference that if attitudes have changed, changes in behaviour will follow.

ACTION PLAN REVIEW

The application of action planning in an evaluation context is akin to the use of the critical incident method. In essence, it is an assessment of what trained persons have done differently in their jobs, as a result of the training and as enshrined in a formalized action plan that they have drawn up as part of the training activity.

Action plan review is a self-report technique and therefore always carries the risk of self-interested responses. However, it is usually quite straightforward to verify whether or not judgements of success are grounded in reality and the method can be usefully linked with the cost-benefit analysis technique whenever action plans have led to specific projects and to changes in work practices. Action plan review may be combined with scheduled follow-up sessions that are an ongoing part of the training itself and this, together with the comparatively simple focus of attention (usually a self-contained project of some kind), makes this a low-cost technique.

REACTIONNAIRE

These simple, end of course questionnaires are used to gather immediate feedback on training activities. They may be employed after a complete course or session by session, depending on the needs of the evaluator. An effective reactionnaire is not to be confused with the ubiquitous 'happy sheet' that asks about trainees' enjoyment of the training and the training environment.

A well-designed reactionnaire will gather reasonably reliable data about such matters as the acceptability of particular learning methods, the performance skills of the trainers, and the match (or mismatch) of training to expectations, but it cannot provide reliable information about the amount of learning achieved, nor will it predict application of learning to job tasks. The reactionnaire provides a quick check against any gross failings that participants have identified in the training event; it should not be invested with any more significance than that.

WRITTEN TEST

Written tests provide an objective measure of the ability of trained persons to restate the things they have been taught. Such tests are appropriate where factual knowledge (including procedural knowledge) is being tested; they are, at best, a very poor substitute for practical testing or behaviour observation methods where skills are to be tested.

Written tests can be used for pre-training diagnosis of needs, pre/post assessment of learning gain, and for ongoing assessment (and reinforcement) of learning within a training event. Tests are easily administered to large numbers of trainees, are comparatively inexpensive to develop and use, and yield precise evaluation data if used appropriately.

PRACTICAL TEST

Practical testing occurs almost exclusively within training events, to give trainees feedback on their learning attainment and to measure end of training competence for purposes of training evaluation or formal accreditation. Practical tests can also be used as an initial diagnostic tool.

Practical tests should be used whenever trainees need to be able to translate knowledge into application. The test may measure the quality of a finished task, for example, accuracy, completeness, or the manner of its performance – speed or planning ability. A single task may be assessed, or a sequence of tasks forming a procedure.

Well-designed tests provide reliable, quantifiable data about training effectiveness. The cost of practical testing can be high where special test equipment needs to be constructed to simulate faults found in operational situations.

BEHAVIOUR ANALYSIS

These techniques are conceptually similar to practical tests, requiring the trained person to demonstrate that he or she can perform the skill for which training has been provided. The distinction is one of convenience, applying practical tests to technical skills and behaviour analysis to interpersonal skills. Typical applications include selling skills, telephone use, participation in meetings, supervision, and customer service.

Behaviour analysis is concerned with the accurate, systematic observation of verbal and physical behaviour, before, during and after training. It is often most usefully employed back at work, following training, and is a technique that often depends on the involvement of managers or supervisors of those trained. Behaviour analysis requires careful preparation, including training of observers, though subsequent data analysis is usually quite straightforward. The great value of the technique is that it concentrates on observable behaviour, not inferred attitudes, and thereby achieves both greater objectivity and reinforcement of behavioural learning objectives.

COST-BENEFIT ANALYSIS

A distinction is made between cost-benefit analysis (CBA) and cost-effectiveness analysis (CEA). The former refers to evaluations where both inputs and outputs of training can have monetary values applied to them. CEA refers to situations where inputs can be priced and outputs quantified, but not readily or meaningfully priced.

THE BENEFITS OF EVALUATION

Constructive, practical evaluation is a tool available to anyone with a serious interest in training. In general, the benefits substantially outweigh the costs. Six direct benefits can be identified.

QUALITY CONTROL

Quality control is concerned with whether a product or service is fit for the purpose. In a training context, that calls for an assessment of the extent to which work-related results can be demonstrated to arise from the training. The successful elements of training can be identified and reinforced and the ineffective elements scrapped or revised. If results cannot be demonstrated, it becomes hard to justify any commitment of resources to that activity and training resources can then be reallocated to where they will do most good.

EFFICIENT TRAINING DESIGN

Two core processes reinforce each other here: defining the training objectives on which the learning activities will be based and setting criteria by which those activities are to be evaluated. These form two sides of the same coin – identifying measurement criteria or performance standards for the objective ('How will we know they can do it?') forces clear thinking about the learning tasks that will be required ('What do they need to learn?'). It puts a premium upon behavioural change rather than awareness objectives and the end-product is clearly specified training objectives with observable outcomes.

There is also a considerable economy of effort achieved when design of objectives and design of evaluation measures proceed hand-in-hand. It is invariably less costly of design time and yields more fruitful information to build evaluation into training design from the beginning, rather than add it on as an afterthought when the design has been finalized and implemented.

PROFESSIONAL SELF-ESTEEM

Trainers can gain an enhanced and merited stature from reliance on systematic evaluation data rather than intuitive assessments of their performance. Most organizations have some kind of appraisal system, but training staff sometimes fall outside its scope because relevant measures are believed to be unavailable. Evaluation can provide this missing input, as well as a better alternative to less meaningful performance measures such as number of training contact hours, or body counts of trainees, which measure effort rather than results. Performance-linked appraisal puts the training department on the same footing as other organizational functions and can thus help to break down the 'them and us' barrier that arises when trainers claim that the nature of their work does not lend itself to measured assessment.

TRACK RECORD

Evaluation makes it possible to demonstrate a track record of relevant, successful and cost-effective training over a period of time. When it comes to budget negotiations, nothing is more persuasive than being able to show what training has contributed to the success of the organization. However, it is essential that evaluation systems are in place and operating long before this kind of budgetary justification is required. Experience suggests that most companies need about an 18-month lead time to get a well-devised evaluation system in place.

APPROPRIATE CRITERIA OF ASSESSMENT

Whether or not evaluation is formalized in a particular organization, it is a fact of life that people will make judgements about the training that is provided. Where there is no guidance available on the choice of assessment criteria, people respond in predictable ways. Participants from a training event will typically respond in terms of their 'enjoyment'; managers in terms of how many days will be lost from work by their subordinates; and accountants will make comparisons such as the 'cost per trainee' or the number of 'training days' provided by one organization in comparison with another, or by the same organization at different points in time. Training is evaluated, in one way or another, whether trainers like it or not.

Systematic evaluation pre-empts judgements being made on inappropriate criteria, such as an emphasis on a head-count of trainees rather than on the quality of performance produced by them after training.

INTERVENTION STRATEGY

Evaluation can be used as a vehicle for changing the way that training is integrated into the organization. It offers a framework through which trainers and managers can examine their respective roles in the training process and redefine the boundary between them. It enables the training department to play a more active role in developing policy and opens doors to better identification of needs.

NEGLECT OF EVALUATION

Evaluation is arguably the most important area of training design and certainly the most neglected. The reasons for neglect lie in three areas – training history, academic analysis and trainer anxieties.

During the 1960s and much of the 1970s training was a growth industry in the UK and funding flowed relatively generously from government and corporate sources. Fads came and went, with the spending justified because the ideas were new, or at least newly packaged. Accountability and value for money were not terms often used by trainers. Indeed, training was often redefined as 'development', a higher level activity, almost mystical in the imprecision surrounding its achievements and requiring acts of faith by managers, rather than, say, cost-benefit justifications by trainers. Into the 1980s it was not unusual to find organizations that required a detailed capital expenditure analysis before purchasing, say, a £5000 computer yet the same organizations would spend as much as £20,000 (in fees, expenses, salary and consequential costs) to send a manager to a business school course, in the belief that it was a 'good thing', or even as a perk of the job. However, because such training was little more than froth on the surface of organizational life, it was blown away in the chill winds that followed the first significant rise in oil prices at the end of the 1970s. Training budgets were slashed and, indeed, numbers of large organizations dismantled their training departments whilst the government closed down the majority of the training boards.

A second factor which has contributed to the neglect of evaluation is the lamentable confusion created by writers on the subject. Nearly every writer has developed a new set of terminology to describe the subject.[1] One consequence has been that much of the training of trainers which purports to deal with evaluation is in fact little more than a ritual 'naming of the parts'. This is a sterile exercise. Professional trainers need to learn how to *use* evaluation, in real organizations, and facing real constraints and opportunities.

This terminological confusion has been compounded by the secondary limitation that many academic analysts have been strong on exhortation – telling trainers that evaluation ought to be done – but very weak on practical guidance and examples which show trainers how to do it. Academic researchers also create the impression that evaluation must be conducted in laboratory-like conditions of experimental control. In working organizations such rigour is unattainable and practitioners tend therefore to conclude that evaluation is impossible. However, evaluation is a practical discipline which can be employed at whatever level of technical control can be achieved in the particular circumstances. What is important is that evaluation data should be collected in a systematic way and not arbitrarily; that evidence is gathered in place of surmise; and that data are not twisted to match preconceived answers. Evaluation is always and inherently a process of judgement. What systematic evaluation does is to make that process, and the criteria of judgement used, explicit so that the subjective anecdote cannot be passed off as a universal truth.

The third factor concerns the fear response amongst trainers. This can be understood partly as the tendency of job-holders to avoid performance appraisal unless a positive outcome is guaranteed (which no doubt accounts for the popularity amongst trainers of vacuous end of course 'happy sheets') and partly as a misunderstanding of the nature of evaluation.

THE ROLE OF EVALUATION

Evaluation is often assumed to be negative and destructive in its effects. Certainly, evaluation does make it possible to question training events and methods that have been allowed to continue for years unchecked. Sometimes, too, evaluation shows that cherished training programmes are having absolutely no effect on how participants carry out their work. On the other hand, it also makes it possible for trainers to know that they are doing a competent, professional job; it ensures that finite training resources are concentrated in the most productive applications; and repeat business is more likely from participants who have a measure of the gains in knowledge or skills that they have made. In any event, fear of negative evaluation findings is generally overplayed. Most evaluations produce a mixture of positive and negative results, since few training activities turn out wholly good or wholly bad. Trainers need both results if their training is not to be built upon a quicksand of untested assumptions about what does or does not work.

Above all, avoiding evaluation for fear of what it might reveal is a strategy that offers no insurance against the demands of other people. One day, the chief executive is going to ask 'Just what is achieved by the money we spend on training?' At that point it is too late to do anything about evaluation. Experience suggests that it takes 12 to 18 months to establish a package of systematic evaluation data that proves the effectiveness of training.

The people who control investment in training ought to be able to respond to such questions as:

'Does this event put across the company philosophy?'
'What contribution is training making to the next five years in the growth of this enterprise?'
'If we retrain staff, is that a better way of meeting our needs than changing our recruitment policy, or perhaps redesigning the job?'
'Are people learning the *right* skills for the jobs they do?'

This book will give you the tools to obtain answers to such questions.

NOTE

1. For a detailed survey of this problem, see Bramley, P. and Newby, A. C. (1984), 'The evaluation of training', *Journal of European Industrial Training*, 8 (6 and 7).

4 Getting it right first time

In an ideal world, evaluation would not be necessary because all training would be perfectly designed, skilfully implemented, and thoroughly reinforced in the workplace. In the real world, there is much that the trainer can do to minimize both the need to conduct evaluations and the potential for negative findings. This chapter covers basics of training design, drawing particularly on the lessons of faulty design that I have encountered in a decade of evaluation research and consultancy. The framework for this chapter is that of the systematic cycle in training which was outlined in Chapter 3 and which is illustrated in Figure 3.2, p. 25.

THE MARKETING APPROACH TO TRAINING NEEDS

The marketing approach to training starts from an analysis of what the consumer wants and needs. The consumer may be a manager who buys training for others, the individuals who take part in training activities, or the organization as a whole represented, for example, by the MD, the director of personnel or some form of joint management-employee board. Training needs analysis is the equivalent of market research for consumer products.

The most common results of inadequate needs analysis are last-minute withdrawals from courses, people attending part-time, or a half-hearted 'tourist' attitude to the content: 'I'm only here to see if this is of interest for other people.' What all these responses have in common is a lack of commitment because the learner has not been involved in the diagnostic stage of training design.

Training needs arise in only two ways:

1. A person is under-performing due to a knowledge or skill deficiency – a *remedial* need to perform existing tasks better.
2. A person is expected to perform tasks in the near future for which that person lacks the required knowledge or skills – a *developmental* need to perform new tasks.

A related point is that non-training alternatives should always be considered. Given a

37

problem or a need for something to change, there may be several options available: redesign of the job (e.g. deskilling); recruitment of people with the required competence; redefinition of the problem (e.g. a training need in subordinate staff may actually reflect a performance deficiency in the supervisor or manager); and of course training itself. Sometimes an organizational problem is labelled as 'training' when it is actually a management 'hot potato' for which nobody wants to take responsibility. Until a job-focused needs analysis is conducted the trainer has no way of getting to grips with this kind of political issue.

Developmental needs pose one special concern: how far ahead should a training need be anticipated? Sometimes, people receive training which relates to a future job for which they have prospects of promotion. A balance is required between providing skills in readiness for the future job and providing them too early so that most of the learning has been forgotten by the time that it is needed. Retention of new knowledge and skills depends to a large extent on whether or not there are opportunities to use them.

The essence of a training need, then, is a gap between what exists and what is wanted. When a piece of training is designed in response to such a need, several positive results follow:

- Training content relates to job realities rather than to abstract principles.
- People undergoing training are much more likely to see the activity as useful and relevant – and therefore learn more readily.
- On-job performance improves.
- Measurement of improved performance becomes more feasible.

One of the best pay offs from needs analysis comes in the form of management involvement in training. If training is to make a real contribution to corporate success it cannot operate in a vacuum. It is a political and a professional mistake for trainers to put up 'keep out' signs around their territory. Successful training is a partnership in which trainers and managers play complementary reinforcing roles. Managers are able to feel involved in the diagnostic process and have a sense of ownership of the training events that result. Following on from this, managers are more likely to play a positive role in the key stages pre- and post-training that do so much to reinforce – or undermine – the trainer's contribution. Trainers also get much better information on which to base training design. Line managers and supervisors are the people most closely involved with the workplace situation to which the needs analysis is being addressed.

A second very substantial benefit from thorough needs analysis is that evaluation is made easier. The connection between evaluation and objectives works two ways. Well-defined objectives contain their own criterion by which the trainer can evaluate the extent to which the objective has been met through the training event. The trainer's decision to evaluate – and the consequent need to specify standards for assessing worth – itself helps to sharpen up the writing of training objectives. It is a very useful test of how well a training objective has been drawn to ask 'How will I know when this objective has been achieved?' Setting objectives and defining evaluation criteria in parallel is also more economical of trainers' time than adding evaluation retrospectively to existing training designs.

DETERMINING PRIORITIES

Between the needs analysis stage and the setting of learning objectives, a process of selecting priorities is often necessary. Training budgets are rarely so open-ended that all training needs can be met at once. Priorities amongst training needs should, logically, reflect the relative importance of the elements of corporate strategy to which the needs relate. In practice, the five most usual influences on priority-setting are as follows:

- The money available.
- Legal requirements (e.g. safety training).
- Policy (i.e. selecting training options most closely related to organizational strategy).
- Organizational politics (who shouts loudest, gets most).
- Trainer preferences (running the courses they most enjoy).

Quite often, the basis on which priorities are set for allocation of training funds is not made explicit. This opens the way for distortion of training needs: certain departments grab the lion's share of available funds; places on external courses are purchased on the basis of their prestige value and recreational potential; and trainers promote and run the courses they enjoy most, rather than those which are most needed.

While training is conducted at arm's length from management, little can change. Conversely, when there is close cooperation between trainers and managers, and training is treated as an integral part of organizational life, the allocation of money between competing training projects can be treated like any other investment decision.

SETTING LEARNING OBJECTIVES

An identified training need pinpoints an area where change is required. Learning objectives specify what a person will be able to do differently as a result of training. Training is like any other organizational activity: the clearer the picture of what you want to achieve, the easier it becomes to plan the means, and the greater the prospects of achieving success. Ineffective training adopts a scattergun approach, rather than pinpointing the target. It is characterized by learning objectives which use weasel-phrases such as

'... will gain an awareness of ...'
'... should understand ...'

THE ROLE OF EVALUATION

Effective training designs are characterized by objectives that *state clearly what trained persons will be able to do when back in the workplace*. A well-stated training objective conveys the same message to the learner, the trainer and to the nominating manager. It will specify without ambiguity what benefits to job performance are likely to result from that training. The quality of the objectives is the first criteria that any buyer of training – whether it is in-house or external course – should apply critically.

Even where a thorough needs analysis has been conducted, there can be a weak linkage between identified needs and training content. What may happen is that the trainer, having identified a real need for, say, delegation skills training, then scours the available textbooks on 'delegation' for anything that might be included in a training course on the subject. The training event that results will be *syllabus-led* rather than *needs-driven*. The consequence is that much of the content has little relevance to participants. Delegation skills (for example) are taught in general terms – almost as if it were an academic subject – thus losing sight of the actual delegating activities of participants.

A key skill for training designers is to translate identified needs into clear learning objectives and only then into content. Clear objectives provide a signpost to where the training is headed. Without them, anything goes. Finally, objectives are essential if you want to evaluate the effectiveness of training. Learning objectives are closely linked to the criteria for evaluating the training which has been based upon those objectives.

Well-drafted training objectives are written to conform to a standard three-part structure:

1. The behaviour to be demonstrated after training.
2. The standard of performance to be attained.
3. The conditions under which performance is to occur.

There are two points to note about this specification. First, 'behaviour' includes not only interpersonal activities but also such observable activities as speaking, writing, and so forth. Second, 'behaviour' specifically excludes non-observable phenomena such as attitudes or motivation, and largely unchangeable features of the individual such as personality traits. The connection between attitudes and behaviour has been debated at length in psychological research. Each can be shown, sometimes, but not always, to influence the other and the strategy offered here is a pragmatic one.

As trainers we can directly influence and observe behaviour; as managers we can see what our staff are doing and can reward good performance, or correct bad. What we cannot do is obtain direct access to other people's thought processes. We have to rely either on the other person's willingness and capacity for introspection, or on our own guesses, which in turn can only be based on behavioural evidence. The difficulty involved in changing attitudes against the subject's will should be caution enough. Furthermore, people can and do behave in ways that contradict the attitudes they hold.

As individuals we may feel more comfortable if we believe that other people hold the particular attitudes which we would prefer them to hold. If, however, we look at the question in terms of indicators of effective performance, what matters is what people *do*, not what they think. There is a considerable economy of effort, and a much higher probability of positive benefits, to be achieved by trainers when they concentrate on developing appropriate and skilful *behaviours* in learners.

'Should objectives be set for "developmental" training?' is a common question. The process of personal development can progress in many different directions: from the same developmental learning experience some people may be inspired to become chief executives of their own enterprises whilst others may decide with equal determination to take up transcendental meditation. Clearly, we cannot evaluate against a criterion of achieving a pre-defined end-state. However, we may wish to evaluate on a criterion of the use made of what has been learned. A suitably formulated objective-cum-criterion for a life/career development workshop might be: *'Within one month of completion of the learning activity, participants will be able to draw up a life-career plan which specifies personal goals and provides estimates of the timescale within which those goals will be achieved'*. The first stage of evaluation would be to review the extent to which participants had started to apply the techniques and perspectives of life-career planning. A longer term evaluation would review the extent to which the plans had been put into practice.

There is no substitute for objectives-based training design, but for some particular purposes there can be evaluation which does not depend on measuring against objectives themselves.

a) It is important when conducting post-training evaluations to be aware of possible unanticipated effects (good or bad) caused by the learning. These will be unanticipated precisely because they do not reflect objectives, but they can sometimes yield key insights into the learning process. This kind of 'goal-free' evaluation can be best carried out by an evaluator who has been insulated from any prior knowledge of the training event. The evaluator is then able to gather information without any preconceptions concerning what participants were intended to learn.

b) In some kinds of programme it will be appropriate to extend the formal training objectives to include individual objectives which participants bring to the event. (It is also important that personal objectives are not at cross purposes with formal objectives.) Where personal objectives differ from the job-related formal training objectives, the evaluator has three options. The first is to indicate the need for a substantial redesign of the programme or a change in the process by which participants are selected. The second is to apply weightings to the valuations placed upon the training by the different parties. The third option is to produce a multiple evaluation report which reflects the interests of the various parties without attempting the inevitably arbitrary comparison of areas of conflict. Where divergent valuations rest on different criteria this can only be resolved at the level of organizational politics and policy-making.

c) Where the evaluator's interest concerns the process of learning rather than its outcomes then a method known as 'illuminative evaluation' may be appropriate. This method seeks to provide insights into how learners approach the learning task and what factors influence their use of the learning materials. The emphasis of the evaluation is on the ways in which changes occur in the quality of the learner's understanding of key concepts in the programme.

CONTENT DESIGN

The design of the content of a training activity consists of three elements:
1. The curriculum, or subject matter to be conveyed to the learners.
2. The methods by which the curriculum is to be presented (e.g. group discussion, role play, etc.).
3. The supporting media employed (such as overhead projector slides, video or computer).

It is in the choice of methods and media that a great deal of training starts and finishes. Design of training activities without prior analysis of needs, or subsequent evaluation of worth, is the commonest cause of low-impact training.

Design development should proceed in three steps. First, the training objectives are translated into appropriate methods. If possible, methods should also be matched to the people who will receive the training. For example, a training objective which concerns development of a skill – whether a physical skill like operating a lathe, or an interpersonal skill like selling – will not be taught effectively by passive methods such as listening to a lecture or watching a film, however entertaining. Skill acquisition demands practice.

Even where the training objectives concern only knowledge acquisition (e.g. information to salespeople concerning a new product) the traditional lecture presentation is not the most effective method to adopt. Group discussion combined with discovery learning (exploring the product individually) will give better absorption of information.

For every training objective and its related method, the second step is to prepare the content. Content may be in the form of a briefing note outlining a character in a role-play. It may be a detailed case study for analysis, or a set of memos and documents for an in-tray exercise. Or it may be a specification for machining a piece of metal, or joining two cables. What matters is that the content is relevant and credible, so that, say, insurance salesmen are not presented with case studies based on petrol retailing.

The third step is to consider the appropriate use of supporting media. One of the most common design errors is to treat an audio-visual aid (e.g. a film) as an end in itself. A second common failing is the 'chips with everything' syndrome where a training department over-invests in a particular approach (such as computer-based learning, or videodisc) and then uses that approach for every training activity, regardless of appropriateness or cost.

Content design is also concerned with the sequencing of materials and with planning for reinforcement of learning and correction of errors. Design should take account of the preferred learning styles of course participants. Not least, the design stage should include the preparation of evaluation instruments to assess the amount of learning that occurs and the extent to which that learning transfers into workplace practice.

The content design stage raises questions about three distinct areas of training skill:

- How is learning made effective?
- What methods of training exist, when should each be used, and how is each to be employed?
- What media are useful adjuncts to particular methods, and how is each one used for best effect?

IMPLEMENTATION OF TRAINING

This stage of the training cycle concerns the ability of the trainer to deliver the training product. It is here that training is most often judged 'good' or 'bad', on the strength of the trainer's performance skill in creating end of course euphoria. Broadly, these implementation skills form three groups:

1. Presentation and facilitation skills.
2. The ability to handle conflict in appropriate ways.
3. The ability to generate participation amongst trainees.

Presentation skills include planning, preparation of materials, public speaking, discussion-leading, and use of audio-visual aids. These skills matter; unless supported by competent presentation skills, even the best designed training events will flop. The first requirement for learning is that the audience continues to pay attention to the trainer.

Conflict handling, too, is a large subject. At the classroom level there are ways in which trainers can respond constructively to conflict between themselves and trainees, or to conflicts amongst the participants themselves. Beyond this, conflict itself can be made the main subject of training events, for example working on conflict within work teams or between different groups or departments. In both classroom and workplace, minor disagreements can easily escalate into serious confrontations which subvert good learning or working practices.

Learning how to generate participation is linked to presentation skills, and to skills of handling conflict. Developing rapport with course members, using questions skilfully in the classroom, and of course creating training designs that encourage active involvement rather than passive listening are key skills to increase participation. The price paid for low participation is not only a low level of learning but damaged self-esteem and confidence in the trainer.

THE TRAINING INFRASTRUCTURE

There are a number of elements which, to a varying extent impinge upon training design:

- The design of training facilities.
- The system for training budgets and training expenditure accounting.
- The efficiency of course administration (e.g. ensuring that facilities are booked, issuing joining instructions, and looking after follow-up evaluation).
- The measures taken to strengthen off-job training by pre-briefings and preparatory work and by post-training reinforcement.

When these infrastructure matters are neglected, trainers find themselves with courses containing unbriefed participants, people on the wrong course, or people turning up at the wrong location. Budgets may be overcommitted on hardware or on fun events of marginal value to the organization. Training premises may have inadequate electricity supplies, poor lighting and ventilation, and a lack of sound-proofing. Clerical procedures can break down with such consequences as over-booking of facilities, failure to provide joining instructions, or lack of course evaluation.

MANAGER-TRAINER PARTNERSHIP: WHAT GOES WRONG?

'Prepare my staff for training courses – most certainly! I make sure that I personally give them instructions on how to reach the training centre, and I wish them luck as they leave.'

'Of course I leave it to the training department – they're the specialists.'

'Well, it's really quite difficult to pin down specific changes in their work after training. What sort of things did you expect?'

Remarks such as these are not uncommon from managers who send their staff on training courses. Involvement in the training process is limited, by and large, to signing the nomination form beforehand and approving the travelling expenses afterwards.

On the other side of this divide trainers often reinforce this non-communication. Course brochures are written for trainers rather than for recipients of training: courses are described in trainer jargon. Often the course content is listed, but rarely the *benefits* that should be expected from the event. This not only discourages discussion between manager and participant, it also reinforces the impression that 'training' happens in a

GETTING IT RIGHT FIRST TIME

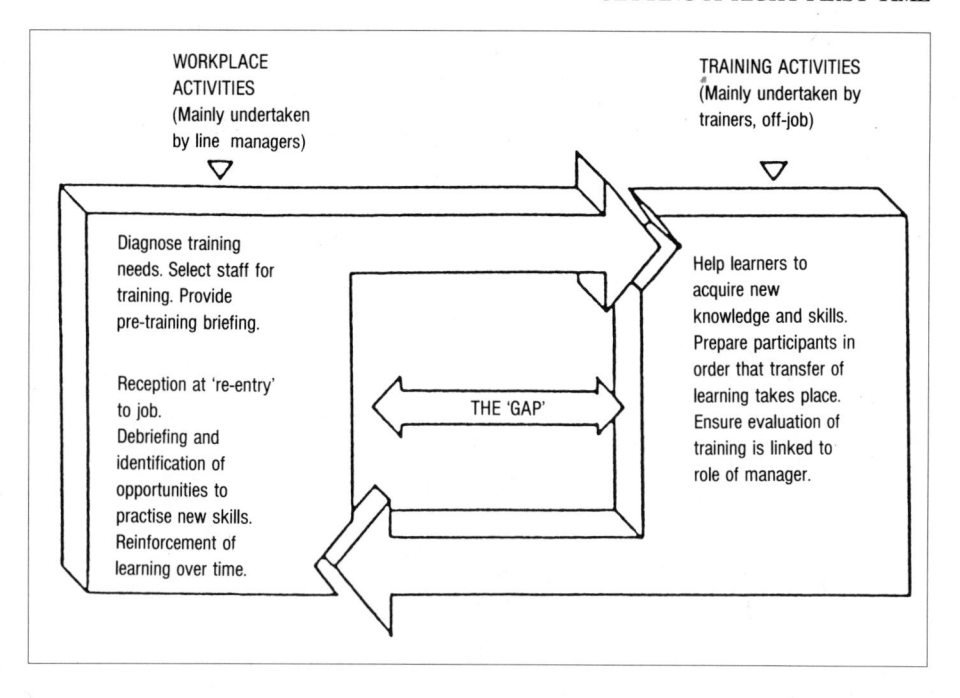

```
WORKPLACE                              TRAINING ACTIVITIES
ACTIVITIES                             (Mainly undertaken by
(Mainly undertaken                     trainers, off-job)
by line managers)

Diagnose training                      Help learners to
needs. Select staff for                acquire new
training. Provide                      knowledge and skills.
pre-training briefing.                 Prepare participants in
                                       order that transfer of
Reception at 're-entry'                learning takes place.
to job.              THE 'GAP'         Ensure evaluation of
Debriefing and                         training is linked to
identification of                      role of manager.
opportunities to
practise new skills.
Reinforcement of
learning over time.
```

Figure 4.1 **The manager-trainer partnership: getting it right**

vacuum, sealed off from real life. But training is meant to make an identifiable impact on work performance: once again, it is the difference between the marketing and the selling approaches to training. So what can be done to close the gap between training and management? Figure 4.1 shows a framework for tackling this issue. What the framework reveals is the importance of management actions before and after off-job training: workplace activities are just as important as training activities.

We can summarize the positive role that a manager can play in training as follows:

1. Diagnose learning needs.
2. Match the right people to the right training.
3. Make sure subordinates know what benefits the manager expects the training to produce.
4. Allow subordinates to do things differently and to take some risks.
5. Provide constructive feedback on subordinates' performance and supportive reinforcement when they employ new knowledge and skills.
6. Act as a model for effective behaviour and as a guiding mentor and coach.

EVALUATION

Evaluation and needs analysis are perhaps the most important stages in the cycle of training. All too often, training is treated as a linear sequence that ends with implementation of the learning activity. Evaluation provides the feedback loops that make training a cyclical process.

The loops shown in the training cycle diagram (reproduced here as Figure 4.2) provide feedback on the different stages, as follows:

Loop A assesses the extent and impact of post-training support and/or workplace obstacles to using new knowledge and skills.

Loop B assesses the quality of the training experience and the performance of the training presenters.

Loop C is concerned with the appropriateness of the training methods to the learning objectives and to the trainees' own preferred learning styles.

Loop D reviews whether or not the right people have been selected for the particular training activity.

Loop E measures the extent to which new knowledge or skills have been acquired, that is, to what extent learning objectives have been met.

Loop F enables judgements to be made about the correctness of the priorities set for training and the policy implications of this.

Loop G examines whether the learning achieved through the training activity matches needs for competent performance of work tasks, that is, to what extent are the *correct* learning objectives being pursued.

As the main theme of this book is evaluation no more details of the subject are required in this introductory chapter on the principles of good training design. We turn now to the issues involved when evaluation is first introduced into the organization as a part of the total training process.

CREATING THE ORGANIZATIONAL FRAMEWORK FOR EVALUATION

The introduction of systematic evaluation is a form of culture change, just as much as programmes to change management style or to introduce 'quality'. As with all organizational change, there is much forward momentum to overcome in order to make even small shifts of direction, as exemplified in the Latin proverb 'make haste slowly'. However, making change by careful evolutionary steps, rather than opting for the revolutionary gesture, is not the same as finding excuses for inaction. Readers of Eric Berne will be familiar with the game of 'Yes, but' and its cousin from organizational life 'Not invented here'.

'That sounds a good idea, but . . .'

'Of course, we do it differently here so you can't really make the parallel with . . .'

GETTING IT RIGHT FIRST TIME

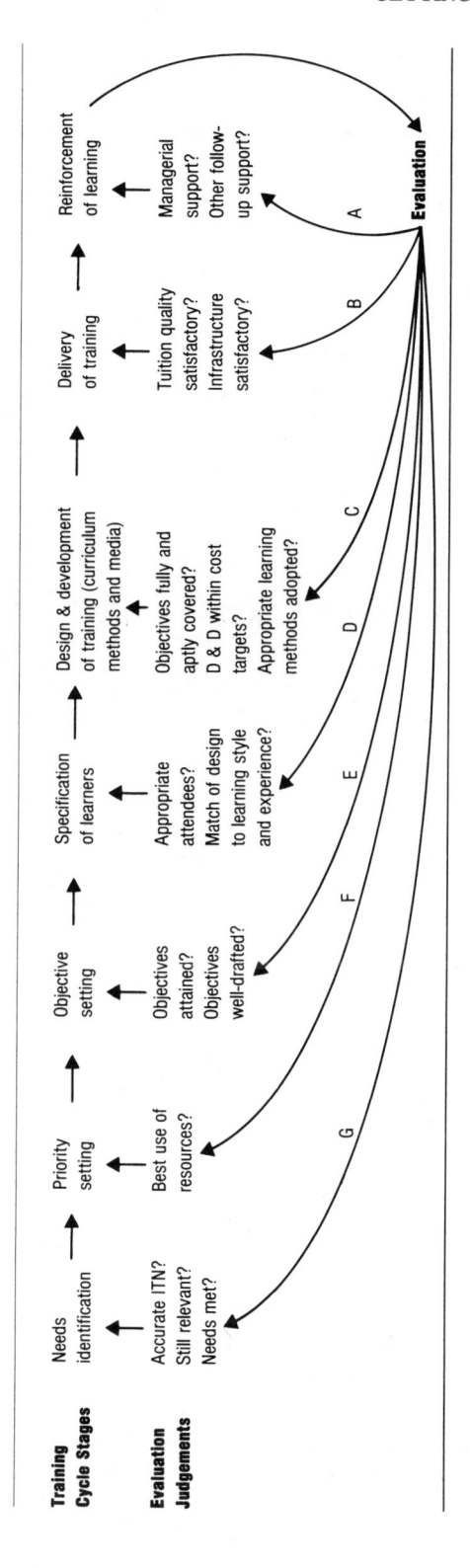

Training Cycle Stages	Needs identification	Priority setting	Objective setting	Specification of learners	Design & development of training (curriculum methods and media)	Delivery of training	Reinforcement of learning
Evaluation Judgements	Accurate ITN? Still relevant? Needs met?	Best use of resources?	Objectives attained? Objectives well-drafted?	Appropriate attendees? Match of design to learning style and experience?	Objectives fully and aptly covered? D & D within cost targets? Appropriate learning methods adopted?	Tuition quality satisfactory? Infrastructure satisfactory?	Managerial support? Other follow-up support?

Arrows from Evaluation labelled A, B, C, D, E, F, G feed back to each stage.

Figure 4.2 The systematic cycle in training

THE ROLE OF EVALUATION

Making change happen is partly a matter of deciding where you want to go and partly a matter of political skills such as persuasion, influencing people and building alliances. The evaluator often works as a catalyst of change and this requires a number of key skills:

- Entry skills that enable you to get access to the people who have the information you need or whom you need to influence.
- Developing relationships – getting rapport with people, understanding their points of view and needs.
- Diagnostic abilities that enable you to analyse the situation facing you, especially the skills of active listening and unbiased questioning.
- Support-building – getting commitments to action and generating resources.
- Evaluating the ongoing process and its outcomes, and providing constructive feedback to those involved.

FROM VICIOUS CIRCLE TO BENIGN CIRCLE

One option for people with a responsibility for training is to move towards becoming an internal consultant who plays a more active part in shaping policy issues and long-term organizational change. Evaluation of training is a powerful lever for the person taking that direction: it brings close involvement with corporate strategy and with functional responsibilities. What is more, in the cost-conscious 1990s, evaluation is an intervention strategy that is more likely to gain the internal consultant allies and rewards than such 1970s hangovers as 'OD' or 'Quality of Working Life'. The 'vicious' and 'benign' circles of Figure 4.3 show the difference that systematic evaluation can make to the corporate climate within which training can wither or flourish.

The situation outlined in the 'vicious' circle can drift on for years, with low expectations on the one hand balancing poor training provision on the other. The circle can become a spiral of decline which resolves itself when the training department is disbanded. The benign spiral is the mirror image of this. Evaluation data (both positive and negative) build up the credibility of the training function. Negative data show that the trainers are serious in their intention to create effective training. A measure of honesty about previous performance, combined with a clear intention to do better, is a far more credible position from which to seek support from the rest of the organization, than a pretence that nothing requires changing or improving. The problem is to break the self-reinforcing pattern of the vicious circle. Systematic evaluation is a powerful tool for the job, which may be reinforced at the start by the use of an external consultant, who can bring fresh ideas to bear on a static, 'taken for granted' situation.

The benign and vicious circles are of course idealized models and many organizations will exhibit symptoms somewhere in-between the two. However, these cycles do

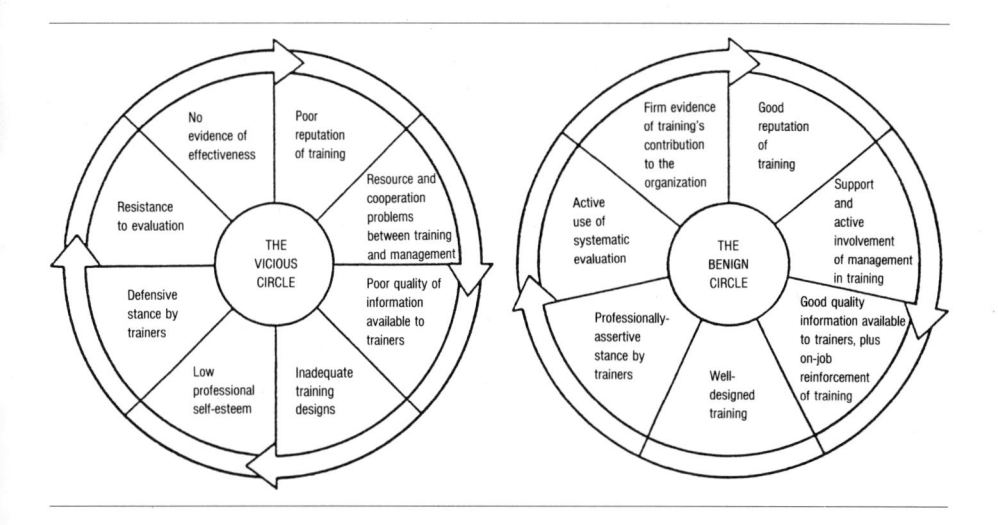

Figure 4.3 The vicious circle and the benign circle

reflect processes frequently observed in real life so the key question for managers and trainers must be 'How do we move our situation closer to the benign circle?'

Sometimes the change is taken out of the trainer's hands. The training unit may be 'privatized' so that it has to compete for the organization's training. Zero-based budgeting may impose new requirements to justify training investment. The training manager may pre-empt such actions by presenting evidence that training has a positive worth to the enterprise.

STARTING TO EVALUATE

The benefits of systematic evaluation are more likely to be obtained where effort is concentrated rather than spread thinly. Evaluation is more likely to take root if the majority of people in a particular training unit or training department are working within a common frame of reference and shared goals. It is less likely to succeed where token, isolated individuals are trained to use evaluation techniques within an organizational culture that is essentialy unchanged. There is a lot to be said for concentrating on forthcoming, rather than well-established programmes. In particular, trainers are more likely to treat evaluation in a spirit of disinterested inquiry ('Does this course do what we want it to') than one of defensiveness about a status quo to which they have been committed for some time ('Nobody has complained before'). On the other hand, an evaluation which establishes that an existing programme is of little value ('shooting sacred cows') can provide a salutary shock.

The 'intervention' role of evaluation is very important in the early stages, when opposition or lack of enthusiasm are common. Different organizations will have very

THE ROLE OF EVALUATION

different levels of receptivity to the idea of evaluation. These differences reflect opinions concerning the feasibility and desirability of evaluation and specific policy pressures and priorities. This diversity must be recognized and accommodated: it is futile to try to introduce systematic evaluation in the face of hostility or 'active apathy'. People take time to absorb new ideas. This has two implications: one is for the timescale over which evaluation ideas are scheduled, the other is for training managers who must act positively to build and maintain the momentum of changed practice. It is a sound principle to build on strengths and to concentrate initial efforts at evaluation where people are most receptive and the benefits are likely to be greatest. Ownership of evaluation projects is important. In the learning stages, it is better that people work on the evaluation of training activities for which they personally have some responsibility.

In many organizations, the first step will itself be an intervention aimed at unfreezing set attitudes – particularly defensiveness about evaluation, and also the common perception that evaluation is a good idea in theory, but too difficult in practice.

'People in organizations do whatever they are rewarded for doing'

Senior managers quite often make remarks that are intended to support training. They may make them because of a sincere belief in training or because they feel the remarks are expected of them, but they then go on to undermine the value of their words by demonstrating behaviour that contradicts the message. We are back to the problem of moving beyond lip-service support of training and into practical support. The commitment of senior policy-makers to a training strategy is valuable, but it is many times more useful if it translates into influence and rewards that encourage middle and junior managers to play an active role in the training partnership.

Managers are busy and fairly rational people. They usually put their energy into the activities that will bring them most rewards. When top management rewards people for keeping the wheels turning, for highly visible fire-fighting, for taking a short-term perspective, then these are the things that will take priority. When middle managers are appraised for, say, production results but not for staff development, only the former will be taken seriously.

An organization that puts emphasis on results, quality of performance and accountability is much more receptive to the ideas of training strategy and evaluation. It is likely to want training that makes a difference and it will want to know whether that difference has been achieved. It is more likely to recognize that the occasional half-hour that a manager invests in assessing training needs, briefing people to attend training activities, and reviewing and reinforcing the outcomes of training will pay for itself in improved work performance. Figure 4.4 will help bring some of these issues into focus.

LEARNING EVALUATION SKILLS

Two processes need to develop in parallel over the period of time (typically, a few months) during which systematic evaluation is being introduced. The trainers who

This is a short quiz, addressed mainly to managers: there is no time limit for completing the quiz. Getting the answers right, however, may be a matter of urgency.

1. Is there a strategy statement which links training provision to corporate aims?
2. Is the training strategy reviewed regularly?
3. Is senior manager involvement more than formal statements of support, and opening (or closing) remarks at training events? If so, what forms does it take?
4. What training and development do senior managers undertake to maintain or improve their own knowledge and skills? How are the benefits of this assessed?
5. What do senior managers do to ensure appropriate training and development of their immediate staff?
6. What do senior managers do to ensure that middle-level managers make appropriate training provision for their subordinates?
7. Do managers at all levels actively collaborate with trainers and reinforce learning through pre- and post-training briefings?
8. How well thought-of are the organization's trainers?
9. Is a period of secondment in training regarded as a positive career move – or as a dead end?
10. When business is declining, does the training budget get cut or increased?
11. Is the training department generally seen to be a provider of courses, or a problem-solving resource and a catalyst of change in the organization?
12. How is the training budget determined?
13. What kinds of justification are given for training expenditure?
14. Is training generally regarded as a cost or an investment?
15. Does the training department apply quality control measures to its own products and those it buys in from external providers of training?
16. What data do senior managers receive concerning the effectiveness of training activities?
17. Does the company's annual report include any statement about investment in training and development?

Figure 4.4 Corporate commitment to training

will employ evaluation techniques must themselves become skilled in their use. At the same time, changes are often needed at the level of policy leadership to create a climate in which evaluation is valued and given positive encouragement. The part played by the head of the training department in *actively* promoting systematic evaluation is very important.

The framework outlined in Figure 4.5 has proved successful in organizations where there are several trainers who can learn evaluation skills as a group. This learning approach can, of course, be adapted to the needs of the individual trainer and training manager.

Skills development	Organizational context

Initial workshop to open up debate and establish pilot evaluation projects.	*Policy measures*
	    Gaining commitment from policy-makers
	    Creating or re-targeting a dialogue with functional managers

In-depth acquisition of evaluation skills, especially by trainers responsible for course design.	Reviewing training strategy Establishing administrative procedures

Routine practice of systematic evaluation, plus updating of skills as necessary	*Leadership*
	    Active goal-setting
	    Rewarding evaluation activities
	    Acting on evaluation results

Figure 4.5 Introducing evaluation into an organization

APPRAISAL SYSTEMS

Formal systems of performance appraisal can sometimes provide a useful adjunct to training. Appraisal can be the opportunity for a constructive dialogue between manager and subordinate which can spotlight training and development needs. Appraisal subsequent to training can be an opportunity to review the outcomes from that activity. On the positive side, appraisal can help to make training a natural element of staff management.

The negative aspect of appraisal comes from two directions. The first is that appraisal may occur formally only once a year or even every two years. Of course, it is a sound principle that there should be no surprises in an annual appraisal, because in theory it reviews issues which will already have been discussed on an ad hoc basis as part of daily worklife. Nevertheless, there can be a tendency for discussion of training needs to be stored up for an annual binge. This may create an excessive lead time between the successive steps illustrated below:

> problem arises → appraisal occurs → training provided

The annual appraisal may also fall prey to 'menu-bashing'. Instead of emphasis on a diagnosis of learning needs, appraisal may be seen as an opportunity to browse through course brochures to pick out those events which have not yet been attended. This temptation increases where the appraisal itself is conducted badly, especially where appraisal concentrates on personal character traits rather than job-performance behaviours.

CONCLUSION

Considered design is central to effective training. Professional training uses a range of methods and media, and uses them in a way which rests on sound learning strategies.

However, it is equally imperative that the design stage is not mistaken for the *whole* of training preparation. Successful design rests upon accurately diagnosed needs and upon careful evaluation of what works well and what requires redesign. The judicious use of evaluation as a catalytic intervention strategy can lead to such quality improvements in the training delivered to the organization that further evaluation is required only on a low level of routine quality control. Effective evaluators can thus work themselves out of a job.

Part II
EVALUATION TECHNIQUES

5 Designing the evaluation project

There are several ways that the organization can set about gathering evaluation data. The least satisfactory, in the long-term, is to hand over the whole task to an external agent, either a consultant or an academic. The impact is usually limited to the particular training event that is examined, and the organizational culture remains unchanged. The trainers themselves may have a very limited sense of ownership of the evaluation, and may give little commitment to implementing changes based on its findings. More positively, the use of an external consultant means that the evaluation is more likely to be free from the bias of vested interests. For the smaller training function, external resourcing may be the only way to get the job done.

The academic may have a contribution to make through long-term research into evaluation methods and findings. The specialist consultant (and genuine evaluation specialists are only slightly less rare than hens' teeth) has a key role to play in training company staff to use evaluation techniques on a day-to-day basis. Both academics and consultants succeed to the extent that they help the client organization to continue to use evaluation routinely over a period of time, and do not merely carry out a token evaluation project which is then shelved to gather dust.

IS EVALUATION REALLY NECESSARY?

Can trainers or managers make do without evaluation of the worth of training? The question needs to be asked, because evaluation requires a commitment of resources and energy and may mean less time for training. Evaluation is never quite as scientifically objective as we might wish. Sometimes, too, organizational politics undermine the best-designed of studies. That said, even partially successful evaluation of training is usually worthwhile. Without it, trainers and managers are in the position of running hard without ever knowing how close the tape is – or even whether they are heading in the right direction. The process of starting evaluation offers real benefits both for the training department and for the organization itself: it is a perfect example of a win-win opportunity. And, not least, if trainers do not conduct serious evaluations of their work then others will do it for them.

WHERE TO BEGIN?

Organisations who have started to work seriously on evaluation have generally followed one of two patterns. Some larger training departments have established a small unit with overall responsibility for quality control in training. Others devolve responsibility for evaluation to each individual trainer or to specialist groups such as course designers. In either case, part of the evaluation responsibility may be placed with line management.

Managers need support in this role, from direct trainers or from an evaluation unit or evaluation consultant. This support can be part of a wider process of helping managers to play a more active joint role with trainers. Such collaboration helps to bridge the gap between learning activities and workplace practice. Action planning and critical incident analysis are evaluation techniques that are especially useful for involving managers in both the training itself and its evaluation.

In a third case, the training manager takes on the quality control role, often using evaluation as part of a process of upgrading the skills of field trainers, and making use of an external consultant as expert resource and catalyst.

HOW MUCH EVALUATION DO YOU NEED?

Time spent on evaluation is time taken away from course design or presentation. It is useful therefore to remember that not everything needs evaluating, nor does it need evaluating all the time. It is always worth asking 'Will the benefits gained from evaluating this training activity justify the effort?' However, if particular training activities are not working well and resources are going to waste, until some evaluation is made, you do not know with any accuracy how good or bad is the situation. There are some guidelines for deciding amongst priorities for evaluation. The key criteria are discussed below.

IMPORTANCE

What is the disaster potential if the training is not successful? For example, what might be the consequences of failing to test whether or not your safety training was effective?

FREQUENCY

How often will the training event that you are thinking of evaluating be run? Will the evaluation data arrive too late to be used to modify the activity? If the evaluation relates to a one-off event, is there useful information to be gathered which can be applied to different events, for example insights into the participants' preferred methods of learning. Projected trainee-hours or trainee-days for different training activities provide a 'frequency' measure for comparing alternative evaluation projects.

COST

This concerns the cost of the training activity (and the potential loss if the training is faulty) compared to the cost of evaluation. More extensive information usually means greater expense in its gathering and analysis. On the other hand, the law of diminishing returns may apply to the benefits from that information. Some information can be gathered quite inexpensively (e.g. by postal questionnaire), but will not answer the sort of question that requires the more costly use of interviews to gather adequate responses.

IMPACT

Will this evaluation project act as a catalyst for change or will it be greeted with yawns and 'we told you so'? When first introducing evaluation into an organization, there is a fine balance to be struck between the higher risk, higher impact approach of evaluating one of the 'sacred cows' of current training provision, against the lower risk but bland results of an uncontroversial evaluation subject.

On balance, when first starting to use evaluation systematically, it makes sense to begin evaluation with a relatively modest, fairly low-risk project which stands a good chance of succeeding. It is then easier to build on the momentum of success when you come to tackle more ambitious evaluation projects. The latter are essential if evaluation is to be a catalyst of change in management and training practices.

The concept of sampling can be adapted to the question of 'How much evaluation?' You can sample from the population of training courses of a particular type, for example, evaluating 1 in 4; you can operate a rolling programme that evaluates all training over a cycle of perhaps three years (any longer and the evaluation results will probably be too late to be useful).

THE POLITICS OF EVALUATION

An evaluator needs to be sensitive to organizational pressures. Sometimes it may be more important for an evaluation to be seen to be 'fair' than 'objective'. Political issues are inevitably involved in evaluation studies because evaluation data can always be

EVALUATION TECHNIQUES

used as a source of power. How the findings are used and to whom they are delivered can determine who will benefit and who will lose. This is particularly true where the purpose of the evaluation is control, for example management-commissioned evaluation of training, central evaluation of decentralized activities, or an evaluation of programmes run by an educational or training organization which is commissioned by the funding organization. Evaluation data should be presented in a way that makes it useful rather than threatening, but it is generally unrealistic to assert that the training product can be evaluated without also judging the trainer responsible. This probably accounts for much of the defensiveness among training practitioners when faced with proposals for evaluation.

Figure 5.1 provides a questionnaire to be used to review the 'political' issues affecting evaluation in your own organization.

STARTING TO DESIGN AN EVALUATION PROJECT

The components of any evaluation project are as follows:

1. For whom is the evaluation being undertaken? ('the client')
2. Which training activity is to be evaluated? ('the course' or other learning process)
3. What kind of judgement does the client want to make about the course? ('the criterion of worth', e.g. learning gain, behaviour change)
4. Who is likely to have information relevant to that criterion? ('the subjects', e.g. trainees, managers, customers)
5. What is the best technique you can use in the prevailing circumstances in order to gather the relevant information from the subjects and convey it in a useful form to the client? ('the technique', e.g. interview, questionnaire)
6. How long after the training should the evaluation occur – is it an immediate check on learning gain at the end of a course, or, say, a six-month follow-up on the use that has been made of the training back on the job? ('the timing')

These questions are summarized in Figure 5.2 which can be used as a working document.

PLANNING THE EVALUATION PROJECT

Figure 5.3 provides a detailed overview of the process of designing and implementing an evaluation project in flow chart form. The following commentary takes you through the process step-by-step.

Discuss the questions with colleagues and/or your manager. Revise your answers in the light of these discussions. (You may also wish to review your answers when you reach the end of this chapter.)

1. What benefits do you anticipate from the introduction of systematic evaluation

   a) in the short-term?

   b) in the long-term?

2. Who will be formally responsible for

   a) carrying out evaluation?

   b) acting on evaluation findings?

3. What part will the training manager/personnel manager/or equivalent be playing in the evaluation process?

4. Who (in training and/or in management) is enthusiastic or at least interested to see systematic evaluation of training carried out?

5. How many person days per year will each of the parties listed at 2, 3 and 4 allocate to evaluation activities?

6. What areas of training and evaluation do you see as offering an early, low-risk pay off?

7. How much evaluation is needed in your target areas (importance/frequency/cost/impact criteria)?

8. What obstacles do you anticipate to achieving your evaluation goals listed at 6?

9. What resources (people/materials/influence, etc.) are already available – or might be acquired – in order to overcome the obstacles listed at 8?

Figure 5.1 Planning the introduction of evaluation into an organization (continued)

EVALUATION TECHNIQUES

10. What would be more ambitious, longer term goals for evaluation?

11. What obstacles do you anticipate to achieving your longer term evaluation goals?

12. What resources are available – or might be acquired – in order to overcome the obstacles to your longer term evaluation goals?

13. Indicate realistic timescales for implementing various stages of evaluation:

    a) Initial pilot project(s)

    b) Developing competence in evaluation techniques

    c) Wider application of evaluation methods

Figure 5.1 Planning the introduction of evaluation into an organization (concluded)

1. For whom are you doing it?
2. Which particular training activity will provide the subject for the evaluation project?
3. What part of the training process do you want to assess?
4. Who is likely to have answers to your assessment questions?
5. What will be the appropriate evaluation technique for you to use?
6. What will be the best time to carry out the evaluation?

Figure 5.2 Evaluation projects – design issues

STEP 1

If you can see no benefits from carrying out evaluation then you have no incentive to put effort into it. You may find it useful to re-read the section on the benefits of

DESIGNING THE EVALUATION PROJECT

1. Do you anticipate any benefits from introducing evaluation in your own organization?
   - YES → 3
   - NO → 2. Stop here. Review the position in a few months times.

3. What are the main anticipated benefits?
4. Who are the principal audiences for evaluation?
5. Which criteria for judging the worth of training are significant to each of these audiences?
6. Do your audiences need to acquire an overview of evaluation concepts?
   - YES → 7. Organize an evaluation introductory workshop.
   - NO → 8
8. Who can most appropriately make judgements using the chosen criteria?
9. Who is formally responsible for training evaluation?
10. Are there any conflicts of responsibility to be resolved?
    - NO → 12
    - YES → 11. Organize an evaluation introductory workshop.
12. Who and what did you identify as resources for the evaluation process?
13. Are resources adequate to get started?
    - 1st NO → 14. Organize an evaluation introductory workshop for key decision-makers; lobby for resources.
    - 2nd NO → 15. Review formal responsibility for evaluation. Check anticipated benefits and the reality of the organization's commitment to evaluation. Lobby for the resources you need.
    - 3rd NO → 16. Reduce your ambitions or give up. Review the situation in a few months.
    - YES → 24

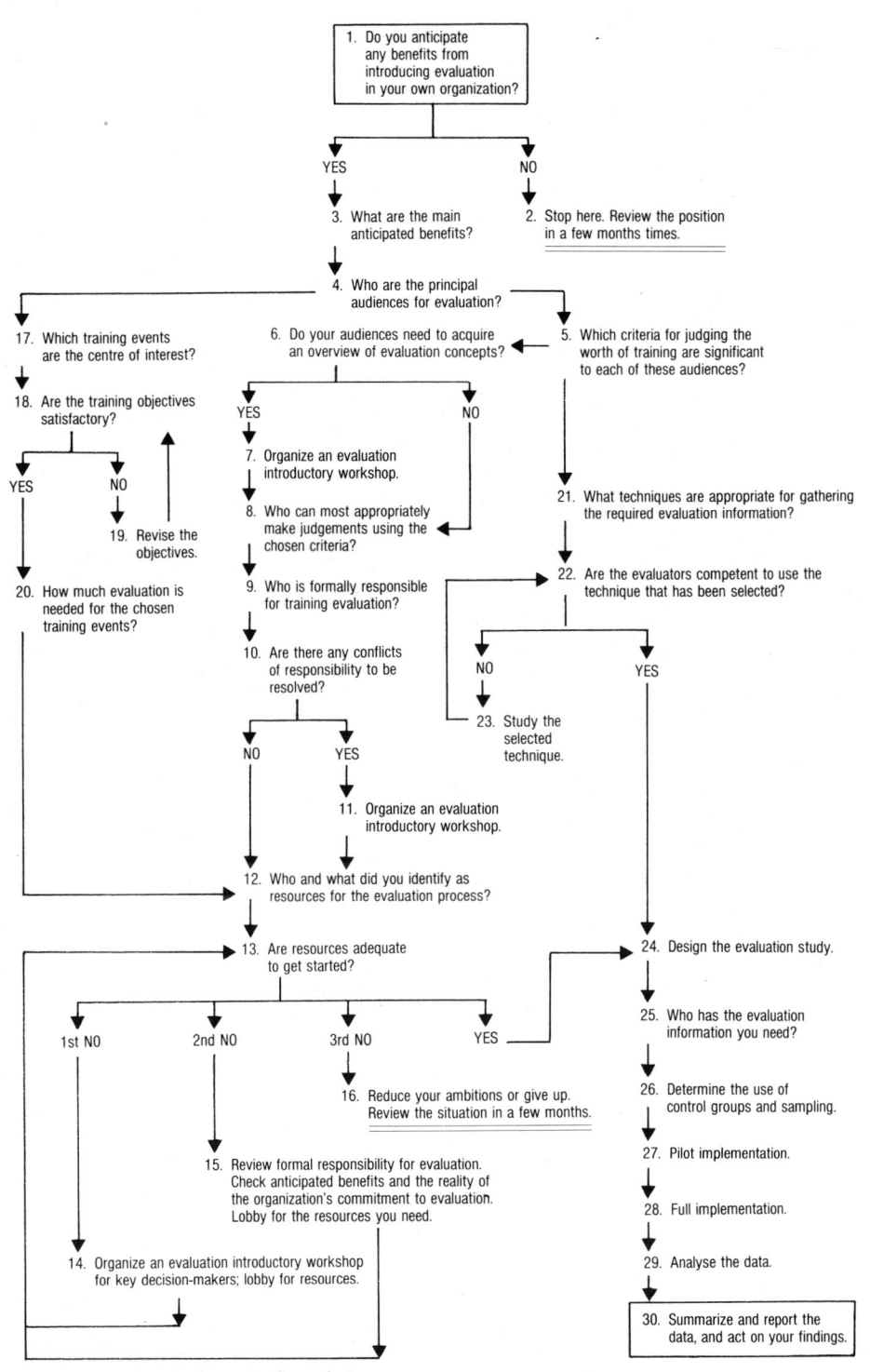

17. Which training events are the centre of interest?
18. Are the training objectives satisfactory?
    - YES → 20
    - NO → 19. Revise the objectives.
20. How much evaluation is needed for the chosen training events?

21. What techniques are appropriate for gathering the required evaluation information?
22. Are the evaluators competent to use the technique that has been selected?
    - NO → 23. Study the selected technique.
    - YES → 24
24. Design the evaluation study.
25. Who has the evaluation information you need?
26. Determine the use of control groups and sampling.
27. Pilot implementation.
28. Full implementation.
29. Analyse the data.
30. Summarize and report the data, and act on your findings.

Figure 5.3 Planning the evaluation project

evaluating training (p. 33–4). Consider the potential value to your own position from introducing systematic evaluation which you control. This pre-empts evaluation by other people on what may be inappropriate criteria.

STEP 2

It is advisable at regular intervals to review your decision not to evaluate. The climate of indulgence towards training in your organization may change quite suddenly – a new chief executive may bring a more rigorous attitude towards training budgets. Competitive difficulties may call for arbitrary cut-backs.

From a tactical point of view, the worst possible time to start systematic evaluation is *after* the value of training has come into question. A strong defence of training budgets requires an established track record, not a last desperate throw.

STEPS 3 AND 4

Using Figure 5.1 you have compiled a list of anticipated benefits and noted who would be the beneficiaries. This list will help you to decide where to focus evaluation efforts for maximum impact, for example trainers will be most interested in receiving the benefits of feedback on course content and methods; the safety officer will want to know how effective training has been in reducing unsafe working practices; the sales manager may be concerned about the level of sales or the mix of products sold.

STEP 5

For each beneficiary (or client) you have identified, determine what criteria they apply when judging the worth of training. Table 3.1 (p. 27) provides a summary of criteria, but it is a good practice – and also reinforces managers' and others' involvement in the training process – to ask people what criteria they wish to apply. Refer to Tables 3.1 and 3.2 (p. 27–8) to ensure that there are no mismatches between your clients, their criteria of worth, and the particular focus of evaluation with which you intend to work. Judgements about the effectiveness and worth of the training can be made within any of four frameworks:

a) Assessments of worth within the training event, for example 'How much has been learned?' or 'Have the chosen learning methods worked well?' These questions provide information of value to trainers, but also to trainees themselves.

b) Assessments made in the workplace after the training event, for example 'What new skills can the trained person demonstrate' or 'What helps or hinders the transfer into work behaviour of what was learnt?'

c) Assessments of the value of training in terms of indices of performance: operational indices (e.g. reduced wastage, improved quality); financial indices

DESIGNING THE EVALUATION PROJECT

(e.g. increased output for given resources); and personnel indices (e.g. fewer grievance claims, improved time-keeping).

d) Assessments of worth on criteria of social, moral, political, or philosophical values, for example an evaluation of an equal opportunities programme.

STEPS 6 AND 7

It is common for potential audiences for evaluation data to have a very limited view of the range of evaluation criteria that may be relevant, and to see evaluation entirely in terms of end of course reactions, or else in terms of an idealized cost-benefit analysis. The evaluator can broaden the basis of evaluation discussions and at the same time generate resources and support for what is to be done, by running a short workshop on the broad principles of training evaluation.

STEP 8

Given your audience and their criteria for the value of training, establish who is in the best position to make the judgements. For example, job-transfer effects of training often can only be assessed by the learner's line manager or, sometimes, by colleagues or subordinates. End of course feedback on the training event itself is better provided by the learners than the trainers. (It is also better if someone other than the trainers collects the end of course information). Table 3.1 provides a summary of who can best judge what.

STEP 9

Formal responsibility for evaluation should be clearly vested in particular individuals. Who is responsible for design, for gathering data, for analysis, for acting on the findings? Figure 5.1 clarified these questions for you.

Much depends on the scale of training activity in the organization. Large training units may have a specialist individual or even a section devoted to evaluation work. Others may designate one, usually senior member of the training staff as the specialist resource and adviser on evaluation matters. In other situations, every trainer may be given the responsibility for building evaluation into his or her programmes. At the other end of the scale, the one-person training department will need to do everything – design, administer, run and evaluate training.

STEPS 10 AND 11

If there are disagreements over any aspects of responsibility for evaluation these must be resolved before going any further or they will return time and again to undermine evaluation efforts. An introductory evaluation seminar is a good vehicle for airing the issues and clarifying responsibilities.

EVALUATION TECHNIQUES

STEPS 12, 13 AND 20

With the help of Figure 5.1 you have identified whatever resources are available to you to help implement evaluation. Review your list of resources, taking into account the decisions you have reached about how much evaluation is required and which priority areas will yield fairly low-risk and rapid returns. Resourcing of evaluation is the issue, more than any other, which sorts the organizations that are serious about evaluation from those which pay lip-service to it.

STEP 14

In Figure 5.3, it is possible to pass Step 13 three times (each time with diminishing expectations and rising cynicism). The first occasion on which you determine that resources are inadequate is one of the best opportunities to arise in the process of introducing evaluation. It is an opportunity precisely because it creates a basis for involving line managers and policy-makers in the evaluation process. It gives you the justification to run introductory workshops on evaluation strategy and the chance to build commitment and resources for your proposals.

Following such a workshop (or workshops), again review the adequacy of your resources. It is quite likely that the workshop will have articulated and clarified other people's expectations and you may need to revise your resource requirements because perceived needs have changed.

STEP 15

If you conclude for the second time that resource provision is totally unrealistic for what you want to achieve or for what the organization is asking you to do there is evidently some mismatch in expectation.

Review the formal responsibility for evaluation. Are there other people who could usefully become involved? Do the people who want to see evaluation data hold different views to the people who control finance?

Check whether the anticipated benefits of evaluation still fit the situation. Lobby the people who stand to benefit the most. If you appear to be the sole beneficiary, then you have probably not taken the step beyond looking at evaluation in terms of how it improves the quality of the trainer's output, to show that better training has benefits for other parts of the organization. Again, lobby for the resources you need.

STEP 16

If you are still facing seriously inadequate resourcing, *give up*. Your organization does not care whether or not its training is effective or represents value for money. You have put a lot of energy into getting this far and no blame should attach to you. The place where you work is not ready to grasp the benefits you can offer.

However, do not despair. In six months time, some of the seeds you have sown will probably begin to sprout. Experience suggests that with something as new as systematic evaluation most organizations need some time to digest the ideas and come to terms with their practical implications. Meanwhile you can make progress within the areas that you control. You can run one or two low-resource projects, review the design of your end of course reactionnaires, and continue to build support amongst line managers. Your own development as a professional trainer need not stop. You can make yourself completely familiar with the whole range of evaluation techniques that are open to you.

In parallel with the sequence of stages from (3) to (16), there are two other activity routes which need to be followed. One is the sequence (17) to (20) and the other is stages (21) to (30).

STEP 17

As well as the need to identify your principal clients for evaluation data and the criteria of worth that are significant to each, you also need to identify specific training activities which will provide a vehicle for evaluation efforts. The importance of the training and the frequency with which it will recur are the key considerations. However, there may also be political considerations which create pressure to work on a particular programme which would otherwise be a low priority for evaluation, or, conversely, *not* to evaluate a programme which would be a good candidate for the process. Evaluation, like politics, is the art of the possible.

STEP 18

Once the target training activities have been specified, you need to review whether the objectives are sufficiently precise to allow evaluation. This is the point at which the retrospective addition of evaluation to an existing programme can become a rather laborious business, if the objectives are inadequately specified and now have to be revised. It really is a great economy of effort to build evaluation into training activities at the earliest point in the design process.

STEP 19

This stage involves revising objectives. The golden rule is this: if a person of average intelligence (who is not a training specialist) cannot grasp from the statement of objectives what it is that the training is intended to achieve, then evaluation of learning outcomes will prove exceedingly difficult.

STEP 20

Review the depth of evaluation you require for each targeted training activity. You may require a large sample to be asked a few basic questions. Others may need quite lengthy interviews with a small, selected sample. It depends on what kinds of information are required, that is, on who your audiences are and what are their criteria of worth.

STEP 21

Table 5.1 enables you to cross-refer from the selected area of evaluation to one or more appropriate techniques. The main evaluation techniques covered in Part II are indicated by capitals.

STEP 22 AND 23

If the technique is one familiar to the person carrying out the evaluation, then the task can progress to the design stage. If it is unfamiliar, for each technique step-by-step guidelines on how it is to be implemented are provided in the relevant chapter of this book. These can be employed as self-study guides or as the basis for a practical workshop for a group of trainers.

STEPS 24 TO 30

The final sequence of stages will vary in content according to the techniques chosen and the emphasis of the evaluation. The order of events from (24) through to (30) is however, common to all techniques, and there are a few general points to consider.

STEP 25

Before embarking on any survey or assessment, reflect on whether your questions are being addressed to the people who are most likely to have answers to give you. Sometimes these people will be managers, sometimes the trainees, or third parties such as customers or colleagues.

STEP 27

The value of pilot implementation is considerable: a critical appraisal of an initial small-scale use of an evaluation instrument often enables 'bugs' to be eliminated which would otherwise undermine the value of the main application.

Where a questionnaire, interview schedule or test is piloted, the pilot use must be a valid indication of what is likely to happen in the general use of the evaluation instrument. Individual questions and test items are sometimes applied to training activities which are different to the activities for which the item was designed originally. This must be undertaken with caution: each item has to be considered on its merits. Evaluation instruments cannot be transferred from one subject of training to another without careful review and any necessary modification.

DESIGNING THE EVALUATION PROJECT

Table 5.1 Component elements of evaluation and techniques

Areas of evaluation and their component elements	Techniques*
1. *Within the training event*	
a) Judgements about the quality of the trainees' experience during training	SESSIONAL REACTIONNAIRES; EVENT REACTIONNAIRES; group discussion; individual comment
b) Feedback to trainees concerning their learning achievement	WRITTEN TESTS; BEHAVIOUR OBSERVATION; REPERTORY GRID; PRACTICAL TESTS; video/audio recording; programmed learning; computer-based training
c) Measures of change during training	Pre/post use of WRITTEN TESTS, BEHAVIOUR OBSERVATION, PRACTICAL TESTS; REPERTORY GRID; attitude scales
d) Feedback to trainers concerning learning methods	SESSIONAL REACTIONS FORMS; TESTS OF LEARNING GAIN (FROM 1.a) or 1.c)); EVALUATION INTERVIEW
e) Assessment of terminal competence	OBJECTIVE TESTS; BEHAVIOUR OBSERVATION; PRACTICAL TEST; ESSAY; oral examination
2. *In the workplace*	
a) Matching the learning goals to the needs originally specified	QUESTIONNAIRE; performance appraisal reviews; EVALUATION INTERVIEWS
b) Use of learning or changes in work task behaviours	ACTION PLANNING; BEHAVIOUR OBSERVATION; CRITICAL INCIDENT ANALYSIS; EVALUATION INTERVIEWS; QUESTIONNAIRES; appraisal performance review; self-apprisal; pre/post sampling of work activities, work quality, and/or quantity; participant observation
c) Feedback to trainers on learning methods and training strategy	Data from 1.d) combined with EVALUATION INTERVIEW; COMPARATIVE ANALYSIS OF COST-EFFECTIVENESS OF ALTERNATIVES; QUESTIONNAIRES
d) Factors affecting the use made of learning in the workplace	Data from 2.b) combined with EVALUATION INTERVIEW
e) Individual learning & development	EVALUATION INTERVIEW; REPERTORY GRID; self-analysis; personality inventories
3. *Organizational effectiveness*	
a) Changes in organizational performance	ANALYSES OF PERFORMANCE INDICES – operational measures (e.g. output quality or quantity, wastage or spoilage, sales volume, equipment downtime, accident rates, expressed customer satisfaction, reduced complaints); financial measures (e.g. unit costs, return on investment); manpower measures (e.g. turnover, absenteeism, organizational climate)
b) Trainee implementation of individual action plans or projects	REVIEWS (INDIVIDUAL OR GROUP-BASED) OF PROGRESS IN IMPLEMENTING PLANS OR PROJECTS (this may usefully be combined with evaluation activity 2.d)
c) Cost-effectiveness of training	COSTING; COST-BENEFIT ANALYSIS; COST-EFFECTIVENESS ANALYSIS
d) Congruence of training and organizational mission/strategies	INTERVIEW; content analysis of formal and operative policies
4. *Social, cultural (etc.)*	
a) Contribution of training to national prosperity	COST-BENEFIT ANALYSIS
b) Social costs and benefits	COST-BENEFIT ANALYSIS, values analysis
c) Ethical, philosophical, or political rationales for training	Surveys of organizational climate; statistical indicators of socio-economic change; human resource accounting

Note: *Techniques covered in Part II of this book are shown in capitals.

STEP 28

The timing of evaluation is a question to be resolved for each specific application. If a follow-up study occurs too soon after the course, people may have had little or no opportunity to practise new skills; too late, and the course learning may have been forgotten unless it has been reinforced through regular practice. The follow-up survey on a course should determine the number of occasions on which participants have had an opportunity to use what was learned, and how long an interval elapsed between the course and that use. The former has implications for who receives training, the latter for when the training should, optimally, be given.

STEP 29

How you will analyse the data is something that should be considered at an early planning stage, for example so that questionnaire responses can be used as direct input to computer analysis. Guidance on data analysis is provided later in this chapter.

STEP 30

Finally, the most important of all stages, action. The evaluation findings should be acted upon – and be seen to be acted upon. Nothing contributes more to cynicism about evaluation than the collection of data which then merely gathers dust.

CHOOSING EVALUATION TECHNIQUES

APTNESS FOR PURPOSE

The choice of evaluation technique is firstly decided by the aptness of the technique for the intended evaluation purpose. For example, to assess the ability to do a technical task, a practical test is likely to be the appropriate means; to assess an interpersonal skill, some form of behaviour observation; to arrive at an understanding of how a person has made use of a training activity, only interview is likely to allow the necessary exploration of the trainee's thought processes.

Conversely, it would not be the most appropriate means to use a written test to assess interpersonal behaviour or a written questionnaire to gather sensitive feedback such as comments about managerial support post-training. The linkages between different areas of evaluation and appropriate techniques is summarized in Table 5.1. A different way of making these linkages is provided by Table 5.2 which correlates evaluation techniques with the type of training to be assessed.

EVALUATOR SKILLS

A second important consideration is the skill of the evaluator. This is an issue of particular concern whenever evaluation calls for a skill that is superficially similar to,

Table 5.2 Types of training subject and evaluation techniques

Training subject	Evaluation technique
Knowledge of facts	Written tests
Knowledge of procedures	Practical test Behaviour observation
Interpersonal skills	Behaviour observation Critical incident method Repertory grid
Psycho-motor skills	Practical tests
Application of knowledge or skills at work	Action planning review Critical incident method Performance indices Questionnaire

but not in fact the same as a skill used in other kinds of personnel or training work. For example, the ability to conduct an effective job selection interview is not a reliable indicator of the ability to conduct a non-directive evaluation interview. Training of evaluators must always be a consideration when planning projects.

The skill issue also comes to the fore when the evaluation process is delegated to people other than the evaluation designer – whether to other trainers or to line managers. Effort must be made to 'fool-proof' the design through pilot testing, and to ensure that the evaluation agents conform to instructions. There is a tendency for other people's agendas to creep into the evaluation process, especially where a method such as interview is used, with the result that the evaluation questions may be subverted or subordinated to the concerns and needs of the agent.

Sometimes agents are anxious not to upset people whom they see as key clients (or to whom they defer as influential seniors) and therefore steer away from awkward questions. Sometimes agents will add in wholly unrelated questions of their own because the interview has allowed them access to people with whom they normally do not have contact. Agents with low ownership of the project may argue against the answers given by interviewees; I have even encountered situations where agents have told interviewees that they do not agree with the purpose of the evaluation and have then proceeded to substitute the agent's own view of that purpose. In other instances, agents have created their own summaries of data that neither conform to the required format for further analysis, nor even reflect accurately what has been said to them.

ACCEPTABILITY TO SUBJECTS

The technique chosen – and the way in which the technique is used – must not alienate the subjects of the study (most commonly, the trainees). The evaluator needs to take account of the subjects' literacy, verbal facility, command of English, their capacity to

EVALUATION TECHNIQUES

be introspective about their learning experiences, their ability to think in behavioural terms and their capacity for making subtle distinctions (or their lack of such). For example, there may be occasions when interview has to be substituted for questionnaire, simply because of illiteracy amongst respondents. Sometimes a pictorial method of conveying test information may be necessary, rather than a word-based test.

ACCEPTABILITY TO THE ORGANIZATION

The chosen technique needs to reflect culture, previous history, industrial relations climate, and any previous exposure to either evaluation or to the technique in question. It does not help response rates if your evaluation questionnaire is the fourth questionnaire-type document to arrive from head office this month.

RESOURCING

The choice of technique also depends upon the resources available to the evaluator, for example, the choice between evaluation interviews which require much skilled labour and questionnaires which require much semi-skilled labour.

SECONDARY BENEFITS

Although it should not be the primary factor determining choice of technique, it is sometimes worth weighing the secondary benefits from a particular evaluation tool. For example, pre-tests can act as an aid to needs analysis, as can repertory grid. Action plans not only provide a basis for follow-up evaluation but also for follow-up reinforcement of learning. Field interviewing for evaluation purposes sometimes carries a valuable public relations bonus for trainers who are seen to be 'getting out and about' and to be listening to feedback.

MULTIPLE TECHNIQUES

Sometimes more than one technique will be needed. The evaluator may want to know whether or not the training itself is working – requiring a pre/post assessment of learning – and whether or not newly acquired skills are transferring into work practice – for which behaviour observation might be an appropriate response. The assessment can then be taken a further stage by conducting a cost-benefit analysis to judge whether what has been achieved is worthwhile.

ANALYSING THE DATA

Except when dealing with very small numbers of people at a purely anecdotal level, the evaluator needs to be able to summarize and analyse the data that has been collected. Always give some thought at the project design stage to the question of how

DESIGNING THE EVALUATION PROJECT

Question: Did you receive any pre-course briefing?

Responses:	Briefing by manager	8
	Briefing by training department	15
	Briefing by other person	3
	No briefing received	6

(Example assumes that 32 questionnaires were returned)

Figure 5.4 Simple frequency analysis (I)

Question: How many months have you been employed in your present job?

Less than 12	12–35	36–59	60 & over
4	5	4	8

Figure 5.5 Simple frequency analysis (II)

you intend to analyse the data that you are intending to collect. The worst time to contemplate this question is when you are already knee-deep in returned questionnaires or facing a hundred hours of interview tapes. Design your instruments so that it will be easy to read off responses. If your computer system permits it and the material consists of closed multi-choice type items, consider the use of bar codes printed alongside the questionnaire or test answers; linked to a suitable statistical package, you can easily get rapid data analysis and summary of test results.

In the case of test material, the data summary will usually be the test score itself, based upon the marking scheme, and further analysis may then be applied (as described in Appendix II, p. 245) to compare individual or group scores, or to analyse the effectiveness of the test items themselves. In the case of data collected by methods such as interview, action plan review, critical incident, and questionnaire, the summary of data cannot be simply a matter of adding up the number of responses of a particular type. First, the actual responses, or raw data provided by respondents must be sorted and classified before proceeding to frequency counts and statistical analyses. The data matrix provides a tool for doing this. At its simplest, the matrix summarizes the number of responses given for each possible answer (see Figure 5.4).

The matrix can be made more complex and the analysis more informative by distinguishing amongst the categories of respondents as well as amongst the types of response (see Figures 5.5 and 5.6). The two examples can then be combined into a single matrix such as that shown in Table 5.3.

73

EVALUATION TECHNIQUES

Question: Please indicate the extent of any briefing that subordinates receive before attending training events.

Responses:	I brief them	9
	Someone else briefs them	5
	No briefing is given	7

Figure 5.6 Simple frequency analysis (III)

	\multicolumn{4}{c}{Length of service (months)}
	Under 12	12–35	36–59	60+
Manager provides briefing	4	3	1	1
Other person provides briefing	0	0	2	3
No briefing provided	0	2	1	4

Figure 5.7 More complex analysis (combining II and III)

When coding raw data into the data matrix, there are two steps which will reduce errors in classifying information. The first is to use what is called a coding frame and the second is to ensure inter-coder reliability. A coding frame is a set of rules that specify how raw data are to be classified into categories for subsequent numerical analysis. The set of categories represents the alternative ways of classifying all possible acceptable answers to a given question. The categories must follow from the concepts that underlie each of the questions in the evaluation study (or, put more plainly, the way you sort the answers must reflect the reasons why you asked the question).

For any one question, the categories into which responses are to be classified must meet two criteria:

1. The categories must be mutually exclusive, that is to say, there must be no overlap of meaning or content between one category and another, no ambiguity about the boundaries between categories.
2. The set of categories for each question must exhaust all possible options for acceptable answers (a requirement which will often be covered by an option to answer 'other – please specify').

'Inter-coder reliability' refers to the importance of ensuring that, where more than one person is involved in classifying raw data, the different people involved with all categorize the data in the same way. The categories should be drawn up in such a way as to eliminate scope for individual interpretation; the coders should be trained so that they understand the meaning of each question and of the acceptable response options.

Especially when codifying answers to open questions, a proportion of responses should be independently 'double-marked'. Any discrepant interpretations should be examined and the cause eliminated.

Categorizing the responses to open questions is helped by working within the following rules:

1. Begin by categorizing one or two tapes (or response sheets) and then ask someone else independently to analyse the same raw data; compare interpretations and categorization.
2. Use respondents' actual words or short phrases, even sentences, as a prelude to categorization; take care not to distort the subject's views either by over-simplifying or by imposing (consciously or not) your own opinions, or your expectations of what the subject would be 'likely' to say.
3. Group key phrases identified at Step 2 into internally consistent categories that then form part of the data matrix.
4. Occasionally carry out further double-analyses as a check that coding remains consistent and accurate.
5. Never ignore any differences of interpretation – the probability is that such differences reflect different, as yet unidentified, categories. Clarity and precision are essential to meaningful evaluation and blurred categories are as misleading and futile as traditional happy sheets.

DESCRIPTIVE STATISTICS

Sometimes evaluation data will be used without further statistical analysis as descriptive case studies or as simple reports of test scores. More usually, it is useful to apply statistical analysis in order to make statements about how 'typical', how 'varied', etc. might be any example drawn from the surveyed population. The calculation of the various kinds of measure is described in Appendix II, p. 245. Figure 5.8 summarizes the types of descriptive statistic that may be useful to the evaluator.

THE EVALUATION REPORT

The evaluation report should be in a format that encourages people to read it and to act upon its conclusions. Clear, concise, plain English should be the rule. A straightforward 'middlebrow' journalistic style is preferable to ponderous formality or pseudo-academicism. Jargon, evasion and ambiguity should be avoided: there should be no doubt about what the report says and what are the implications of those conclusions. Facts and opinions should be clearly distinguished and labelled as such.

EVALUATION TECHNIQUES

---

1. Measures of what is 'typical' of the sample:
   1.1 If the category has been measured on an *equal interval* scale then the artihmetic mean is appropriate.
   1.2 If the response categories can be put in *order of magnitude*, but do not form an equal interval scale, then the median (midpoint value) should be used.
   1.3 If the response categories do not form a scale from lesser to greater (a *nominal scale*) as, for example, with multi-choice alternatives, the proper measure is the mode (or most frequent value).

2. Measures of how widely individual people or cases within a group vary from the 'average':
   2.1 The extremes of the variation are shown by the range.
   2.2 Quartile deviation (based on the medium) shows those points within which the central half of cases fall.
   2.3 The average deviation of any individual case from the group mean is calculated using the formula for standard deviation.

3. Measures of how individual cases are distributed in relation to another variable:
   3.1 Graphing the distribution curve which may reveal the 'normal' bell-shaped curve, an asymmetrically skewed pattern, or a straight-line relationship.

4. Measures of the way in which changes in one or more variables produce changes in another variable:
   4.1 Calculation of the Pearson correlation coefficient.

5. Measures of the differences between sets of frequencies (such as test results, occurrences of behaviour, etc.):
   5.1 Application of the chi-squared test to the data.

6. Measure of the limitations of generalizing from a sample to the population from which it has been drawn:
   6.1 Tests of significance.

Figure 5.8 Summary of descriptive statistics

A suggested framework for the evaluation report is as follows:

1. Contents list, followed by any general introductory preface (e.g. a statement of endorsement by a senior manager).
2. A brief summary of the main conclusions and recommendations.
3. A short statement summarizing the core elements of the project – who the client is, which training activity forms the focus of attention, what evaluation criteria are significant for the client, what evaluation technique(s) have been employed, who has conducted the evaluation.
4. The main text of the report, comprising:
   a) a summary of each finding;
   b) an interpretation of that finding;
   c) a proposal for action arising from each finding.
5. Concluding remarks: possibly including general observations upon the process of conducting evaluation in that organization; comments on the value to be obtained from systematic evaluation; exhortations to managers to mend their wicked ways; etc.

DESIGNING THE EVALUATION PROJECT

6. Appendices. It depends upon the amount of detailed information that you wish to convey to your audience (and also upon the impression of 'weight' you wish to create) as to whether or not methodological descriptions and raw data are to be included in the document. Optional appendix material may include the following:

   a) A description of the techniques used for gathering data, including the evaluation instruments used, details of sample size and similar technical issues.
   b) The raw data from which the analytical summaries have been drawn (but note here the importance of maintaining guarantees of anonymity given to respondents when collecting the data).
   c) Where applicable, extended case studies drawn from the data.

Having completed the report, there remains the task of building support for the changes proposed as a result of the study. Useful questions to ask are:

- Who might benefit from the proposals?
- What are the financial benefits from the proposals?
- What are the formal lines of authority on your proposal?
- What are the anticipated obstacles?
- What might be done to overcome or work around such obstacles?

Achieving organizational change on the basis of evaluation studies is ultimately no different to achieving it from any other starting point. Although evaluation data will give you a rational underpinning from which to promote change, the process of achieving it is still a political one that involves all the usual issues of vested interests, resourcing, lobbying, and use of the informal structure of communications and influence.

6 The questionnaire

The evaluation questionnaire and the evaluation interview are often thought of as alternative ways of gathering the same kinds of evaluation data. The choice of technique is then regarded as a pragmatic weighing of available time and preferred style of working. However, each method has its own strengths in particular applications, and its balancing limitations. These pros and cons are summarized in Tables 6.1 and 6.2.

Fitness for purpose should be the deciding criterion. The choice of method should be determined by the kind of evaluation data that you need to collect, albeit tempered on occasion by expediency. Most commonly, shortage of time, or lack of relevant experience, will steer evaluators away from use of interview. Conversely, in organizational cultures which exhibit a strong antipathy to paperwork, questionnaires may be ignored, and interview may be the only way to acquire adequate data.

In some situations the two methods should both be used in order to gather complementary aspects of the data. For example, a questionnaire may be used to collect basic information from a sample of trainees. It may then be supplemented by interviews which focus on particular issues or follow up in-depth certain of the answers to the questionnaires. Another joint application of the two techniques is to employ interviews as a way of refining draft questions before they are included in a questionnaire.

Telephone interviewing is a variant form that shares some of the advantages and some of the disadvantages of both methods. It is relatively cheap to administer and avoids the costs and travel time incurred by interviewing. Response rates are usually good and the data is gathered relatively quickly. However, it is much harder to establish rapport with the interviewee and most of the non-verbal clues to a respondent's opinions and feelings are lost. It is usually difficult to sustain a telephone interview for as long as a face-to-face interview so the range of questions used tends of necessity to be narrower and the opportunities for follow-up probing are diminished.

WHEN TO USE QUESTIONNAIRES

Questionnaires may be used in the following applications:

Table 6.1 Comparison of strengths of questionnaire and interview

Questionnaire	Face-to-face interview	Telephone interview
Comparatively low unit cost	Better response levels can be achieved, though usually on smaller samples	Comparatively low unit cost
Allows responses to be gathered from large samples	Allows unanticipated lines of enquiry to be pursued	Enables use of a larger sample within a given timescale
More straightforward coding of data	Most suitable method where open questions are needed	Convenient where respondents are geographically scattered
Greater anonymity is possible		Can yield better response levels than questionnaire
Comparatively quickly administered: can be made machine readable		Does allow some probing and follow-up to questions
Convenient where respondents are geographically scattered		Questions can be explained and understanding checked
May avoid interviewer bias: selective questioning and listening errors		
Most suitable method where closed questions are needed		

Table 6.2 Limitations of questionnaire and interview

Questionnaire	Interview	Telephone interview
May yield a low rate of response and/or require much follow up 'chasing' to recover data	Comparatively high cost	More time-consuming than questionnaire at data-collection and data-analysis stages
Information depends on respondents' abilities to analyse their own situation and their personal attributes and mental processes: they must possess fairly clear views which can be expressed simply	Time-consuming to conduct interviews and to analyse the data: this usually restricts sample size	Harder for interviewers to establish a good rapport with respondents
Questions must be restricted to those which do not exceed the level of literacy possessed by respondents	Depends upon the skills of the interviewer to draw out responses	
Inflexibility: it is less easy to change the content of an established questionnaire design		
There is a risk of over-simplifying data and of losing useful insights that may be excluded by the closed question designs that are to be preferred in questionnaires		
The design of effective questions and the pilot testing of questionnaires is time consuming		

- Reviewing the match between training objectives and job tasks.
- Assessing application of new knowledge or skills to the trained person's work.
- Obtaining feedback on the preferred learning methods of participants and their opinions of the effectiveness of the trainer's chosen strategy and methods.

Once the decision has been made to employ a questionnaire as the most appropriate evaluation technique there are six steps to be followed:

1. Decide what you want to know.
2. Draft the questionnaire.
3. Pilot the draft instrument and redraft it as necessary.
4. Implement fully, with a defined sample drawn from the total relevant population.
5. Analyse the data.
6. Report the findings.

WHAT DO YOU WANT TO KNOW?

The question you should ask yourself is *'What do I really need to know?'* One important factor which affects the response to questionnaires is length: more is less; shorter questionnaires produce higher response rates, other things being equal. When you have drawn up your initial list of questions go through it and ruthlessly prune the number of items.

It is usually a mistake to include 'nice to know' questions. There is quite a lot of work involved in producing and distributing a questionnaire, and therefore it is tempting to put in extra questions on subjects not directly connected with the evaluation. However, the questionnaire should always be kept as short and specific as possible if respondents' resistance to completing it is to be minimized.

Watch out for questions that seek the same information using different words. It is a useful test to ask yourself what sorts of answer you expect to get from each of your questions. This will help pinpoint overlapping questions, as well as any ambiguously worded item. Occasionally, you may wish to retain duplicated questions: more or less equivalent questions do allow you to check for the consistency of responses. However, they inevitably make the document longer and respondents may notice the similarity of certain questions and resent your attempt to catch them out.

The kinds of information you are seeking must be information which your respondents (the people who complete the questionnaire) are in fact able to give you. There is no point in asking people questions on matters outside their knowledge and experience. When drafting and piloting the questionnaire be sensitive to regional, occupational, or social class differences of vocabulary. Also recognize that individuals differ in their capacity for abstract thought.

Your choice of questions will also reflect the criteria of worth that are important to the client for whom you are conducting the evaluation.

DRAFTING THE QUESTIONNAIRE

There are three aspects to the design of a questionnaire: the sequencing of the questionnaire, the way in which questions are formulated, and the substantive content of questions. First, one general point about layout: design the questionnaire so that it can be used as a direct input document to your computer system. Bar-coding of response alternatives will ease the number-crunching aspects of data analysis.

SEQUENCING

The first thing a respondent should see is an explanation of the reasons for his or her involvement in the enquiry. Postal surveys require a covering letter. A standard verbal introduction should precede supervised completion of the questionnaire. The purpose is to encourage the cooperation of respondents so that they will answer the questionnaire seriously. If respondents believe that their contribution matters – it will be taken seriously and not just filed away – they are more likely to put some serious thought into their answers.

The next item in sequence is the instructions for completion of the questionnaire. Instructions should be clear and concise. Sources of potential confusion must be checked. For example, sometimes an instruction will appear part way through a questionnaire to guide respondents past certain questions which are not relevant to them. The positioning of such an instruction is critical.

The order in which the questions themselves are placed can affect response content and response rates. It is a good general rule to move from more general to more specific questions on each particular theme and from the more familiar to the less familiar. It is also advisable to start a questionnaire with fairly innocuous questions, for example biographical and job information. Responses to earlier questions tend to be less reliable; the same is true of later questions in a long questionnaire where responses may become mechanical or inaccurate. In a long questionnaire it can help to break up the questions into different sections, with varying layouts to introduce some visual relief.

Questions that concern one particular aspect of the training under evaluation should be grouped together. Within each grouping the questions should follow an order that makes psychological sense to respondents. It is often easier for a respondent to answer a question about attitudes after the specific facts to which the attitude relates have been established. Questions that follow the time sequence of past events can help recall.

Where a group of questions applies selectively to only some respondents, the first question in the group should be drafted so as to differentiate between those who need to answer the rest of that group and those who can jump to the next item relevant to themselves.

FORMULATING QUESTIONS: GENERAL GUIDELINES

It is valuable at the drafting stage to hold a few loosely structured interviews with people who closely resemble the target group for the proposed questionnaire. The benefit of an interview is that it helps you to explore in an open-ended way what sorts of response are likely, given the subject of your evaluation. It enables you to convert *open questions* (which as a rule are better handled in an interview) into *closed questions* (which are the type most suited to questionnaires).

Open-ended questions present an invitation to the respondent to state whatever facts and opinions appear relevant and significant to the topic in question. They are necessary when the range of possible alternative answers is not known. Analysis of open-ended questions is much more time-consuming than analysis of closed questions, precisely because of the variety of potential answers. Closed questions are designed so as to obtain a single specific answer (or choice amongst several specified options). Closed questions are more easily answered and analysed.

Open questions should whenever possible be converted to closed questions for use in questionnaires. For example:

Open

How much experience do you have as a customer service engineer?

Closed

How much experience do you have as a customer service engineer?		
Under 6 months	☐	
Over 6 months and under 1 year	☐	*(tick*
1–2 years	☐	*one*
3–4 years	☐	*box)*
Over 4 years	☐	

The questions you include should be relevant to the purpose of the evaluation. Do resist the temptation to add extra questions that are not central to the task in hand.

The way in which you word your questions must be absolutely clear and unambiguous. Never take it for granted that someone else will understand by your question the same ideas that you understand it to cover. Even before pilot implementation of a questionnaire try out your draft questions on colleagues and trainees. Make a note of everything you find you have to clarify or discuss; the final questionnaire will have to stand (or fall) on the printed word alone.

EVALUATION TECHNIQUES

Aim for precision and specificity in your questions. Words such as 'frequently', 'most', 'sometimes' will without fail be interpreted differently by different respondents.

Avoid negative questions and, of course, double negatives. Instead of asking 'Why do you not carry out preventive maintenance?', ask 'Do you carry out preventive maintenance: Yes/No?' and 'What determines whether you carry out preventive maintenance?'

Use impersonal language with no emotional overtones that would bias the replies. Loaded questions contain an implicit bias either in the choice of wording, or (a common problem in multiple-choice designs) in the choice of permitted alternatives. For example, the question 'Which of the following routine aspects of your job benefited from the training event?' contains two loaded presuppositions: first, that the respondent does in fact see the job tasks as 'routine' and, second, that the training produced benefits. A multiple-choice question might ask:

How useful did you find the training session on marketing policy?

Very useful	☐	(*tick*
Useful	☐	*one*
Moderately useful	☐	*box*)

However, the significant response here might be the number of people who – given the choice – would have selected the excluded option 'Not at all useful'.

Some words are loaded with external associations that affect responses to the subject in question – words like 'independent', 'working class', 'practical or theoretical', 'interference'. Give respondents *clear permission* to say what *they* want to say, not what you (or your client) thinks they ought to say.

Beware of double-barrelled questions. These are questions where the respondent may wish to answer one way, e.g. 'yes' (or 'badly') to one part of the question and 'no' (or 'well') to the other part. If the two parts are combined it is difficult to give any answer and equally difficult to make sense of the responses that are given. An example of a double question would be: 'When you make file amendments are you closely supervised or do you rely on system checks?'

One significant source of resistance to evaluation by learners is a belief that their responses are being manipulated to produce outcomes which match the trainer's requirements. Leading questions must be resisted. These are questions which lead the person to complete the questionnaire in a particular direction. Phrases which give away the leading nature of a question include 'Wouldn't you agree that . . .' and 'Most people think . . .'.

THE QUESTIONNAIRE

TYPES OF QUESTION FORMAT

The simplest form of question requires a choice between two options, indicated by circling one or deleting the other. For example:

Do you currently use evaluation techniques in your job?
Yes/No   (*circle your answer*)

Sometimes there may be several items, each of which requires yes/no options. These can be listed in tabular form. For example:

Do you ever use the following equipment?

	Yes	No	
Overhead projector	☐	☐	
Film projector	☐	☐	(*tick*
Slide projector	☐	☐	*appropriate*
Sound cassette recorder	☐	☐	*boxes*)
Video cassette recorder	☐	☐	
CBT terminal	☐	☐	

Some questions require a choice to be made between several alternatives. It is desirable that all possible options are listed. Where this is not practicable (either because the list would be too long for convenience or because there are some alternatives which cannot be predicted) then an 'Other' category should be provided. It is often useful to supplement an 'Other' tick box by a short open-ended question which asks the respondent to state what 'Other' represents. Over a period of time, a pattern may emerge which permits some of the other items to be listed under a specific category heading. For example:

EVALUATION TECHNIQUES

To what extent are you involved in identification of training needs?

Not involved	☐
Conduct detailed analysis	☐
Rely on managers' identifications of needs	☐
Assist senior trainer to conduct analysis	☐
Other	☐

(tick one box)

If you have ticked the 'Other' box please give a brief description of your role in training needs analysis.

A step beyond simple yes/no choices is to rate items on some form of scale. For many training evaluation purposes a three- or five-point scale will provide an adequate spread of responses. However, you should note that terms like 'very', 'fairly', 'quite' and so on are imprecise: different respondents will interpret them in different ways. Examples of questions using three- and five-point scaling are shown below.

Please indicate the importance of these topics to success in your own job

Topics	*Importance*		
	None	*Some*	*A Lot*
1. Handling face-to-face customer inquiries 2. Handling customer telephone inquiries 3. Etc.			

THE QUESTIONNAIRE

Rate the performance of salesperson when carrying out the following work tasks	Poor	Fair	Satisfactory	Good	Excellent
1. Preparing a sales call					
2. Establishing rapport with customer					
3. Etc.					

It is preferable that ratings of this kind are made as specific as possible. Thus in the first example, 'importance' can be defined in terms of frequency of occurrence:

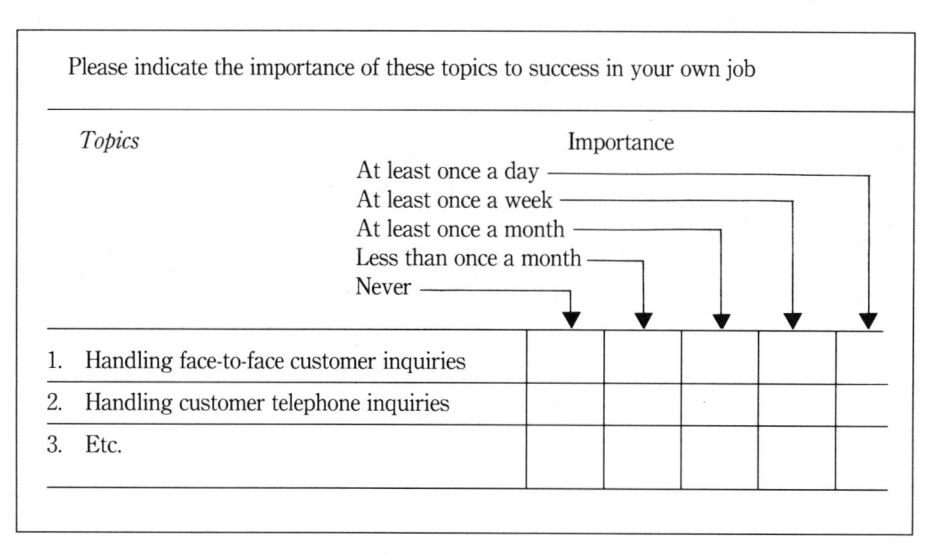

Please indicate the importance of these topics to success in your own job

Topics	Importance — At least once a day / At least once a week / At least once a month / Less than once a month / Never
1. Handling face-to-face customer inquiries	
2. Handling customer telephone inquiries	
3. Etc.	

Scales may be used to gather evaluation data on the attitudes of respondents. Ideally, a scale consists of two opposite 'poles' (which may be single words or descriptive phrases) and a number of graduations in between. For example:

87

EVALUATION TECHNIQUES

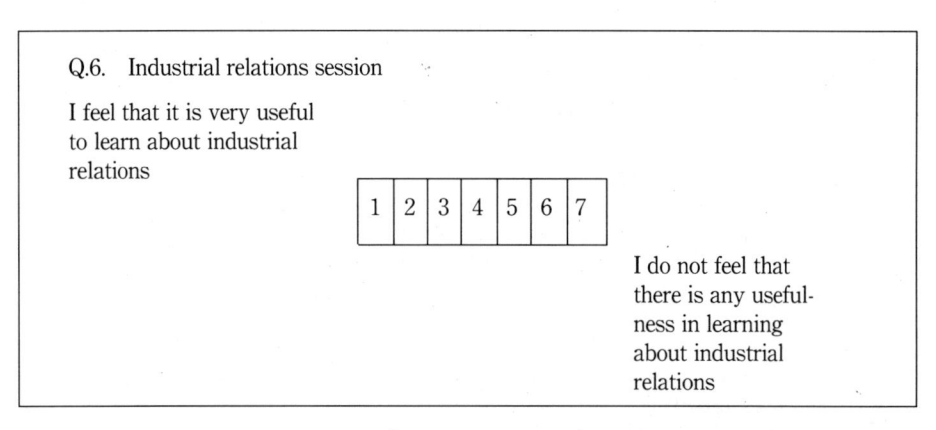

> Q.6. Industrial relations session
>
> I feel that it is very useful to learn about industrial relations
>
> | 1 | 2 | 3 | 4 | 5 | 6 | 7 |
>
> I do not feel that there is any usefulness in learning about industrial relations

Instead of numbers, the boxes may be labelled 'very useful', 'quite useful', etc. Of course, different individuals will interpret these items differently, just as different individuals will put different weights on the numbers in the numerical scale. The assumption that has to be made is that with enough responses, the *group* average will show a pattern that is a useful indicator of overall ratings on the particular issue.

Note too, in this example that the scale is provided with boxes. With a numerical scale, it would be adequate to ask respondents to circle their preferred number. However, with descriptors attached to each point this becomes cumbersome and boxes should be provided for the respondent to tick. What should be avoided is the kind of ambiguous scale that is exemplified below:

Low ⟝⎯⎯⎯⎯⎯⎯⟞ High

Respondents may treat this as a seven-point scale and mark it as, for example, at X. Alternatively, it may be read as an eight-point scale and marked as, for example, by the circle above. Ambiguity is avoided either by boxing the scale points, or by anchoring each point with a descriptive label. For example:

Low ☐☐☐☐☐☐☐ High

1 2 3 4 5 6 7 8
⟝⎯⎯⎯⎯⎯⎯⟞

Where unambiguously opposing poles are not readily available, the rating scale may be written as a single descriptive statement followed by a scale to show degrees of agreement or disagreement with the statement. For example

Please indicate your agreement or disagreement with the following statements by placing a tick in the appropriate box

	Strongly agree	Agree	Undecided	Disagree	Strongly disagree
1. I would like to see self-development exercises introduced into the course					
2. Etc.					

PILOTING THE QUESTIONNAIRE

It is essential that your questionnaire is given a test-run before it is fully implemented. The critical reactions of other people are often invaluable in refining your design. There are two groups with whom you should check your draft: subject experts such as fellow trainers or managers, and people who are similar to those who will be asked to complete the questionnaire.

Individuals should complete the questionnaire under the supervision of the evaluator. After completing each question it should be discussed to check the following points:

1. What did the respondent understand by the question?
2. What difficulties were there in answering?
3. What (if any) further ideas did the respondent have on the subject that had not been brought out by the question?
4. How would the *respondent* have asked that question?

At this stage some new questions may be added and some existing ones deleted. Some open questions can now be converted to closed multi-choice items.

The questionnaire is then given a trial run under the same conditions that will apply during full implementation. Any difficulties are noted and appropriate amendments made.

EVALUATION TECHNIQUES

Dear . . . .

We would like your help to review the effectiveness of the Advisory Skills programme.

You have been selected randomly from the total group of people who have taken part in the programme during the last two years. Your opinions about the course and your experiences in using the course content as part of your job will provide us with feedback about the effectiveness of the programme which we cannot obtain from any other group of people. All replies will be treated in confidence. Please do *not* put your name or any other identification on the questionnaire.

The questionnaire requires about 30 minutes to complete. Detailed instructions appear in the text of the questionnaire. Please return the completed document in the addressed envelope provided.

Thank you for your cooperation.

Your sincerely,

Training Department

Figure 6.1   Specimen covering letter for questionnaire

FULL-SCALE IMPLEMENTATION

Questionnaires can be administered in two ways: by direct (postal) delivery to the respondent or by some kind of supervised completion. Direct postal delivery is most common and, of course, most economical. Supervised completion virtually amounts to conducting a very structured interview with all of the costs and none of the flexibility of an interview. However, supervised completion may increase response rates and it lessens the problems of giving very clear and comprehensive instructions in a covering letter. Supervision may be provided by the evaluator or by the respondent's line manager. The involvement of the latter is good in terms of helping transfer of learning from training to work practice, but does carry the risk that non-controversial responses may be given.

A good covering letter is particularly important with the postal questionnaire because it will usually be the only medium by which the evaluator can influence response rates. It is not unknown for payment of training expenses to a course participant to be made conditional upon completion of a post-course questionnaire. However, there is a risk that respondents will only go through the motions of completion because of that threat.

The covering letter should aim to establish rapport with the respondent. It must explain the purpose of the questionnaire and the potential value to be obtained from considered responses. The letter should state clearly what guarantee of confidentiality is being offered to respondents and should be brief and to the point. Detailed guidelines on completion of the questionnaire should appear in the text itself. A specimen covering letter is shown in Figure 6.1.

The covering letter is one of a number of factors which affect response rates, most of which lie within the control of the evaluator. Response is conditioned by the following factors:

- The layout and visual attraction of the questionnaire.
- Its length.
- The impression created by the covering letter.
- The status of the person who is formally sponsoring the evaluation (endorsement by a senior manager will lend authority to the request).
- How easy or difficult it is to complete.
- How easy it has been made to mail back the completed questionnaires.
- Inducements to reply (e.g. a gift).
- The kind of people to whom the questionnaire is sent, in particular their literacy, and also their attitudes towards either the training function or the sponsor of the evaluation.
- Whether or not respondents regard the questionnaire as being of interest.
- Whether or not respondents expect that the questionnaire data will be acted upon.
- Follow-up letters and telephone calls to known non-respondents.

Within the overall response rates, there are likely to be individual variations in willingness to answer particular questions. In general, willingness to answer questions can be broken down into three categories:

1. No resistance: the respondent sees no personal disadvantage in replying to the question – typically a question about technical or professional matters.
2. Resistance: questions are perceived to conflict with the respondent's interests – typically, questions which probe for instances of error in work performance.
3. Willing response: questions which provide an opportunity to express opinions, articulate needs and wishes, and describe personal achievements.

Instructions for completion of the questionnaire need to be developed and pilot-tested in just the same way as the questions themselves. The instructions must be clear to the least alert of your potential respondents.

Where the questionnaire is lengthy, or divided into sections, it will often be desirable to spread the instructions through the documents. Some instructions may attach to a single question, for example the instruction 'Please tick one box'. Where the respondent possibly needs to refer back to the instructions from time to time, these may usefully be printed on a loose insert sheet or a fold-out page of the document.

ANALYSIS OF DATA AND REPORTING THE FINDINGS

The tasks to be performed in analysing the data and reporting your findings are common to questionnaire and interview (as are the guidelines on sampling). These

EVALUATION TECHNIQUES

topics are therefore presented as separate sections at the end of Chapter 7, 'The interview' (see p. 109).

SPECIMEN QUESTIONS

Examples of questions are provided in this section to cover a number of issues commonly raised in follow-up questionnaires. Your own questions and the structure of your questionnaire should always be designed to do a specific job in your own organization. It is never advisable simply to repeat other people's questions, unless you first check their relevance to your purpose and adapt the wording to the content of your training and the nature of your respondents.

Are you carrying out work on X? [where X is a skill, piece of equipment, etc. covered by the training event]

Yes/No

About what percentage of an average week do you spend working on X?

None	some but less than 5%	6–10%	11–30%	31–65%	66–100%
☐	☐	☐	☐	☐	☐

(*please tick one box*)

Did the course meet your expectations?

Yes/No   (*delete as applicable*)

Please add any comments

THE QUESTIONNAIRE

In relation to the work you do, was the timing of the course

Too late/About right/Too soon

(circle your preferred response)

How frequently do you make use of the technical reference materials provided on the course?

At least once a day	At least once a week	At least once a month	At least once a year	Never
☐	☐	☐	☐	☐

(please tick one box)

Please give three examples of how you have used the course reference materials

1.
2.
3.

Have you received any other training on X either before or after the course?

Yes/No

Please give brief details of other training on X

Please list any problems in maintaining X that you feel were not adequately covered on the training course

EVALUATION TECHNIQUES

Please indicate what kind of pre-course briefing you received (if any)

No briefing	☐
Joining instructions only (letter, etc.)	☐
Verbal briefing by training staff	☐
Verbal briefing by line manager	☐
Discussion with ex-participant of course	☐
Written briefing document	☐

(tick as many boxes as apply to you)

Comments

How useful to your job performance were the practical sessions?
(Circle your preferred response)

Very useful   6   5   4   3   2   1   Not at all useful

Please state any problems you had with accommodation, travel, or the workshop facilities

---

List any topics which you think should be omitted from the programme. Please add any explanatory comments which you feel would be helpful

List any topics which you think should be added to the programme. Please add any explanatory remarks which you feel would be helpful

THE QUESTIONNAIRE

Which of the following methods would you most prefer to use in order to learn about X?

- Tutor-led course with lectures, demonstrations, and discussion ☐
- Practical project based in your own workplace ☐
- Self-paced tuition using a computer-based learning package ☐
- Reading the reference materials on your own ☐
- Other ☐

If you have ticked 'Other' please state your preferred learning method

---

The objectives of the course are listed below. For each one, indicate your assessment of the extent to which it was achieved by you

		Fully achieved 6	5	4	3	2	1	Not achieved at all
1.	Will be able to							
2.	Etc.							
3.	Etc.							

(tick the rating which most closely matches your assessment)

7 The interview

Interview is an appropriate method to adopt for a number of evaluation purposes:

- Exploration of learners' responses to particular training designs or learning methods.
- Assessing the extent to which training aims and content are perceived to be relevant to the learners' job activities.
- Examining the extent to which training content has been applied to work practices.
- Identifying workplace factors which affect the extent of learning transfer.
- Gaining information about learners' feelings and attitudes.
- Providing learners with a vehicle to consider their own personal development goals and achievements.
- Comparing the congruence between organizational strategy and training provision.
- As a preparatory aid in the drafting of questionnaires.

Although interviewing has been described quite aptly as 'holding a conversation with a purpose' it is a technique which requires skill and preparation far beyond the levels required for a casual chat. It may be informal in tone but the interview is carefully structured to ensure that relevant information is collected from the interviewee and that the interviewer creates as little bias as possible in the replies. The quality of design and the skill of the interviewer make a significant difference to the quality of the data collected. A difficult problem to guard against is that poor interviewers are often not aware of the effect they have in obtaining superficial or distorted information. On the positive side, it is fair to say that people are not born interviewers: interviewing is a skill which can be acquired and practised like any other skill.

The stages through which the interview method proceeds are quite similar to those for questionnaire design:

1. Decide what kinds of information you need.
2. Draft the interview schedule.
3. Pilot the draft instrument and redraft as necessary.

4. Full-scale implementation.
5. Analyse the data.
6. Report the findings

WHAT KINDS OF INFORMATION DO YOU REQUIRE?

The recommendations made in Chapter 6 concerning questionnaires apply with equal force to interviews and will not be repeated here. However, the *number* of questions is a matter that does require extra emphasis. Interview questions are typically open-ended and respondents will more often ramble on at length than clam up tight. Twenty to forty minutes is a reasonable length to aim for, both in terms of the demand on the interviewee's time, and in terms of the evaluator's span of concentration. Serious listening is quite hard work. About 6 to 12 questions is a realistic maximum for that amount of time: more questions will mean that the interview becomes simply a verbal questionnaire and any depth in the responses will be lost.

DRAFTING THE INTERVIEW SCHEDULE

GENERAL REMARKS

The interview schedule consists of the list of questions which the evaluator will ask the interviewee. The point of having a schedule is to ensure *consistency*. The same questions will be asked every time, using the same words. However, the interview schedule should not be a strait-jacket for the interviewer. One of the particular strengths of interview as a method is the scope it creates for a two-way conversation with respondents. Thus, the main questions in the schedule will usually be supplemented both by prepared follow-up questions which probe for additional information and by off-the-cuff questions that arise naturally in the course of the interview. These questions which arise spontaneously may later be incorporated formally in the schedule, or they may prove to be specific to only one or two respondents.

SEQUENCING

The interview should start with an explanation of the purpose of the interview, the roles of the interviewer and interviewee, the sponsorship of the study, and the extent to which the interview will be confidential. This is also the point at which to reach agreement on the method of recording the interview, whether pencil and paper or tape.

Sequencing of questions should follow the same principles as for questionnaires: group together those questions that concern a similar theme; move from the general and the innocuous to the specific and the controversial; build the questions into an

EVALUATION TECHNIQUES

order that makes psychological sense to interviewees; ask questions which help respondents to recall the pertinent facts before you ask questions about their feelings towards those facts.

TYPES OF QUESTION

There are two kinds of questions which should be avoided: leading questions and rhetorical questions. Both are more easily committed in the free-flow of an interview than in the more controlled context of a questionnaire.

Rhetorical questions

These are comparatively easy to avoid. They are statements, made in the form of a question, but which do not expect an answer. Typically, the person who poses the rhetorical question then goes on to provide her or his own answer, for example:

'Can we afford not to exhibit at Birmingham . . .?'

'Is this the face that launched a thousand quips?'

Leading questions

These are often similar in form to rhetorical questions but the intention is different. Leading questions are posed so as to get someone else to answer in the way preferred by the questioner, for example:

'Do you really think that we can justify that sort of expenditure on training?'

'Most people think that the right way to conduct training is like this. What is your view?'

'T-group training is often unpopular with participants, isn't it?'

There are two types of question commonly used in both questionnaire and interview – open and closed questions – and one type that is specific to interviewing: the reflective question.

Open questions

These are most commonly used in interviews and their use should be minimized in questionnaires. Open questions are valuable as a way to get an interviewee to talk ('Please tell me about the kinds of work you do') and as a way to discover the opinions, assessments and personal frame of reference of the respondent ('How did you feel about a training experience of that kind?'). A mixture of open and closed questions allows the interviewer to explore a complex subject by means of a series of questions that gradually narrow the focus of attention, without, however, leading the respondent into any preferred answer. For example:

Q8. 'Did you draw up any sort of plan – either on paper, or informally in your own mind – to put into practice things that you learned on the course?'

(closed question)

THE INTERVIEW

(if 'yes')
Q8.1. 'Please give me some specific examples of things from your plan that you have implemented in your job?'

(open question)

(if examples given)
Q8.2. 'Do you think these changes have made any difference to how effective you are in your job?'

(closed question)

(if 'yes')
Q8.2.1. 'What changes in your job effectiveness can you identify?' (If necessary, probe for specific instances.)

(open question)

(if 'no')
Q8.2.2. 'How do you feel about the fact that those changes you made seem to have made no difference to your job effectiveness?'

(open question)

It should be evident from these examples that the key feature of an open question is that there is no single answer to be expected from it, and answers will rarely be brief. It is because open questions can generate a range of responses that they are invaluable as a preliminary step towards design of closed multiple-choice type questions for use in questionnaires. An open question such as 'Please tell me about any preparatory briefing you received before the training event' may produce answers that build in to a multiple-choice item such as that which follows:

Q16. Indicate the nature of any pre-course briefing

No briefing	☐	*(tick as*
Written joining instructions	☐	*many*
Discussion with training staff	☐	*boxes*
Discussion with line manager	☐	*as are*
Discussion with ex-participant of course	☐	*appropriate)*

Open questions carry a risk that the interviewee will use them as an opportunity to evade the question. Supplementary questions which probe for specific details will help to keep the interviewee on the subject in hand. They will also help to distinguish between those who are making general statements of good intent or wishful thinking and those who are talking about real actions and concrete events.

Closed questions

These questions are drafted in such a way that there can only be a short, very specific answer of a particular kind. For example:

'What is your job title?'

EVALUATION TECHNIQUES

'How old are you?'

'Male/Female (*delete one*)'

'When did you attend the negotiating skills course?'
1981 ☐
1982 ☐ (*tick one*
1983 ☐ *box*)
1984 ☐

A limitation of closed questions is that 'yes/no' type answers do not allow the respondent to qualify or expand the answer. Their value is, first, that very specific and unambiguous information is obtained and, second, that analysis of data is easier.

When drafting closed questions it is important to check that you are not creating either false dichotomies or 'leading' options. A false dichotomy arises where you might ask:

> 'When you identify training needs, do you mainly rely on job analysis or do you mainly respond to managers' requests for training?'

This question excludes valid alternative methods of needs identification, for example critical incident analysis. A closed leading question might ask, for example:

Q19. Please indicate how useful you found the session on 'selling to major accounts'
      Very useful ☐
      Useful ☐
      Moderately useful ☐

This example excludes the possible response 'Not at all useful' and leads the respondent towards the biased conclusion that the session *must* have been useful in some degree.

The comments on design of questions for use in questionnaires (pp. 82–9) apply with equal force to interviews and will not be repeated here. The advice on double-barrelled questions is worth re-emphasizing, however, because it is easier to create multiple questions in the free conversational flow of an interview than in written form ('Did you make any changes following the course, and what did your boss think about it – was it all worthwhile?').

Reflective questions

These form a useful part of the interviewer's repertoire. A reflective question consists of a brief re-statement of something that the interviewee has said, given with a questioning intonation in the voice. For example:

> 'You said that there were some problems with individual reactions to the trainers . . .?'

'It will sometimes be advisable to phrase the reflective statement tentatively so that the interviewee does not feel threatened:

> 'I think you said there may have been some disagreement with your boss about your attendance on that particular course . . .?'

Reflective questions are useful in three ways. First, they are a relatively subtle way of probing into potentially controversial areas. Second, they allow interviewers to check whether or not they have correctly understood the respondent's statements. The reflective paraphrase gives the respondent the chance to correct any misunderstandings. Third, the reflective question demonstrates that the interviewer is paying attention to the respondent.

One final point on design of questions: it is a good rule to rely on Rudyard Kipling's 'honest serving men': What, Where, When, Who, and How[1]. It is generally advisable to avoid 'why'. The difficulty with questions that begin 'why' is that very often the respondent will fall back on defensive explanations and rationalizations, rather than provide useful factual information about the circumstances under which something has occurred. Do not ask

> 'Why did you not make use of course learning back in your job?'

This will commonly produce answers that begin 'I have been too busy . . .' or 'It was all very well in theory but . . .' or the almost traditional response of 'My boss won't let me . . .'. Instead ask

> What factors in your own work situation have affected how you are making use of the course learning?'

THE INTERVIEW SCHEDULE: TWO EXAMPLES

Although there is no universally-applicable interview schedule, many questions will be common to different evaluation situations and can be easily adapted to match your own requirements from the examples given in Figures 7.1 and 7.2. However, you should always be prepared to draft your own questions so that you can gather data that will be relevant to the particular interests and criteria of worth of your audiences for evaluation.

PILOTING THE DRAFT SCHEDULE

DEVELOPING INTERVIEWING SKILLS

Interviewing is, of course, a practical skill. You will get better by doing it and by reflecting on your successes and the inevitable mistakes that arise. There are some general principles to guide you and two exercises are provided (Figures 7.3 and 7.4) for you to try out in a 'safe' environment.

The golden rule of interviewing is to *listen*, not talk. At least 95 per cent of the verbal

EVALUATION TECHNIQUES

---

1. Please give me a brief outline of your job.
2. Have you taken part in any other training activities during the last three years? (*if yes*)

    2.1 Looking back over the various training activities you have taken part in, can you tell me what you take into consideration when you decide whether or not an event was good, bad, or whatever?

3. If you think back to before you attended course X, can you recall what you hoped to gain from it?
4. What, if anything, do you think you actually gained?
5. Can you describe any actual event – preferably recent – in which you acted differently because of what you learnt on the course? (*if not*)

    5.1 Does that mean there have been no changes in your job behaviour following the training? (*Probe: Do these answers appear to contradict answers given to Question 4?*) (*if yes*)

    5.2 What exactly happened? (*Probe: Who was involved; when; where; what was significant?*)

6. Do you see that course as having any impact on how effectively you do your job? (*if yes*)

    6.1 Can you please describe some specific examples where this has happened?

7. Did your manager do anything to prepare you for your attendance at the training event (*Probe for specifics*)
8. Did your manager do anything after the course to help you make use of the course content?
9. Are there any other aspects of your job where you feel training might be useful? (*Probe for details*)
10. What are your views on the methods the trainers employed during event X? (*Probe for details*)
11. Is there anything else about that course on which you would like to comment?

Figure 7.1   Specimen interview schedule questions: to ex-participants

---

1. Can I first confirm that you nominate members of your staff for various training events?
2. Can you please think about the range of training events for which you make nominations, and tell me what you take into consideration when you decide to nominate someone for a particular event?
3. Thinking specifically about course X, do you recall what you hoped – before the event – would be the benefits for the person you nominated?
4. Did you do anything before the course to prepare that person for it?
5. Did you do anything after the event to review what they had learned (*if yes*)

    5.1 Did you discuss how they might put the things they had learned into practice?

6. Do you feel that the time and money that course X incurred were a good investment or a waste of resources?

    6.1 Can you tell me what you took into account in making that judgement?

7. Is there anything else that you would like to comment on regarding course X?

Figure 7.2   Specimen interview schedule questions: to nominating managers

---

This exercise requires that you work with someone else – a colleague, friend, or partner. It is preferable to select someone with whom you have worked before and with whom you will not feel anxious.

The purpose of the exercise is to improve your listening skills by providing you with an opportunity to listen to views with which you will strongly disagree.

1. Name a subject about which you hold strong opinions. It should not be a technically specialized issue, requiring a high level of expertise, but should be a controversial matter of general knowledge or 'current affairs'.

2. Your partner should now prepare to talk for three or four minutes, arguing the case *against* your preferred opinion as strongly and convincingly as possible. As your partner delivers this statement you should listen, without comment, and make mental notes of all the significant points.

3. When your partner has finished, give a full and unbiased summary of what your partner has said. Ask your partner to tell you frankly how accurate you have been. Discuss your own feelings whilst listening to the point of view with which you strongly disagreed, and any difficulties these feelings created for you when you were required to provide an objective summary (and not a counter-argument).

Figure 7.3 Hearing what you don't want to hear

output should come from the interviewee. Interviewers should restrict their statements to the scheduled questions plus follow-ups and probes. Although the interview should start with a brief description of the purpose of the evaluation, this should never extend to offering comments on the anticipated outcomes of the research. Nor should the interviewer be drawn into debating views which the respondent advances. People are generally adept at telling you what you apparently want to hear. Do not give away clues.

Effective listening is a far from passive activity. It requires the interviewer not just to hear but to confirm the accuracy of his or her understanding, to clarify any ambiguities, and to explore – with a delicate touch – any apparently contradictory statements. Reflective summaries are invaluable for these purposes.

Effective listening also means hearing the bad as well as the good. To succeed as an interviewer you need to be willing to explore the respondent's point of view without letting your own biases and preconceptions act as filters. Figure 7.3 presents an Exercise, 'Hearing what you don't want to hear', which sets out a structure to practise listening to views with which you would usually disagree.

Tape-recording of interviews is often thought to be a controversial technique. The objections, in my experience, are far more likely to come from inexperienced interviewers than from interviewees. A handful of refusals in a decade of interviewing does suggest that taping is usually acceptable provided it is introduced in the right way. The initial contract of confidentiality must be talked through, before taping starts. It is usually easier to give credible guarantees of anonymity when the evaluator is recognized to be an independent outsider rather than a member of, say, the corporate personnel department. It is particularly important to state explicitly who has access to the recorded tape (preferably only the interviewer) and what will happen to the tape itself when the evaluation is completed. The norm should be that tapes are electronically wiped after data analysis; tapes should never be made available to the client if promises have been made to protect the identity of respondents.

EVALUATION TECHNIQUES

The advantages of taping are as follows:

- Better attention and eye contact.
- The ability to capture all data, including nuances of tone and emphasis.
- Much greater freedom for the interviewer to follow up responses with supplementary questions – instead of busily writing notes, the interviewer can be an active participant in a two-way dialogue.

The main disadvantage of taping is cost – principally the time that is required to make even selective transcriptions of what has been said in the interview. When transcribing tapes allow yourself two to three times as long as the time occupied by the interview itself.

Listening goes hand-in-hand with using the power of silence. When you have asked a question, do not say another word. Wait. Silence *always* seems longer and more uncomfortable for the person asking the question than it does for the interviewee. Silence gives the interviewee time to think about the answer; it creates a pressure to give an answer. Resist the urge to restate the question or, worse still, to start to answer it yourself. Only if the interviewee explicitly asks for clarification should you restate or paraphrase the question. Finally, remember during silences to look attentive, maintain eye contact and create the impression that you are keen to receive the interviewee's reply.

There is a second consideration on the subject of silence: make it a rule not to interrupt the flow of the interviewee's replies. Interruptions can easily irritate the respondent. They are also likely to interfere with a line of thought which then gets lost beneath the new conversational direction. The only exceptions when interruption may be necessary are where the person has either misunderstood the question or is rambling in an unambiguously irrelevant fashion. More usually, simply make non-committal, vaguely encouraging noises of the 'Mmmm' kind.

One final observation on the importance of listening: the greatest value of the interview technique is its flexibility. You can probe and explore in response to what the interviewee says. Often the clues to valuable insights and opinions may be quite tentatively stated. There may be a passing allusion, a 'throwaway remark' which can be easily missed or disregarded. Careful listening – noting the tone as well as the words, the hints and undercurrents, even the things that do not get said – is essential if the more subtle kinds of interview data are to be gathered.

TESTING THE SCHEDULE

The interview schedule should be tried out on both subject matter experts and on a few people who are similar to your target interviewees. As the pilot interviews proceed, check what the respondents understand by the question and how they feel about answering it. Find out how respondents would have asked that question. Probe to discover whether your question has fully covered the subject. Delete and revise

THE INTERVIEW

1. Form a group with two other people to practise your interviewing skills. Use the schedule which you have drafted ready for pilot implementation. You will act as interviewer, one of your colleagues will be the interviewee and the other will act as observer. Set a time limit of 15–30 minutes (depending on the length of your draft schedule).
2. Conduct an interview in as realistic a manner as possible. The observer should make notes as the activity proceeds, using the checklist which follows.
3. When the interview is completed, invite both the interviewee and the observer to give you feedback on your performance. Discuss any problems arising.
4. *Write down without argument* any suggestions for how you can improve your interviewing technique. Resist the urge to play 'Yes, but. . .'. You are doing this in order to make yourself a highly professional evaluator. Welcome constructive criticism. 'The wise man always throws himself on the side of his assailants. It is more his interest than it is theirs to find his weak point' (Emerson).
5. Reflect later on the comments you have received. Not all of them will be accurate or helpful, but some almost certainly will be.
6. Repeat the exercise with a different interviewer and perhaps a different observer.

Observer's Checklist

Use of questions	Frequency of use	Specific instances
Open		
Closed		
Reflective		
Leading		
Other		

Use of interview behaviour	Frequency of use	Specific instances
Inaccurate listening		
Reflective summarizing		
Use of silence		
Interrupting the interviewee		
Clarification of ambiguity or contradictions		

Figure 7.4 Interview practice

questions as necessary. Remember that an interview schedule cannot include the number of questions that are possible with a written questionnaire.

Interviewers should also note their own reactions during the interview. What difficulties of access to interviewees were encountered? Was the reception unfriendly? Did certain questions provoke resistance or embarrassment? Were there any problems in maintaining a good working relationship with the interviewee? Were there any signs of irritation, impatience, or boredom in the interviewee? Was there a tendency to argue or talk too much on the part of the interviewer? Were there problems in recording data during the interview?

FULL-SCALE IMPLEMENTATION

ADMINISTRATIVE ASPECTS

Interviewing is best conducted on the interviewee's home ground. Prior appointment is essential. Travelling time and possibly overnight accommodation must be included in plans. An evaluation interview is normally held on a one-to-one basis: it should not be confused with a group discussion. Even where both manager and subordinate are interviewed concerning the latter's participation in a training event, they should be seen individually.

An introductory letter should be sent to potential interviewees, even before appointments are fixed, to inform them of the purpose of the evaluation study and to explain their own role within it. The letter should invite their participation rather than assume it. Few things are more futile than conducting an interview with an unwilling and hostile respondent. The introductory letter should also discuss the question of confidentiality of information.

A confirmatory letter may be sent when the interview has been agreed in principle and a date fixed. This letter, or a similar telephone communication, should mention the importance of being able to talk in private, rather than in an open office. It is imperative that the interviewee is cut off from his or her telephone for the duration of the meeting: few things are worse than the telephone for interrupting a line of thought or for interfering with the rapport established between the two parties.

At this initial stage the interviewee should be given a fair indication of the length of the meeting. This will be known quite accurately as a result of the pilot testing of the schedule. As a rule, you should stick to the maximum length you have quoted, unless the interviewee expressly indicates a willingness to continue. Respondents do vary in their talkativeness but you should over-run only rarely provided the piloting was done with representative subjects.

OPENING THE INTERVIEW

The first thirty seconds of any one-to-one encounter are critical in determining the direction in which it proceeds thereafter. Greet the interviewee by name, smile, introduce yourself, and allow the interviewee time to invite you to sit down. It is a sensible precaution to match your own style of dress to that of the interviewee: people tend to like people who appear like themselves. In some situations age, sex, or ethnicity may present potential barriers and these occasions may call for interviewers with characteristics that match those of the respondents.

A few minor pleasantries break the ice and help to start the interviewee talking. You may then remind the interviewee of the purpose of the evaluation study and the agreement on confidentiality. A form of words that covers many evaluation interviews is:

> 'What you say will be used to help me compile a report to (the training manager) on (the supervisory skills programme). However, nothing you say will be used in a way that identifies the source of the information. Our discussion today is confidential in the sense that no one else will be able to find out what you have said.'

If you are using a tape-recorder, you may add (after discussing the use of the apparatus):

> 'Nobody but me will hear the tape and all the tapes are electronically wiped once I have transcribed the data I require.'

It is often very easy to move on the conversation from the statement of confidentiality to the idea of tape-recording it. There is far less resistance to use of recorders than you perhaps imagine and there are three very persuasive reasons to employ them. The first is that tape-recording allows interviewers to give all their attention to the respondent – maintaining eye contact and an attentive posture, instead of hiding behind a clipboard and scribbling away furiously. It seems likely that the sight of every word being painstakingly noted is rather more inhibiting than a discretely positioned, small, directional microphone linked to a miniature tape-recorder.

The second advantage of taping is that you capture *all* the data. With note-taking, you are constantly under pressure to keep up. Consequently, you tend to note the statements that fit into the preconceived framework of ideas with which you arrived at the interview. It is very easy to miss significant issues if they do not fit in with your expectations about the kinds of answer you will receive. A tape can be played back without this pressure and all ideas, even the unexpected, can be transcribed.

The third advantage of taping is that you can listen full-time to the interviewee and therefore can probe and clarify as the need arises. You can also be more sensitive to nuances of tone or content which hint at issues that need to be explored more fully.

THE MAIN BODY OF THE INTERVIEW

Work your way through the interview schedule in sequence of questions. It is not uncommon for respondents to answer a question that you have not yet reached, in the course of answering one you have asked. Where this happens, it is advisable to ask the later question anyway, when you come to that point in the schedule. You might

EVALUATION TECHNIQUES

sometimes add an informal comment such as: 'I think we may have covered some of this ground already, but I'd like to ask the next question to be sure.'

The central skills of the interview are listening and maintaining a good relationship or 'rapport' with the interviewee. Rapport is very quickly dissipated if you start to argue about things the respondent has said, or if you pass judgements on them. Rapport is also lost if your attention is seen to be wandering or you look bored or irritated.

Rapport is strengthened by eye contact and by verbal support, both in the form of encouraging noises ('Uh-Huh', 'Yes ...', etc.) and in the form of short reflective summaries of what the interviewee has said. Rapport is strengthened in particular by your expressed acceptance at face value of what the interviewee says. Clear discrepancies in what is said at different points in the interview should be tactfully clarified. Catching-out untruths, or expressing disbelief in the interviewee's statements very rapidly undermines the working relationship and leads to defensive formality or termination of the interview.

However, it is also necessary to gather data that will illuminate the truthfulness (or lack of it) in the interviewee's answers. This can be done least threateningly by asking for concrete examples of situations that illustrate a particular claim to competence. This probing can be presented as a request for clarification or for additional detail. Be sensitive to three indicators of truthfulness in respondents' answers:

- Internal consistency – statements do not contradict each other.
- Balance – personally unfavourable information is provided, as well as that which puts the interviewee in a good light.
- Exaggeration – personal achievements are overstated or overvalued.

Last, remember that the guidelines on effective listening (pp. 103–04) apply to 'real' as well as pilot interviews.

When asking supplementary and probing questions, it sounds less interrogatory to preface your questions with 'May I ask ...' and similar phrases. Take care with off-the-cuff questions that you do not ask confusing, double-barrelled questions such as 'Did you find the lectures helpful or would you have preferred more role plays?' Be particularly careful that you do not inadvertently ask leading questions – when improvising probes, it is very easily done.

TERMINATING THE INTERVIEW

It is advisable to end with a broad 'catch-all' open question that gives the interviewee a chance to say anything that has not been covered previously. This question might be as broadly phrased as 'Is there anything else you want to say?' It may probe for topics missing from the schedule: 'Is there anything else that you think I should have asked you on this subject?'

The interviewee should be given an opportunity to ask any more questions about the purpose of the evaluation, confidentiality, and the like.

Lastly, interviewees should be thanked for their cooperation and the thought they have put into their answers. A modest exaggeration of the value of individual contributions may be justified for the goodwill it establishes towards the evaluation project.

DATA ANALYSIS AND REPORTING YOUR FINDINGS

These topics are considered in relation to the analysis of data from questionnaires and from interviews.

There are four kinds of conclusion that an evaluation study using questionnaire or interview may yield:

- Illustrative insights (typically arising from an individual's descriptive anecdote, or constituting a case study).
- Frequency statements (compiled from questionnaires or interviews, using a data matrix).
- Statements of co-variance (obtained by a cross-tabulation of different variables within the study).
- Statements of causal relationship (based on statistical, logical and factual evidence).

ILLUSTRATIVE INSIGHTS

These can be of great value to the training evaluator. The value of an idea lies in its fruitfulness – its potential utility. A good idea never needs to be 'representative' in any statistical sense.

It is when the evaluator is exploring trainee or manager perceptions, attitudes, feelings and beliefs about a particular learning event, or learning method, that this kind of insight is most likely to arise. It is characteristic of interview and of open-ended questioning.

Very little in the way of analysis is required. Statements or anecdotes may need to be depersonalized in order to respect confidentiality. Where more than one person has the same insight, it may be worth adding a frequency count to the substantive data, but as a rule illustrative insights stand or fall on their intrinsic quality, not their numerical quantity. Incidentally, there is research evidence that descriptive (case-study type) data is particularly influential with policy-makers. Its concrete reality has more persuasive impact than purely statistical information. Certainly, if this data has been collected in a systematic way, there is no reason to apologize for its non-numerical nature.

EVALUATION TECHNIQUES

Please indicate the importance of these topics to success in your own job

		Importance			No
Topics	None	Some	A lot		response
1. Handling face-to-face customer inquiries	~~HHt~~ // (7)	~~HHt HHt HHt~~ // (17)	~~HHt HHt HHt~~ ~~HHt HHt HHt~~ ~~HHt~~ /// (38)		//// (4)
2. Handling customer telephone inquiries	// (2)	~~HHt HHt HHt~~ ~~HHt HHt HHt~~ ~~HHt~~ /// (38)	~~HHt HHt HHt~~ ~~HHt~~ //// (24)		// (2)
3. Etc.					

Figure 7.5 Data matrix (assuming 66 respondents)

FREQUENCY STATEMENTS

Classifying data

The first step in data analysis is to classify and count the responses to questions. With closed questions, the classification categories will be contained in the question, which in turn has been developed from your hypotheses about the training which you are investigating. Categories *must* have the following characteristics:

- They must be defined so that there is no overlap or ambiguity in the border between two categories.
- The set of categories must allow for all possible responses that can occur.

For example if you hypothesized a connection between age and openness to learning new techniques, one of your questions would ask for respondents' ages. A category set in an occupational setting might be:

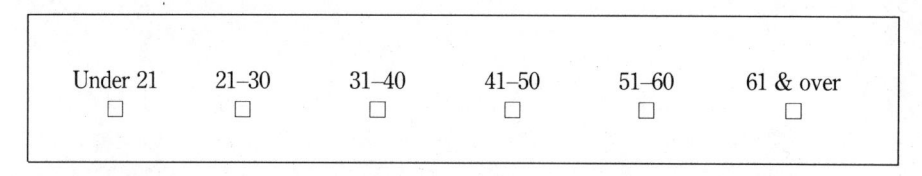

Under 21	21–30	31–40	41–50	51–60	61 & over
☐	☐	☐	☐	☐	☐

The basic tool for creating frequency statements is the data matrix. This combines *variables* with *units of analysis* so that a cell is formed for each combination of a variable with a unit. Into these cells are added the values of the responses you have collected. The data matrix can sometimes be simply created by using a master copy of the questionnaire item, with larger boxes so that you can score response frequencies (see Figure 7.5).

THE INTERVIEW

Ratings of course presentation	(1 = low) (6 = high)	A	B	Respondent C	D	E	etc
1. Clarity of verbal presentation		3	4	4	3	4	
2. Questions answered adequately		4	5	4	3	5	
3. Discussion encouraged		2	3	4	2	5	
4. Opportunities for practice		5	6	5	5	6	
5. etc							

Figure 7.6   Ratings of course presentation

When you use a questionnaire item in this way, do not forget to add an extra column to account for people who do not answer that particular question.

The matrix can be designed so that the analysis provides data on individuals as well as on the evaluation variables and the units of analysis (or ratings) applied to those variables (Figure 7.6).

Averages

Frequency alone may be a significant piece of information: in Figure 7.5 it must be cause for further inquiry as to why there were seven respondents for whom the topic of face-to-face customer relations was perceived to be of no job importance. However, it is also useful to employ the basic data as a way of characterizing what is 'typical' about the group of respondents. There are two measures – the average and the central tendency (the clustering around a midpoint).

In Figure 7.5, there are no grounds for assuming that the three scale items (None/Some/A lot) represent *equal* intervals along a scale. However, they do form an *ordered* measure from lesser to greater quantity. In this instance, the appropriate measure of the average is the *median*. When all scores are placed in order of magnitude, the median is the midpoint position. In Figure 7.5 the midpoint of 66 scores is 33. Adjusting for non-response cases, the median for Topic 1 will be the 31st case ($\frac{66-4}{2}$). Adding the totals in each cell, starting from the left (None) box, the 31st median case is the 7th case in the 'A lot' cell.

In Figure 7.6, the scores may be assumed to be based on an equal interval scale. It is therefore appropriate to use the *arithmetic mean* as the average. The data matrix would of course extend far beyond Respondent E and would include the whole of the sample (sometimes the whole of the population) included in the evaluation. In the simplified illustration here, the arithmetic mean for the first rated item (Clarity of verbal presentation) is 3·6. The mean is arrived at by adding together all the individual

111

EVALUATION TECHNIQUES

To what extent are you involved in identification of training needs?		
a) Not involved	~~HHH~~ /	⑥
b) Conduct detailed analysis	~~HHH~~ ~~HHH~~ ~~HHH~~ ~~HHH~~ //	㉒
c) Rely on managers' identification of needs	~~HHH~~ ~~HHH~~	⑩
d) Assist senior trainer to conduct analysis	~~HHH~~ ~~HHH~~ ~~HHH~~ /	⑯
e) Other	///	③

Figure 7.7 Analysis of nominal scale to illustrate the mode

ratings (3 + 4 + 4 + 3 + 4) and then dividing the total (18) by the number of cases (5 respondents).

The third measure of 'average' is the *mode*. This is the score which occurs most frequently. The mode is used for what are called nominal scales, where the various items do not form any sort of order of magnitude.

In Figure 7.7, the modal response is b) – 'Conduct detailed analysis'.

Dispersion

It is useful to know how widely individual cases vary from the average of a group. There are three measures of this:

1. *Range* is the simplest and states the extreme values of the group scores. In Figure 7.6, the range varies between topics – only 3–4 on Topic 1, and 2–5 on Topic 3, indicating a greater variety of respondent opinions.
2. To establish *quartile deviation* response values are placed in order of magnitude along their scale. Positions known as quartiles fall one-quarter and three-quarters of the way along the distribution. The quartiles are located half-way between the median value and the upper and lower extreme values.

   Quartile deviation is calculated thus:

   $$QD = \frac{Q_3 - Q_1}{2}$$ where Q_3 is the upper quartile and Q_1 the lower.

   The quartile deviation is expressed in terms of the value units which form the ordered distribution. To compare QDs you should calculate the quartile co-efficient of dispersion:

   $$QCD = (\frac{Q_3 - Q_1}{2}) \div (\frac{Q_3 + Q_1}{2})$$

3. *Standard deviation* shows the average distance of individual cases from the group

mean. Thus SD presupposes an equal interval scale is being used. It is calculated by the formula:

$$SD = \sqrt{\frac{\text{Sum of squares of individual deviations from arithmetic mean}}{\text{Number of items}}}$$

For example

Scores	Deviations from AM	Squares of deviations
4	−1	1
7	+2	4
3	−2	4
5	0	0
8	+3	9
2	−3	9
6	+1	1
Total 35		28

AM = 35/7 = 5
No. of scores = 7
$SD = \sqrt{\frac{28}{7}} = 2.0$

Comparing frequencies

A common requirement for evaluators is to compare the responses obtained from one group with those obtained from another. The comparison of scores (e.g. from written tests) is discussed in Appendix II, p. 246. The comparison of response frequencies in the answers to questions is useful as an indication of consistency or of change occurring over time, as between one course group and another. It is only in extreme cases that visual inspection of two sets of frequencies will show clearly that there is a difference between them (or not), and that inspection still would not tell you *how* alike or different the frequencies were.

The technique for comparing frequencies is the chi-square test (pronounced Ky to rhyme with 'eye', and written as χ^2). χ^2 tests whether the frequencies in a distribution differ significantly from some other set of frequencies. It is calculated by the formula:

$$\chi^2 = \sum \frac{(O-E)^2}{E}$$

where O = observed frequency and E = a frequency which could be expected, on the basis of some assumed hypothesis about the subject matter. The calculation proceeds as follows:

Step 1: responses to a question are summarized for two or more groups, as below.

EVALUATION TECHNIQUES

Q16. How frequently do you make use of the technical reference materials provided on the course?				
At least once a day (A)	At least once a week (B)	At least once a month (C)	At least once a year (D)	Never (E)
Group I 1	3	10	4	1
Group II 0	5	7	1	0

Step 2: The row, column and overall totals are calculated, thus:

	A	B	C	D	E	Row totals
Group I	1	3	10	4	1	19
Group II	0	5	7	1	0	13
Column totals	1	8	17	5	1	32

The sum of the row totals equals the sum of the column totals and is referred to as the overall total; 32 in this example.

Step 3: For each cell in the matrix, an 'expected value' is calculated by means of the formula:

$$\frac{\text{Row Total} \times \text{Column Total}}{\text{Overall Total}}$$

For example, for Group I, Column C, the expected value becomes:

$$\frac{19 \times 17}{32} = 10\cdot 09 \text{ (rounded to } 10\cdot 1)$$

Applied to the whole matrix, the expected values are:

		A	B	C	D	E	Row totals
Group I	Observed	1	3	10	4	1	19
	Expected	0·6	4·8	10·1	3	0.6	
Group II	Observed	0	5	7	1	0	13
	Expected	0·4	3·3	6·9	2	0.4	
Column totals		1	8	17	5	1	32

Step 4: Subtract each expected value from its corresponding observed value within its group. Square the result. Then divide that figure by the expected value and total the column.

Observed values	Expected values	O − E	(O − E)²	(O − E)² / E
1	0·6	0·4	1·6	2·67
3	4·8	1·8	3·24	0·68
10	10·1	0·1	0·1	0·009
4	3	1	1	0·34
1	0·6	0·4	1·6	2·67
0	0	0	0	0
0	0·4	0·6	3·6	9
5	3·3	1·7	2·89	0·88
7	6·9	0·1	0·1	0·02
1	2	1	1	0·5
0	0·4	0·4	1·6	4
0	0	0	0	0
			$\chi^2 =$	20.769

Step 5: The χ^2 value of 20·77 gives a measure of the difference between the two groups. This difference may, however, be due to chance and it is important to assess whether or not this is a probable factor in the situation. This is achieved by looking up the critical value for χ^2 in a table of critical values tabulated against 'degrees of freedom'. You obtain the df value thus:

df = (no. of rows minus 1) (no. of columns minus 1)

In the example above, df = (2−1) (5−1) = 4. Tables show a critical value for χ^2 of 9.49 where df = 4, subject to the assumption that there is no worse than a 1 in 20 probability of the results being due to chance. It depends on how important it is for your confidence in the results as to whether you select a 5 per cent level of confidence, a

EVALUATION TECHNIQUES

1 per cent, or even an 0.1 per cent level (i.e. a value of χ^2 that would be exceeded by chance only once in a thousand similar analyses). There are published tables for χ^2 values which show critical values for a range of levels. At the 5 per cent level for df 1 to df 20 the values are as follows:

df	Critical value for χ^2
1	3.84
2	5.99
3	7.81
4	9.49
5	11.07
6	12.59
7	14.07
8	15.51
9	16.92
10	18.31
11	19.68
12	21.03
13	22.36
14	23.68
15	25.00
16	26.30
17	27.59
18	28.87
19	30.14
20	31.41

In the worked example, χ^2 was calculated as 20.77. This puts it well above the critical value of 9.49 and enables you to state that the two frequencies are different, with no more than a 1 in 20 probability that the differences are due to chance.

STATEMENTS OF CO-VARIATION

Statistical correlation arises where two or more groups of values vary together, either directly or inversely. The coefficient of correlation gives a measure of this co-variance. The formula can be summarized as:

$$\frac{\text{The mean product of the deviations from the mean}}{\text{(The standard deviation of the 1st group)(The SD of the 2nd)}}$$

or as:

$$r = \frac{n \sum XY - \sum X . \sum Y}{\sqrt{[n \sum X^2 - (\sum X)^2][n \sum Y^2 - (\sum Y)^2]}}$$

where r is the Pearson correlation coefficient
n is the number of cases

X is the first set of values attaching to the cases
Y is the second set of values attaching to the cases

If the correlation is perfect and direct, the coefficient will be +1. A perfect inverse correlation yields −1. A coefficient of 0 suggests a wholly random connection between the two sets of values. Most coefficients will fall in the mid-range between −1 and +1. If a coefficient has a value of 0.30 or less then the correlation is weak. A level of 0.50 or higher should be required before making statements of correlation. For a worked example of the calculation of the coefficient of correlation see Appendix II, p. 254).

A common use of correlation is to show that some aspect of training, for example test scores, varies directly with some characteristic of the learners, for example level of previous education. However, it is a misconception of the nature of correlation then to state that the level of previous education determines or causes the level of test scores. Correlations permit a prediction but do not prove a causal connection.

STATEMENTS OF CAUSALITY

If you wish to say that X causes Y (e.g. that exposure to higher education leads to the use of impenetrable jargon), you have to satisfy three conditions:

1. That X and Y vary together (values of X and Y can be correlated); and the way in which they vary together can be specified from your hypothesis about that relationship.
2. That Y (the effect) occurred later in time than X (the cause).
3. That there were not other factors in the situation, besides X, that caused Y.

Requirement 1 has been discussed in the previous sections. Requirement 2 is a matter of observation. Requirement 3 is tackled by applying existing knowledge and logic to the hypothesized relationship of causality ('does "X causes Y" make sense in terms of what we know of the world?'). You must actively search for other explanations and in particular for spurious relationships. These arise where the apparent connection between X and Y is in fact due to both co-varying with a third variable W:

$$W \swarrow \searrow$$
$$X \quad Y$$

ANALYSING RESPONSES TO OPEN-ENDED QUESTIONS

Step 1

Review the raw data. If it was collected in an interview, read through your notes or (preferably) play-back the tape of what was said. If the data consists of answers to open questions on a questionnaire, read through the answers.

EVALUATION TECHNIQUES

Step 2

Look for key words or phrases which accurately summarize what the respondent is saying. Be very careful if you have to provide your own summarizing word for a lengthy description given by the respondent. The risk is that you will end up analysing your own opinions rather than those of the respondent.

Step 3

Key words should directly relate to the question and hence to your purpose in conducting the evaluation. As you proceed through the data, start to group the words you have highlighted into categories (which must, of course, be both internally coherent and mutually exclusive).

Step 4

With clear response categories established you can proceed with data analysis as described in the preceding sections.

REPORTING YOUR FINDINGS

Reports on evaluation of training are, by the nature of the subject, rarely wholly favourable or wholly unfavourable. Reality often turns out to be a bit fuzzy around the edges. The practical effect of this is that there can be some tension between decision-makers' preferences for clear-cut findings, and an evaluation report which is accurate but qualified by some reservations or by a proportion of mixed conclusions. It is therefore most important that the evaluation has been conducted with a clear grasp of the specific criteria of worth which are significant to the decision-makers.

Begin an evaluation project by identifying your audience and their criteria for judging the training activity which you are about to evaluate. You are then unlikely to produce a mismatch between expectations and actual results. This mismatch is common in evaluation projects where the strategy has not been properly developed. It quickly undermines the credibility of evaluation as a worthwhile activity and makes adequate resourcing unlikely.

What this means is that you should start your evaluation report by stating for whom it has been compiled and on what criteria of worth judgements have been made.

The main body of your report will contain the findings of the evaluation study. Some information will be reported as summary statements, as in Figure 7.8. According to your purpose, you might then go on to show correlations between pre-course briefing (or its absence) and amount of learning achieved, or participants' reactions to course methods and content.

Some information may be presented most conveniently in tabular form or using visual summaries such as graphs, pie-charts or histograms.

When you quote summary data, always explain what it signifies in non-technical language. Aim for brevity, clarity and plain English. Wittgenstein said it all with: 'Anything that can be said, can be said clearly.'

THE INTERVIEW

> Interviews were conducted with 61 level D managers who had nominated staff for the 'Contractor liaison and negotiation' programme. This represents 83 per cent of managers who make nominations for this programme.
> When asked about how they prepared staff for participation in the programmes, responses were as follows:
>
> | | | |
> |---|---|---|
> | Discussion at annual appraisal | 8 | (13.1%) |
> | Discussion shortly before the programme | 9 | (14.8%) |
> | No discussion and/or passed formal briefing papers to participant | 30 | (49.2%) |
> | Arranged briefing by training department or by other ex-participant of the programme | 13 | (21.3%) |
> | No answer given | 1 | (1.6%) |
> | | 61 | 100% |

Figure 7.8 Evaluation report summary statement

A SUGGESTED FRAMEWORK FOR THE EVALUATION REPORT

1. Contents, plus introductory remarks
2. Statement of intended audience
3. Statement of evaluation criteria employed
4. Summary of conclusions and recommendations
5. Main text: a) Summary of each finding
   b) Interpretation of each finding
   c) Action implications of finding
6. Concluding remarks
7. Appendices: a) Description of the methods employed to gather data, the sample used, etc.
   b) Raw data from which the summaries have been drawn
   c) Extended case studies (if applicable).

NOTE

1. Kipling, R. (1940, reprinted 1973), 'The Elephant's Child', *Rudyard Kipling's Verse Definitive Edition*, Hodder & Stoughton.

8 Critical incident review

As with several techniques for evaluation, the critical incident method can perform a multiple role: evaluation, needs identification, and reinforcement of management involvement in the training process. This book consistently emphasizes the importance of specifying behavioural changes as the end result of training. Possibly no other technique offers such a close link to key performance behaviours as the critical incident method, in both its needs analysis and evaluation roles.

The critical incident method is a procedure for collecting direct observations of workplace behaviour in situations which have special significance for the people concerned, hence situations which are 'critical' to them. What critical incident analysis yields is a description of the observable behaviours that are of key importance to effective performance in a specified task or role. The incident must happen in a situation where what the person does, and the consequences that follow, whether positive or negative, can be identified as directly affecting job performance. Incidents which are more extreme (whether good or bad) are to be preferred because they are more easily remembered in detail and therefore offer greater validity and reliability.

IMPLEMENTING CRITICAL INCIDENT ANALYSIS

WHO PROVIDES THE DATA?
Anyone who is in a position directly to observe the performance of the subject before and after training can provide the data. Observers may be supervisors, colleagues, or the subjects themselves. Who should act as observer depends first on who is in a position to see what is happening in the incident situation.

Sometimes quite divergent assessments will be made by different observers of the same subject and it will be useful, where this is likely to happen, to record several observers' viewpoints. For example, in an evaluation of assertiveness training, behaviour in work situations was judged assertive, non-assertive, and aggressive by the subjects, their line managers and a nominated colleague, respectively.

WHEN IS THE DATA TO BE COLLECTED?

Two approaches are commonly used: immediate recording, following a critical incident, and recall recording some time afterwards. Both methods have proved reliable. Which method to use is mainly a question of the observer's convenience and any situational constraints that inhibit or help recording. It is sensible to involve the observers closely in the choice of recording time and method so as to increase their commitment to providing reliable data.

HOW IS THE INCIDENT DATA TO BE COLLECTED?

Methods of collecting data are interview; group discussion; questionnaire; diary; and performance appraisal. Principles which contribute to success are as follows:

a) Persons providing their own critical incident data or observing the behaviour of others need make only simple judgements of success or failure about the actions described.
b) Trained observers.
c) *Actual* behaviour must be observed at first hand. The method does not require inferences to be made about what people might do in hypothetical situations, nor judgements about personality or mental states. By basing the method on the observation of behaviour, subjectivity is minimized.
d) As with most evaluation activities, the credibility of the findings will be enhanced if the analysis is combined with appropriate controls and pre/post assessments of change.

Interview

A skilled interviewer works with observers on a one-to-one basis to probe for details of critical incident behaviours. (Interviewing techniques are discussed fully in Chapter 7.) It is desirable that a sample of incidents described in interviews is followed up and the facts confirmed by some other method. This provides a check on the reliability of the observers' reports and on the interviewer's recording of reports.

Interviewing is a time-consuming method and it is always prudent to use it sparingly, as a first step to other more economical techniques such as questionnaire or diary. However, interview is unrivalled as a method which allows a two-way discussion and probing clarification of the significance of incidents. An example of a critical incident interview schedule is shown in Figure 8.1.

Group discussion

Typically this method will be combined with questionnaire or diaries. Observers record incident information on a questionnaire and the group discussion, led by an experienced interviewer, is then used to clarify details, probe for greater specificity, and allow the opportunity for observers to talk through their understanding of particular incidents.

EVALUATION TECHNIQUES

1. Introduction:
    - Purpose of the interview
    - Confidentiality
    - Method of recording replies
    - Establishing rapport with subject

2. Please think about the best member of your staff. Describe something that person did which made you think of them as your best worker. What actual behaviour did you see – what did he or she do and what was the result? (Probe as necessary for more specific and concrete detail)

3. What was the specific behaviour?

4. When did the behaviour occur?

5. What were the circumstances in which the behaviour occurred?

6. What was the outcome of the behaviour?

7. What made this an example of effective performance?

8. What is the job title of the person whose behaviour you are describing?

9. Did you yourself directly observe the behaviour?

10. Did you directly observe the outcomes that followed the behaviour?

Figure 8.1   Critical incident interview schedule

Questionnaire

The use of questionnaires is most appropriate where large numbers of subjects and observers have to be contacted. There are a number of rules of good design which increase the quality of responses (see Chapter 6), in particular clear instructions,

CRITICAL INCIDENT REVIEW

The Central Training Unit is currently reviewing the effectiveness of the Internal Adviser Skills Programme (IASP). We are asking you to complete this short questionnaire because you are one of a sample of ex-participants of IASP from whom we are seeking follow-up data. Please return the completed questionnaire by .... A reply-paid envelope is enclosed.

1. Briefly describe the most difficult situation that you have handled successfully as an Internal Adviser following IASP. (What happened? Who was involved? What was the outcome?)

2. Which particular elements of IASP (if any) helped you to respond in the situation you have described at 1.?

3. What made the situation particularly difficult for you?

4. Briefly describe the situation that you have handled *least* successfully as an Internal Adviser, subsequent to IASP. (What happened? Who was involved? What was the outcome?)

5. Indicate any ways in which inadequate training contributed to your lack of success in the situation described at 4.?

6. How often (daily, weekly, monthly, annually) do you encounter situations like that described at 1. and 2.?

    1. _____
    2. _____

Figure 8.2 Critical incident questionnaire

unambiguous questions and brevity. A sample critical incident questionnaire is shown in Figure 8.2.

Diary

The diary method is useful to monitor the frequency of different critical incidents as well as the nature of the incidents. A common application is in time management training where the subject logs relevant incident data, such as interruptions by the telephone or by subordinates.

Generally, diaries are compiled at the time an incident occurs, or at the end of the day. A standard diary format should be developed which is completed for each

EVALUATION TECHNIQUES

Please complete one form for each occasion when you deal with a situation that is significant in terms of how effectively you do your job. Include situations where things went well and situations where problems were not satisfactorily resolved. Use one diary form for each situation.

1. Briefly describe the situation (What happened? Who was involved? What was the time span? What was the outcome?)

2. Was the outcome satisfactory?   YES/NO
3. What did you take into consideration in answering 'Yes' or 'No' at 2.?

4. Describe any aspect of training you have received (or any lack of training) which you feel contributed to the way you handled the situation?

5. Give the date when this situation arose

Figure 8.3   Critical incident diary form

separate incident. The diary form may sometimes include recording categories that are specific to a particular activity, but in general a layout such as that shown in Figure 8.3 will be suitable for most of the situations to be analysed.

Performance appraisal interview

Regular staff appraisal interviews can be used as a vehicle for collecting critical incident data (which, incidentally, also increases the validity of the appraisal discussion). The supervisor conducting the appraisal may use a checklist of elements that are considered important to the job and which have been covered by a training event attended by the appraisee, as a basis for discussion. That discussion would seek incidents of behaviour relevant to the checklist categories, by inviting the appraisee to recall critical incident situations.

This process may resemble the one-to-one interview discussed above or it may be made more routine in a standard format such as that shown in Example 8.4. The ticked responses on the form would then be followed up by discussion in the appraisal interview.

ANALYSIS OF DATA

When critical incident information has been collected, individual incidents are grouped into categories of similar items. This categorization inevitably involves subjective

CRITICAL INCIDENT REVIEW

Job tasks/training topics	Frequency of use (tick box)					Difficulty in use (tick box)		
	Never	At least				Never difficult	Sometimes difficult	Frequently difficult
		Once a year	Once a month	Once a week	Once a day			
1.								
2.								
3.								
4.								
5.								

Figure 8.4 Appraisal interview: form for analysis of job tasks/training topics

judgements and it is therefore advisable to have it carried out by several independent analysts. This provides a check on the reliability of the classification.

Behavioural incidents should be grouped into thematic areas that could be affected by a specific type of training (when using critical incidents for needs analysis), or into thematic areas that relate back to training objectives of the learning activity under scrutiny (when conducting evaluation).

The analysis proceeds through several stages:

Stage 1

Incidents are sorted into those that provide genuinely behavioural descriptions and those that are vague, general descriptions of non-observable matters.

Stage 2

Incidents are sorted into categories. There should be consensus amongst the evaluators about which incident goes into which category, and each category should avoid any overlap with another.

Stage 3

Inter-rater reliability can be assessed using an appropriate statistical test (see Appendix II).

Stage 4

Behaviours within a category are examined and then collected into narrowly drawn sub-categories. These sub-categories should consist only of examples of behaviour that are so similar as to be virtually identical. For each sub-group a statement of the characteristic behaviour is written.

Stage 5

a) evaluation – the categorized behavioural descriptions are compared to the stated behavioural objectives of the training activity. Similarities and differences can be identified as well as the frequency with which types of behaviour recur. A pre-post assessment can be obtained by comparing behaviour categories drawn from what trained people are doing in their jobs, with the categories developed from critical incidents analysed prior to training. Where training has been effective, the expectation is that behaviour categories will present more positive statements (actions to do right, rather than what to avoid), and the proportion of positive to negative incidents will increase. Trained persons will present evidence to show that they have learned how to apply the incident technique to make themselves more effective problem-solvers.

b) needs analysis – the defined categories of behaviour should be tested by inviting people with no previous involvement in the critical incident analysis to apply the categories to a range of situations. Consistency between the analysts should be tested and any problems in fitting categories to contexts should be identified.

CONCLUSION

The critical incident method has both advantages and limitations. Its great strength is its high face validity: it uses behaviourally defined criteria of effective performance in job settings. Because it is behaviour-oriented, it avoids much of the subjectivity of other rating methods that depend on inference rather than observation. In addition, the technique will allow subjects to report their experiences in their own language and using their own frame of reference, rather than a preconceived point of view imposed by the evaluator. The information subjects provide is usually quite comprehensive in its detail and in the coverage of key work tasks.

The drawbacks of the technique include: reliance on the competence of observers; vulnerability to distortions caused by badly worded questions, or by interviewers who provide illustrative examples of critical incidents which subjects then 'parrot' back. Structuring the incident data into categories is inevitably a subjective process into which errors and bias may enter. The technique is quite costly in the time and energy required, particularly if it is based on use of interviews rather than self-completion measures such as diaries or questionnaires. Lastly, of course, the technique does not provide an assessment of routine elements of a job – only of the critical elements.

9 Repertory grid

Repertory grid can perform several roles: self-development aid, training needs diagnosis, development of training objectives, and, of course, evaluation. Its evaluation applications are as follows:

- Feedback to trainees on their learning.
- Measures of change in attitudes and in the ways in which individuals view particular aspects of their environment.
- Assessment of individual development (in the sense of psychological/personality development).

Repertory grid is a technique developed by the American psychologist George Kelly[1] as part of his theory of personal constructs. Kelly suggested that each individual has a distinctive personal frame of reference – a way of making sense of the world about us. This frame of reference is made up of personal constructs which are ways of categorizing experiences and people.

The constructs indicate how the individual views the particular subject and thus indicate predispositions to act in a particular way. A note of caution is necessary here: attitudes and personal constructs indicate a *predisposition* to act, but people can and do act in contradiction of their attitudes. Thus, repertory grid can provide pre/post indicators of shifts in trainees' perceptions of a subject, but it does not tell you whether learning will transfer into practice. There remains the basic question of whether training based on attitude change – rather than behaviour change – is worth attempting. If, however, you are carrying out training which is aimed at changing the participants' view of the world, then the repertory grid technique is to be recommended.

What is perhaps the unique value of the repertory grid technique is that it enables individuals to identify their *own* constructs for categorizing behaviours. This is achieved without the distorting influence of a trainer's or evaluator's preconceptions of what those categories might be. Questionnaires and interviews always contain the risk that the questions formulated by the evaluator will distort (sometimes very subtly) the answers elicited from respondents. Even an open-ended question implies a certain perspective on events which may differ from that of the respondent. This makes

REPERTORY GRID

repertory grid particularly valuable as a self-development aid: it allows individuals to hold a mirror to their view of the world.

USING REPERTORY GRID

The easiest way to learn this technique is to do it. The technique has the advantage that you can practise it on your own. Simply follow the step-by-step instructions. These are addressed to 'you', as the user of this book, approaching 'repgrid', perhaps for the first time, in order to learn how it works. When you employ repgrid with a group you can use the thirteen steps virtually unchanged as your instructions to the training group.

STEP 1

Decide your topic for analysis. If you are using repertory grid with a training group then your choice of topic will reflect the purpose of that training event. Thus you may wish to examine personal constructs of what distinguishes good and bad salespersons, what does an effective manager do, what behaviours make for good interpersonal skills, what behaviours do customer service clerks show, and similar themes.

If you are using repertory grid on your own, to learn about the technique, choose a theme that interests you (what distinguishes good and bad trainers, spouses, neighbours, shop assistants, or whatever).

STEP 2

Prepare six small pieces of paper or card, about 50 × 50mm each. Make a photocopy of the repgrid form shown in Figure 9.1.

STEP 3

Think about your chosen theme (by way of example, say 'Trainers'). You need to identify six people whom you know well enough to be able to specify the behaviours that each one exhibits whilst acting as a trainer. Furthermore, it is important that your chosen six show a wide spread of ability. Try to select two good, two middling, and two poor trainers for your sample. Six is recommended because users commonly have difficulty thinking of more people whom they know well enough to carry out the analysis. However, eight or ten is possible, though the grid analysis becomes very protracted, and diminishing marginal returns of information should be expected.

Write the name of each of your six chosen people on a slip of paper. It is quite permissible to include yourself as one of the six. It is also possible (and for self-development purposes appropriate) to include yourself twice: as you are now, and as you would like to be, plus four other people whom you know.

Shuffle your six slips of paper which now have a name on each. Label the slips A–F.

EVALUATION TECHNIQUES

THEME: Behaviour as a							
What is *one* behaviour shared by the pair (but not by the third) which characterizes their behaviour as a	A	B	C	D	E	F	What is *one* behaviour that makes the third person different from the pair, when behaving as a ....
	*	*	*				
	*		*	*			
	*			*	*		
	*				*	*	
		*	*	*			
		*		*	*		
		*			*	*	
			*	*	*		
			*		*	*	
				*	*	*	
	*	*		*			
		*	*		*		
			*	*		*	
	*	*			*		
		*	*			*	
	*	*				*	
	*		*		*		
	*			*		*	
	*		*			*	
			*		*		*
Overall effectiveness ranking							

Figure 9.1 Repgrid form

REPERTORY GRID

Note: When you do this with a group, especially one where the members know each other well, you should advise people to write pseudonyms, initials or other identifying symbols on the six cards, rather than names. No one apart from the individual participant and the supervising trainer needs to see the six cards, but in practice it is often easy for one participant to see another's cards. No one apart from the participant needs to know the real identities of the six subjects.

STEP 4

Now you can start to use the repgrid form. You will see that in each horizontal row there are three asterisks. In the first row, these appear in the columns under A, B and C. In the second row, the asterisks appear under the columns A, C and D and so on. For each row in turn, pick out the slips of paper labelled with the letters that head the asterisked columns. For the first row, pick out slips A, B and C.

STEP 5

Place slips A, B and C side-by-side. Think about each of these three people when they are doing whatever it is that the repgrid is concerned with, in this example 'training'. What can you identify in their behaviour that two have in common, which also makes the two different from the third. Try to specify *a single observable behaviour* that is characteristic of the two. Write a word or short phrase describing the pair behaviour in the left-hand box, adjacent to the first row. This description is one of your personal constructs.

Do ensure that you are describing only *one* aspect of behaviour, not several: 'smiles and talks a lot', for example, describes two separate behaviours.

Now turn your attention to the third person. Specify one observable behaviour that makes the third person different from the pair when behaving as a trainer. The specified behaviour may be the simple opposite of the pair's behaviour or it may be a different kind of behaviour, for example

	A	B	C	D	E	F	
ANSWERS QUESTIONS FULLY	★	★	★				EVADES ANSWERING QUESTIONS
DRAWS ON PRACTICAL EXPERIENCE	★		★	★			DRAWS ON TEXTBOOK THEORIES
etc.	★			★	★		

131

EVALUATION TECHNIQUES

Return the three slips to the 'pool'.

Note: at this point you should *not* write anything in the columns under A–F. You do not need to keep any record of which two formed the pair in each trio and which one was the single case.

STEP 6

Repeat the procedure at Step 5 for each of the rows in turn. There are twenty possible combinations of your six people. You will need to know all six very well to complete a row for every combination. In practice, you will often find that some constructs are repeated for different trios: enter these repetitions in the same way as the rest. If you feel that you have exhausted all possible constructs before you complete the twenty rows, that is not a problem. Stop when you run out of ideas.

STEP 7

The repgrid form should now be scored. The first stage in scoring is to rank your six subjects on each of the dimensions (the constructs) that you have identified. In effect you are treating each row as if it were a rating scale with two polar anchors (the left- and the right-hand descriptions of your constructs).

Lay your six slips of paper out in front of you. Which of the six is most like the left-hand description? Suppose this is person D. Put a '1' in column D. Now decide which of your six is most like the right-hand description. Say this is person E. Put a '6' in column E.

Next, choose the person second most like the left-hand description and the person second most like the right-hand description. Allocate these the numbers 2 and 5 respectively, in the appropriate columns. Finally, select the third most like each description: these are allocated 3 and 4 respectively.

There are three points to note: first, the persons who are chosen for the more extreme positions (1 and 6) need not be drawn from the asterisked original trio that you used to identify the constructs. Second, you should start with the extremes and work towards the middle values, because it is easiest to make the necessary rankings where the differences are most obvious. Third, avoid tied positions.

STEP 8

This ranking process should be repeated for each row in turn. It is a good idea to shuffle your slips after each row so that you do not unconsciously impose an ordering which is influenced by the layout of the slips on your desk. Your repgrid form should look something like this:

REPERTORY GRID

	A	B	C	D	E	F	
PREPARES MATERIALS IN DETAIL	★ 4	★ 1	★ 5	3	2	6	OFF-THE-CUFF IMPROVISATION
STICKS TO THE FACTUAL CONTENT	★ 6	3	★ 1	★ 4	2	5	TELLS A LOT OF JOKES
etc.							

STEP 9

The next stage of scoring is to rank all six people in terms of their *overall effectiveness* as trainers (however you conceive of that). Move your six slips about until you feel sure that you have got them ranked in order of overall effectiveness as trainers.

Use the row of boxes at the foot of the columns on the repgrid form to enter your rankings. Put a '1' for the most effective and a '6' for the least. Then rank '2' and '5', lastly '3' and '4'. Your bottom row should now look something like this:

	A	B	C	D	E	F	
REPEATS EXPLANATIONS WHEN ASKED	6	★ 1	2	★ 4	3	★ 5	RUDE TO PEOPLE WHO DON'T UNDERSTAND FIRST TIME
Overall effectiveness ranking	5	1	3	4	2	6	

STEP 10

You now need to discover which (if any) of the personal constructs you have identified correlate with your judgement of the overall effectiveness of the six people whose behaviour you have been scrutinizing.

Take a piece of paper and position it under the 'Overall effectiveness' boxes. Copy the overall effectiveness rankings onto the paper so that the copied numbers exactly match their column positions on the repgrid form, as illustrated overleaf:

EVALUATION TECHNIQUES

Repgrid form

Overlay paper

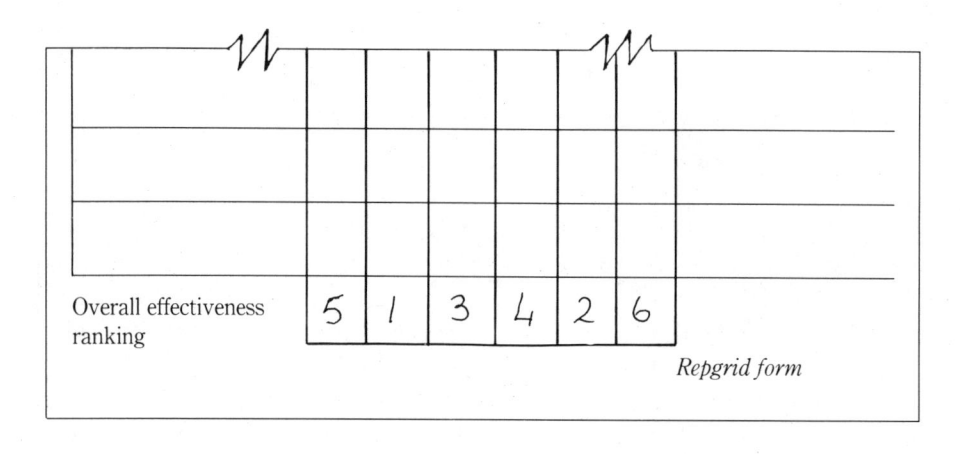

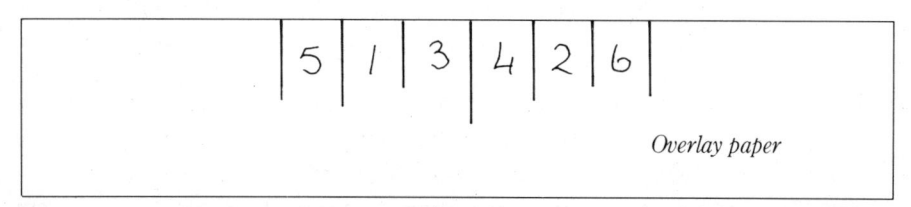

STEP 11

Take the piece of scrap paper and overlay it beneath the first row of rankings on the repgrid form. Within each column, subtract the smaller number from the larger. Add the differences. Write the total in a circle, somewhere in the right hand box. The process looks something like this:

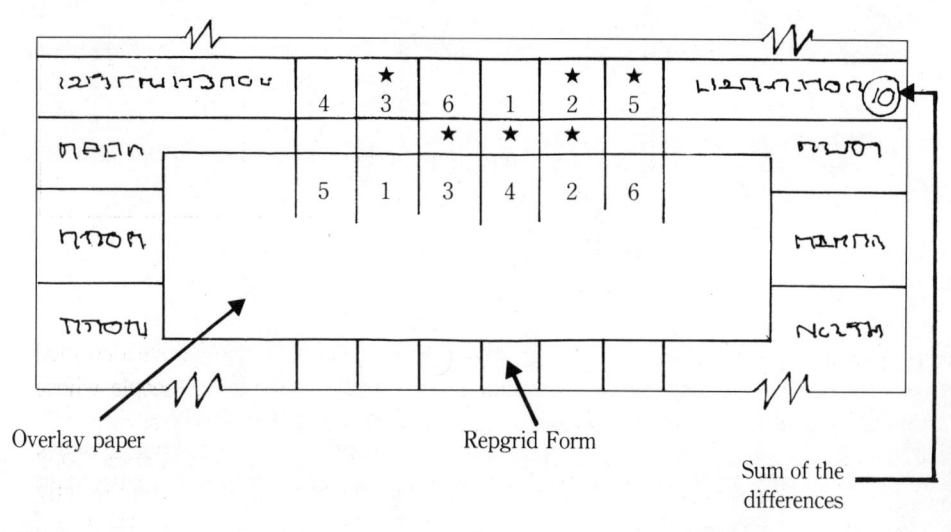

Overlay paper

Repgrid Form

Sum of the differences

In this example the calculations were:

134

```
5 − 4 =   1
3 − 1 =   2
6 − 3 =   3
4 − 1 =   3
2 − 2 =   0
6 − 5 =   1
Total    10
```

Use a piece of scrap paper for running calculations.

STEP 12

Look at the list of circled scores. Are there any high scores (12 and above)? High scores indicate one of two situations. *Either* the constructs used on that row do not have any significance in your judgements of overall effectiveness, *or* it is a row where the pair are linked by a negative behaviour and the single case is distinguished by positive behaviour.

What you should do with high scores is to reverse the scoring. Take your overlay paper with the overall effectiveness rankings on it and reverse the ranking: 1 becomes 6, 2 becomes 5, 3 becomes 4, and so on. Thus the ranking used in the earlier example is transformed from:

```
         5  1  3  4  2  6
to
         2  6  4  3  5  1
```

Now rescore 'high' rows using the reversed ranking on the overlay. This may bring the sum total obtained from the differences down to those low levels which indicate close correlation between the construct and your judgements of overall effectiveness.

STEP 13

Any remaining constructs with scores of 4 and above should now be discarded. Low scores (0, 1, 2, or 3) are indicators that the constructs you have identified on that row are closely linked to your judgements about overall effectiveness.

What you do next depends on what the repgrid is being used for in this instance. If you are using it for analysis of training needs or to clarify behavioural objectives, you should be able to take the low-scoring constructs and apply them. Bear in mind that these are *your* constructs and if the training need is not just a personal need, you should assemble a composite list of low-scoring constructs from a number of people.

To assess pre/post shifts in perceptions of a subject area you will need to run the repgrid activity before and after an individual or a group receives training. As with any pre/post assessment, the trainees should not be reminded of their pre-test results before they complete the post-test. What you may do in this application is compile a list of the lowest-scoring constructs from group members. As a result of training, participants should develop a clearer understanding of the subject area and its relationship to effectiveness in their jobs. In the post-training assessment you would hope to see a number of changes:

- The average score for constructs included in the composite list should fall (more 0, 1 and 2 scores).
- The constructs should be more precise, concretely expressed rather than abstract, and describing observable behaviour rather than personality traits.
- There would be less diversity of views about what 'doing an effective job as a trainer' means.

NOTE

1. Kelly, G. (1955), *The Psychology of Personal Constructs*, Norton.

10 Action planning

The model of training presented in the introductory chapters emphasized the importance of treating training as something which happens within an organizational context. One aspect of this model is that it highlights the importance of successful management of the transition from the learning activity to the workplace. This transition depends in part on the active involvement of the learner's line manager, and in part on the extent to which the training event consciously prepared the participant for the return to work. In this chapter, the focus is upon the latter process.

What can be done within a training event to increase transfer of learning? Part of the answer lies in the design of relevant training, in the use of training materials and activities that the participant recognizes as real and connected to the job situation. It suggests an emphasis on 'need to know' content rather than 'nice to know'.

The other part of the answer, which forms the subject of this chapter, is action planning. Action planning has a dual value to the trainer because it both facilitates application of learning back in the job and provides a job-related evaluation tool. It is especially useful in the many areas of training – interpersonal skills, sales, management, etc. – where the application of newly developed abilities may require some thought. How the skill is to be employed, and when, may need careful planning. This is much less of a problem with technical training where the application is generally clearcut and the solution less dependent on the part played by other people.

USING THE ACTION PLANNING TECHNIQUE

There are several elements to consider within action planning:

- Trainee expectations.
- Tracking learning gains.
- Formalizing a plan for implementing learning.
- Building commitment.
- Involving line management.
- Reviewing achievement.

TRAINEE EXPECTATIONS

The first step is to create the expectation amongst participants in a training activity that what they are going to learn will be of *use* to them. The tourist attitude of 'I'm only here out of interest' should be discouraged. From the start of a programme the trainer should demonstrate the relevance of the learning to participants' back-home situation. Participants should be encouraged to think about and discuss ways of applying what they are learning. This is a continuing emphasis throughout the programme.

TRACKING LEARNING GAINS

Trainees need to keep track of new ideas which strike them as usable. Course handouts will normally cover all the detailed learning content. What is required is a record of ideas for applying that new knowledge or skill – a way of capturing the fleeting insights that can occur at any time, but quickly disappear if they are not recorded. One way of doing this is 'yellow pages' (other colours will do equally well). Participants are given blank sheets of distinctive yellow paper on which they are instructed to note any ideas for applying the course content. At the end of each day's training it is an effective reinforcement of the practice to hold a brief (10 minutes or so) yellow pages review. This allows course members to share their ideas on potential areas of practical application. It also starts accustoming them to making public commitments about their intentions to act on the learning that is occurring.

FORMALIZING AN ACTION PLAN

Daily yellow pages build up over a course and provide an invaluable base for an end of programme action plan. Your training programme needs to be structured to allow about an hour for this activity.

The construction of a formal action plan has three stages:

1. Identifying personal action targets.
2. Deciding individual priorities.
3. Analysing the obstacles and resources that relate to the priority targets.

Stage 1: Personal action targets

The first stage is for each participant to generate a list, drawing on the yellow page records, of things that she or he would like to do differently back at work. Action targets must be specific and tangible. The more concretely that participants can visualize a mental image of themselves acting differently in identifiable workplace situations, the greater the likelihood that transfer of learning will occur. Action targets are never satisfactory when they consist of general statements of good intentions and broad principles. 'I intend to be very careful about wasting time' is less useful as an action target than 'I intend to keep a time-log once a month to check how much time I am wasting.'

ACTION PLANNING

Action targets should resemble good training objectives, with a statement of the desired behaviour, standard to be achieved, and conditions for performance, plus one extra element: a target date for achievement. Trainees can be given lists of behavioural verbs as an aid to compiling action targets that can be made to work.

Some questions that help the learner to think of action targets in a specific way, relating to real life rather than wishful thinking, include:

- Who will carry out the actions?
- Who will be most affected (for better or worse) by them?
- What resources are required: personal skills, equipment, staff, money, authority, time, etc.?
- What obstacles can be anticipated?
- What and who can be mobilized to help?

Depending on the subject matter of the training event, it may make sense to set both short-term and longer term targets, possibly relating to different aspects of the learning.

Stage 2: Prioritizing

Trainees sometimes respond to action planning with excessive zeal and create enormous lists of things to do when they have little prospect of finding the necessary time and resources. It is a useful discipline to reduce the initial list of action targets to, at most, the two or three items seen by the individual as his or her greatest priorities. What is a priority *must* be each participant's own decision – not the trainer's or the peer group's. Central to the concept of action planning is the idea that people should take responsibility for implementing their own learning.

Stage 3: Analysing obstacles and resources

For each priority action target, the learner should list all the potential obstacles to realizing it *and* all the sources of help that might possibly be available. Obstacles typically will include both matters within the individual (e.g. a feeling of powerlessness to influence events) and matters in the work environment (e.g. staffing levels, the boss's attitude, lack of money, and so on).

The trainer's role at this stage is to encourage the action planner to look for positive resources as well as difficulties. Difficulties must not be dismissed or wished away, but they can be counter-balanced by positive factors which encourage the trainee to make an effort to achieve the action targets. The trainer can help the trainee to assess any taken for granted assumptions about what can be done, what will be permitted, what cannot be changed, and so forth. Some obstacles may turn out to be phantoms, others will prove insubstantial, and even those that cannot be eliminated may be neutralized. One common aspect of action planning is planning how to get around immovable objects.

A useful method for opening up possible new directions for the planner is to use group discussion or one-to-one dialogue to examine obstacles and generate lists of potential resources. This often works effectively because members of the group quickly see how many of their obstacles are shared and are not unique problems and also that practical solutions may be generated. The personal action planning form (Figure 10.1) provides a structuring document for one-to-one discussions. The person receiving suggestions to overcome obstacles should note these down and agree to think about them before commenting. Without this restriction, there is a common tendency to play 'yes, but ...' by picking holes in every positive suggestion, instead of picking up its potential and adapting it to personal needs.

The last element in this process is to define strategies for achieving action targets, specify a completion date for each, and decide how progress towards the target can be measured. It is a powerful psychological aid to implementation to persuade participants to make a public statement of their action targets. Better still, participants might set up informal support and progress-monitoring networks under their own control, to help maintain the momentum to implement course learning.

ACTION PLANNING AND EVALUATION

The usefulness of action planning as an evaluation technique is in its direct connection to workplace activities. Action plans provide a focus for two elements of evaluation:

- Transfer of learning: answering the question 'Are people using what they learned?'
- Measure of job performance: answering the question 'What is the value of the action targets the individual has achieved?'

The technique works as follows: former course participants are asked to review their end of course action plans in order to identify the action targets which they have achieved. In addition, the follow-up should probe for any changes in work behaviour that were not included in an action plan, but which relate to the training objectives.

Achieved action targets plus other, untargeted, changes represent the use made of course learning. This information can be grouped and categorized allowing the evaluator to identify patterns of use – and of course patterns of non-use – of the course content. This provides very helpful feedback on the relevance of course objectives to the needs of the participants. If a discrepancy should emerge between intended actions and achievement, this suggests that there are situational factors (organizational climate, line manager, peer group, etc.) which are working against the participant's plans. The follow-up should elicit reasons for any under-achievement of action targets. It should also try to obtain valuations of the changes implemented by the participant. These judgements may be made in money terms (savings achieved, profits increased) or in terms of performance indices (such as increased output for given resources). Cost-benefit analysis techniques are covered in detail in Chapter 15.

Follow-up of action plans may be by questionnaire or interview. Examples of questions to employ in the follow-up are given in Figure 10.2.

ACTION PLANNING

From this training event, there are several things that I particularly want to put into practice in my work. These action targets are:

PRIORITY

Indicate down the right-hand side of your list what the order of importance is amongst the targets you have identified. Select the two (three at most) highest priorities. For each of these, list below several factors that will help you to achieve it, and any obstacles that may have to be overcome.

Action target	Helps (Resources)	Hinders (Obstacles)
1.		
2.		
3.		

Form a pair or trio. Take it in turns to discuss your highest priority target, what you might do to build on the helping factors, and what you can try to do about the obstacles. If time permits, go on to discuss your second or third priority. If time is limited, carry out the exercise for your lower priorities at a later date, either on your own or with a colleague at work. Make notes below of all the positive suggestions that you receive. Try not to play 'Yes, but ...' with the suggestions you receive.

Helping factors (Resources):
Suggestions for strengthening their contribution to the achievement of your action targets.

Hindering factors:
Suggestions for reducing or eliminating obstacles to your action targets.

Action strategy:
Write down below what *specifically* you are going to do to achieve your goal; *when* you will do this; and by *what criterion* you will judge your own success.

Tasks to achieve your action target(s)

Date(s) for achievement of action targets

Criterion/criteria for success

Figure 10.1 Personal action planning form

EVALUATION TECHNIQUES

1. Which, if any, of the priority action targets that you listed on your action plan have now been achieved?

2. Have you made any other changes in the way you do your job that you would attribute to the course?

3. For each change you have made or action target you have achieved, please give an estimate of what it is worth.

4. (Where appropriate) You did not achieve (specified action targets) – please describe what has prevented you from doing what you planned.

5. Are there any other factors that have hindered or helped you in implementing your action plan, (e.g. your boss, colleagues, subordinates, systems, etc.)?

6. In what ways was it useful to have a formal action plan?

7. Would you have achieved the same results without it or preferred some other method?

8. Now you have had some time to put into practice the things learned on the programme, are there any changes you would like to see in the content of the programme to bring it more in line with your work situation?

Figure 10.2 Follow-up schedule

11 Reactionnaires

Trainers need quick feedback on how well individual training sessions are running and whether a particular event has been worthwhile or not. Sometimes, more is needed and the importance of the training need or the frequency with which the event runs will justify the relatively greater investment of time and money required by a broad-based evaluation. Other occasions call for something simpler and more economical: most commonly this is the end of course reactions sheet or questionnaire – the 'reactionnaire'.

A reactionnaire is a tool for gathering, in questionnaire format, on-course feedback about the following themes:

- The trainee's subjective experience of the event.
- How well particular learning methods are felt to have worked.
- How well received are the 'performance skills' of the trainers.
- Whether the event matches formal or individual objectives and expectations.

Reactionnaires yield rapid, though rough and ready, feedback about problems within the training event. They are commonly administered at the end of an event and sometimes at the end of individual sessions. As such they are an essential part of the professional trainer's kitbag though by no means sufficient as a systematic evaluation of the learning activity.

Reactionnaires are generally – and dismissively – known as 'happy sheets'. This description aptly characterizes the end of course feedback forms used in many organizations. The description comes, of course, from the use of questions or rating scales that invite participants to show how much they have enjoyed the event (rather than, say, what they have learned, or how their learning will affect their work performance). Typical happy sheet questions include:

- How interesting did you find the course? (Scale 1–5)
- How much new information did you acquire?
    A lot _____ A little
- Your overall assessment of the course was:
    1 2 3 4 5 6 7

EVALUATION TECHNIQUES

How would you rate the following?	Good	Fair	Poor
content of the sessions	3	2	1
sequence of the sessions	3	2	1
the films shown	3	2	1
the session leaders	3	2	1
seating arrangements	3	2	1

There are a number of faults with questions of this kind. Later in this chapter, several tried-and-tested practical steps will be offered by means of which the professional trainer can substitute cheap and useful reactionnaires for cheap and uninformative happy sheets. It does not require much more time or effort to administer one rather than the other, and the rewards of putting a little thought into your design are considerable.

COMMITMENT AND COOPERATION

It is helpful to consider the reasons why happy sheets fail to deliver. There are two sides to this problem – learners are often reluctant to complete them and trainers themselves are frequently unenthusiastic about their use. The reluctance of learners can be traced to the following factors:

- Trivial questions that do not seem worth an answer.
- Restrictive questions that leave out alternatives that matter to the learner.
- Questions worded so as to produce the answers the trainer wants.
- The belief that nothing is done with the answers that they have provided.

Trainers' lack of enthusiasm is attributable to the following:

- Their lack of involvement in the ritual of 'being seen to do something about evaluation'.
- Personal commitment to particular programmes which leads them to discount criticisms as ill-founded.
- The ambiguous, unspecific, even meaningless answers that many happy sheet questions invite.
- Lack of encouragement from training management and the organizational reward system for putting effort into systematic evaluation.
- Dislike of the effort or upheaval that change involves.
- Fear that negative feedback will have disagreeable consequences for the trainer responsible.

These difficulties can be overcome. Respondents' attitudes towards answering reactionnaires can be very positive when the instrument is well-designed and it is evident that trainers will pay attention to the feedback they receive. The purpose of the reactionnaires must be explained clearly: this will usually be to give the trainers rapid feedback on the way in which the training has been received. By its nature the reactionnaire cannot offer an assessment of the trainees themselves or a measure of learning achieved – and it should never be presented as such.

When trainers present reactionnaires as a quality control device focused on their training product, and state (convincingly) that they are genuinely open to all comments and suggestions, whether favourable or not, then trainees often actively welcome the opportunity to put forward constructive observations. The questions must ask for useful, not trivial, information and there must be nothing that would lead trainees to feel they were being manipulated towards a particular set of responses.

THE LIMITATIONS OF REACTIONNAIRES

There are a number of limitations to what can be achieved with reactionnaires (although trainers often fail to recognize them). These limitations include the following:

- They will not reliably assess the relevance of course content to participants' jobs: relevance often becomes apparent to a participant only after returning to the job and trying to implement what has been learned.
- Reactionnaires give a very limited indication of whether transfer of learning will occur. An action plan in which priorities have been set and possible obstacles reviewed gives a much more convincing indicator of a person's intention to use what has been learned, than does a simple statement within a reactionnaire of 'action to take'.
- They will not provide measures of knowledge acquisition or behaviour change: these require techniques such as written tests or behaviour analysis. At most, reactionnaires can provide a quick impression of how much participants *think* they have learned but this self-rating may be quite inaccurate.
- Reactionnaires certainly do not yield an index of the effectiveness of training (unless of course an organization provides training solely for its recreational value – in which case 'happiness' criteria are ideal). Where participants provide ratings of the 'interest' a course has provided that is useful information for the training unit in terms of public relations or marketing. Levels of interest indicate the extent to which the programme and the trainers are viewed favourably, which has implications for repeat business. However, levels of interest are not a substitute for proper measures of learning gain.

WHAT ARE REACTIONNAIRES USEFUL FOR?

1. Reactionnaires provide a quick check against any significant failings that participants have identified in the training event, for example, where a particular session has gone badly.

EVALUATION TECHNIQUES

2. Reactionnaires are a way of capturing any personal objectives and expectations which course participants hold, complementary to or in conflict with the formal course objectives. These objectives should be identified at the beginning of the event (or before arrival) and the reactionnaire may need to be divided into several sections which are issued at different times.

    Where personal objectives and expectations have been identified, it is essential that there is a follow-up item in the reactionnaire to establish a) whether or not (or to what extent) these objectives have been met, and b) what factors in the training situation have influenced that outcome.

3. A check can be provided on what, if any, pre-course briefing has been given by the participant's line manager (or other appropriate person) and on the perceived quality of pre-course documentation.

4. *If* they are constructed carefully and *if* respondents are prepared to rate many detailed aspects of the learning process, then reactionnaires can provide important information about the acceptability of the learning methods employed in a programme.

5. There is a certain amount of 'happiness' data that does need to be collected. Are participants satisfied with housekeeping arrangements (accommodation, comfort, catering, etc.)? Do they feel dissatisfaction with the programme that would discourage them from coming back for further training?

6. Opinions about the balance of a course – the relative emphases given to different topics, the presence of unnecessary topics and the absence of required inputs – can be collected. Opinions about course content should always be checked against more objective data such as end of course tests: a participant may hold the opinion that a topic is unnecessary but score poorly on a test of competence in that subject area.

7. Reactionnaires allow judgements about the quality of presentation to be collected. It is, of course, essential that the design permits a separate assessment to be made for each presenter and/or each session.

    Judgements should only concern dimensions on which the trainees themselves are competent to make an assessment. Examples would include clarity of speech; willingness to answer questions (or to find out answers); clarity of explanations; and the extent to which the trainer involved the learners through discussions, questions and feedback.

    It would rarely be appropriate (except in the special case of a presentation made to an expert audience) to ask learners to rate the trainer's subject knowledge. It is reasonable for trainees (as consumers of the product) to rate the quality of visual aids and course handouts.

    There is rather less justification in asking trainees to rate the effectiveness of the learning method adopted. This judgement is easily distorted by the entertainment value ascribed to particular learning methods, especially video and, more recently, battle games. That said, trainees can be asked to identify their

preferred learning methods provided they are given a prompt list of the more common alternatives (e.g. lecture, case study, discussion group, film, on-job project, reading a book, role play, computer-based package, etc.).
8. Reactionnaires should collect some basic biographical data on the participants. This will help the evaluator to put individual responses into the context of the person's job and will highlight any anomalies between those attending a training activity and those for whom it was designed. Biographical data could include: job title; nature of work; length of experience; and (sometimes) name, official telephone number and address.

THE DESIGN OF REACTIONNAIRES

This section covers a number of themes by providing examples of good practice. The section which follows, 'Some common problems', provides instances of bad design which are analysed to help you avoid similar mistakes in your own reactionnaires.

STRUCTURE OF THE REACTIONNAIRE

Some information must be collected before a training activity begins, if it is to be collected at all. Other information should be collected on a session-by-session basis (or, possibly, at the end of each day). Some information can only be gathered at the end of an event, looking back on it as a whole. Finally, much important data will only be obtained by use of follow-up questionnaires or interviews sometime after the training event (see Chapter 6 and 7 for detailed guidance).

A convenient solution is to split the programme reactionnaire into several sections which are issued to participants in instalments. This has the bonus of reducing the apparent size of the reactions document – a lengthy document might be found off-putting.

SECTION 1: PRE-TRAINING INFORMATION

Personal objectives and expectations about the course should be written down by participants before their preconceptions are altered by the training experience. Note in Figure 11.1, that as well as expectations, participants are encouraged to say what they hope the training will enable them to *do*.

The preliminary section of the reactionnaire can also be used to collect biographical data and to check on pre-course preparations.

Figure 11.2 asks for the participant's name. In some instances it may be important that anonymity is guaranteed and it will then be appropriate to include a statement at the beginning of the document such as:

EVALUATION TECHNIQUES

> Your responses to this questionnaire will be treated in confidence. Please do *not* put your name or any other personal identification on the document.

MARKETING STRATEGY WORKSHOP: 6–8 FEBRUARY 1992

Please complete Section 1 before you attend the workshop, Section 2 session-by-session as it proceeds, and Section 3 as soon as possible after the event concludes.

Section 1
My own objectives and expectations
The most useful skills that I hope to gain from the workshop are:
1.

I see this as useful because it will enable me to...

2.

I see this as useful because it will enable me to...

3.

I see this as useful because it will enable me to ...

Please continue on a separate piece of paper if you wish to list further expectations concerning the seminar.

Figure 11.1 **Personal learning objectives**

SECTION 2: SESSIONAL FEEDBACK

A balance has to be struck between the number of questions asked and the amount of time that will be taken out of the total available for training purposes. Another consideration is that a large amount of form-filling can become a chore for participants so that the quality of responses declines. It is better to err on the side of simplicity.

Figure 11.3 offers a simple framework for a course where there are a large number of short sessions and only limited time for form-filling. Note that the options to be circled are limited to three: this is quite adequate for quick feedback of this type. The polar terms of the judgements are put in differing orders as a precaution against respondants simply circling all items in one column, without giving thought to their choice.

Where individual sessions are longer, or whole modules of a programme are being assessed, it may be acceptable to use a more detailed sessional reactionnaire as shown in Figure 11.4. In this example, six-point rating scales are used. This form can be

REACTIONNAIRES

---

1. Name

2. Department

3. Job title

4. Please give a brief description of your job tasks

5. Length of service in your present job (*tick box*)
   ☐   ☐   ☐   ☐
   Under   1–3   4–6   Over
   1 year   years   years   6 years
6. Was a pre-course briefing discussion held: YES/NO
7. Who discussed the course with you (if a briefing took place)?

8. Was the pre-course documentation:
   GENERALLY EASY TO UNDERSTAND/GENERALLY DIFFICULT?
9. Was the pre-course documentation:
   TOO MUCH TO READ/ABOUT RIGHT/INSUFFICIENT?

Figure 11.2   General information

employed for a wide variety of training topics. Other reactionnaires need to be designed specifically for particular events, or particular kinds of training method. Extracts from a reactionnaire designed for use with computer-based, distance-learning packages are given in Figure 11.5.

SECTION 3: END OF PROGRAMME REVIEW

Where there has not been a separate set of questions relating to the individual session, a number of the items given in the preceding examples will need to be included in the end of event reactionnaire (Figure 11.6). Participants will be invited to make judgements which span the whole event and this inevitably means that the information gathered will be less specific and less usable. For example, 'Depth of topic coverage was ... inadequate/appropriate/excessive' provides precise *sessional* feedback, but only a broad indication of the adequacy of the training when it is asked of a whole course. Where ratings of tutor performance are asked for, it is essential that the question allows a rating to be given for each individual tutor. A combined rating for several tutors is worthless.

A second area of information which the terminal reactionnaire covers comprises questions which can only be answered by reviewing the whole training event: achieve-

EVALUATION TECHNIQUES

Section 2
Please complete this at the end of each session during the workshop.

Session title	Aspects of the session	Your judgement (please circle preferred item)
Changing environment of retailing 6 Feb. 09.00–10.30	The presenter's explanation of the subject was ...	good/adequate/unclear
	The depth of topic coverage was ...	excessive/appropriate/inadequate
Profit planning 6 Feb. 16.00–17.30	The presenter's explanation of the subject was ...	unclear/adequate/good
	The depth of topic coverage was ...	inadequare/appropriate/excessive
Group work + case discussion 6 Feb. 20.30–22.00 and 7 Feb. 09.00–10.30	I found the case study ...	realistic/moderately realistic/unrealistic
	In relation to my job, the case study was ...	relevant/partly relevant/inappropriate
	From the group work and case study I learned ...	little/a moderate amount/a lot

Figure 11.3 Sessional short reactionnaire

ment of formal and/or personal objectives; identifying major learning points; general critiques of the event and its content. Figures 11.7 and 11.8 provide illustrations.

An alternative format to that in Figure 11.8, appropriate to assessing achievement of formal course objectives rather than personal ones, is shown in Figure 11.9. In this format, the course objectives are listed in full and participants give a rating for their individual and subjective perception of the extent to which each objective has been met. Note that this is *not* a substitute for objective measures of actual learning gain on the course.

Where a standardized end-of-course reactionnaire is in use, specific course objectives can be incorporated using a loose insert for each separate course.

The third category of information that the end of course reactionnaire may collect relates to future activities. Reactionnaire statements about what the individual will implement back in the job are less satisfactory than properly compiled action plans, however, they are better than nothing. Figure 11.10 illustrates these questions. It is advisable always to include a final open-ended 'catch-all' question such as Question 22.

REACTIONNAIRES

Sessional Review Form
Topic: *Training Objectives*

On each of the following scales, please put a circle around the item that best indicates your opinion on that subject. The scales run from 1 (lowest or worst) to 6 (highest or best).

1. How easy was it to understand the tutor's presentation of the topic?

    very difficult   1   2   3   4   5   6   very easy

2. How confident do you now feel about your ability to ...*write a behavioural objective*...

    very confident   6   5   4   3   2   1   very unsure

3. How much of the session do you feel was new information to you?

    a lot   6   5   4   3   2   1   a little

4. How satisfactory did you find the tutor's replies to questions?
   (please tick one box)

Answers were generally clear and complete	☐
Answers were generally clear but not complete	☐
Answers were generally unclear	☐
Questions were generally not answered	☐

For the following items, circle the description which best reflects your feelings about the subject of the question.

5. Was the depth of topic coverage

    Too much/About right/Too little?

6. Did the proportions of theory and practice give you

    Too much theory/About the right mixture/Too much practice?

7. Did the proportions of individual work and group work provide

    Too much group work/About the right mixture/Too much individual work?

Figure 11.4 Sessional longer reactionnaire

QUESTION DESIGN: SOME COMMON PROBLEMS

A number of common errors of question design which are found in reactionnaires are illustrated below, together with a commentary on the principles involved.

1. **How do you rate the trainers' style of instruction?**

    Low   1 2 3 4 5 6   high

EVALUATION TECHNIQUES

---

1. How difficult did you find the use of the keyboard?

    very   1   2   3   4   5   6   not at all

2. How isolated from contact with other trainees did you feel?

    Felt very isolated   1   2   3   4   5   6   Felt it easy to make contact

3. Was the tutor accessible to provide help?

    all the time   1   2   3   4   5   6   never

4. Was the tutor helpful when asked for assistance?

    very helpful   1   2   3   4   5   6   very unhelpful

5. How often did you ask the tutor for assistance?

    ☐ About once an hour   ☐ About once per ½ day   ☐ About once per day   ☐ About once every 2 days   ☐ About once per week

6. Was the pace at which the package progressed

    Too fast/About right/Too slow?

Figure 11.5 Distance learning reactionnaire

Comments

a) It is not useful to provide a composite rating for several trainers.
b) The rating should be made against a specified criterion, for example clarity of speech; adequacy of explanations; adequacy of question-answering. A high/low scale is not informative.

2. How useful were the course handouts?

Very useful   6 5 4 3 2 1   Not useful

Comments

a) Usefulness of reference materials often can be assessed accurately only after a period back in the job.
b) Where handouts are intended to be used as reference guides back in the job it would be useful to have post-training follow-up questions such as 'How often do you refer to the course notes?' and 'In what ways do you find the course notes either helpful or unsatisfactory as an aid to doing your job?'
c) It would provide more precise feedback for the course designers if the question asked 'Describe any difficulties you have experienced in using the handouts.' All that rating scales can do is to highlight that problem areas exist: scales usually need to be supplemented by open questions which probe for more detail about the nature of the problem.

REACTIONNAIRES

---

1. How easy was it to understand the presentation of course topics?

    Very easy   6   5   4   3   2   1   Very difficult

2. How confident do you feel about your ability to put what you have learned on the course into practice in your job?

    Very confident   6   5   4   3   2   1   Very unsure

3. How much of the course content was new to you?

    A little   1   2   3   4   5   6   A lot

4. How helpful did you find the visual aids used in the course (overhead projector slides, films)?

    Very useful   6   5   4   3   2   1   unhelpful

5. How difficult to understand did you find the course handouts?

    Very difficult   1   2   3   4   5   6   Very easy

6. Rate each tutor's contribution on the following scales:

    1. (name)

gave good explanations	6	5	4	3	2	1	Difficult to understand
Answered questions well	6	5	4	3	2	1	Answered questions badly

    2. (name)

Gave good explanations	6	5	4	3	2	1	Difficult to understand
Answered questions well	6	5	4	3	2	1	Answered questions badly

    3. etc.

7. Was the depth of topic coverage generally
    too much/about right/too little?

8. Was the overall pace of the course
    too slow/about right/too fast?

Figure 11.6   Detailed end of event reactionnaire

3. What was good about the course? (or) List three good elements of the course.

Comments

a) Questions should be balanced so that respondents have the option of giving 'good' or 'bad' ratings and descriptions. One-sided questions reflect the trainer's manipulative use of reactionnaires and very quickly demotivate the people asked to complete them.

b) A better formulation of the question would be to ask 'Please list the three elements of the course you most liked and the three you least liked.' Bear in mind, though, that this is largely a happiness rating and it certainly is not a true measure of learning achieved on the course.

EVALUATION TECHNIQUES

---

1. How useful was the pre-course briefing discussion (if you received one) in helping you to make the most of this training event?

   Very useful/Moderately useful/Not useful/No briefing

2. What aspects of the briefing made it more or less useful?

3. What (if any) parts of the programme do you feel should be omitted?

   Why?

4. What (if anything) do you feel should be added to the programme?

   Why?

6. Would you recommend this course to a colleague who does a similar job to your own?

7. Please comment on any unsatisfactory aspects of the course administration, accommodation, training facilities, food, or documentation provided.

Figure 11.7 Short end of event reactionnaire

4. Was the topic covered in sufficient depth for your needs?

$$\text{Low} \quad 1\ 2\ 3\ 4\ 5\ 6 \quad \text{High}$$

Comments

  a) A post-test would allow participants to *demonstrate* their competence, rather than assert it. Furthermore, participants may not yet know how much depth of coverage they do require.
  b) Depth of coverage should be clearly linked to training objectives which themselves are based upon an analysis of the job to which the training relates. In this way a post-test provides an objective measure of whether training coverage was in fact sufficient.
  c) This question provides no indication of whether or not the topic that has been learned will be transferred into work practice. Only a follow-up, post-training, can discover that.

REACTIONNAIRES

Section 3
A. The most important things I have learned from the workshop are:
    1.

    This is important to me because

    2.

    This is important to me because

    3.

    This is important to me because

    (please continue on a separate piece of paper if you wish to)

B. Please comment on any divergence between your expectations of the workshop (as you listed them in Section 1) and the actual learning outcomes you have listed in (A) above.

Figure 11.8 **Assessment of personal course objectives**

The training objectives of the course you have been attending are listed below. Please indicate the extent to which you feel you have achieved each objective. Circle the scale point which best indicates your own position (1 is no achievement; 6 is complete achievement).

Course participants will be able to:
1. Describe four methods of identifying training needs.
    Not achieved   1   2   3   4   5   6   Completely achieved

2. Write behavioural objectives to meet specified training needs.
    Not achieved   1   2   3   4   5   6   Completely achieved

3. State the advantages and disadvantages of six commonly used training methods.
    Not achieved   1   2   3   4   5   6   Completely achieved

etc.

Figure 11.9 **Assessment of formal course objectives**

EVALUATION TECHNIQUES

---

19. When I start to implement specific learning points from the seminar, I anticipate both obstacles and positive opportunities and resources. These are:

What I want to put into practice	Possible obstacles	Opportunities and resources

20. Please list any further information or skill-development needs you can now identify. (We will also contact you in about three months time since some needs may only become apparent over time.)

21. I personally learn best from the learning methods I have circled in the list below:

   Lecture/Case study/Discussion groups/Film/On-job projects/
   Computer-based packages/Reading/Role-play/Business games/
   Other

   If you have ringed 'Other', please specify what method you prefer

22. If there are any other comments you would like to make about the seminar please write or telephone Alf Trainer on 020202 extension 2020.

Figure 11.10 Future activities

---

d) A scale running from low to high is not suitable for this question. A better pair of anchors could be provided by 'fully covered' and 'not covered at all'.

5. Will you be using Method I or Method II when jointing cables?

Yes ☐
No ☐ (*tick box*)

Comments

a) The question is ambiguously worded. If both Method I *and* Method II might be employed, then yes/no alternatives are satisfactory, but the question should read 'Will you be using *either* Method I or Method II . . .?'

b) If only one method or the other will be employed, then the response boxes should be labelled as follows:

Method I ☐
Method II ☐ (*please tick one box*)

REACTIONNAIRES

6. To what extent have you achieved your personal objectives for the course?

Completely   6 5 4 3 2 1   Not at all

Comments

   a)   Whether or not a question about personal objectives is worth asking depends on the purpose and main emphasis of the training event. Where, as is generally the case, training is run for reasons related to job and task performance, personal objectives may not be of significance.

   b)   Where an assessment is required of the extent to which objectives (organizational or pesonal) have been met, then it is necessary to list those objectives. It is probable that some will be achieved and some will not and these differences need to be identified. 'Official' course objectives can be pre-listed on the reactionnaire or included as a loose insert to a standard form. Personal objectives will have to be written in by the participant. This should be done at the beginning of a training event to help the trainers identify individual needs; attainment of objectives is then reviewed at the end of the event.

7. How long have you been carrying out the duties of a distribution engineer?

☐	☐	☐	☐	
Up to 1 year	1–3 years	3–5 years	5 years and over	*(tick one box)*

Comment

   a)   The response categories overlap and this creates confusion for the respondent and the analyst. Non-overlapping categories would be as follows:

☐	☐	☐	☐	
Less then 1 year	1–2 years	3–4 years	5 years and over	*(tick one box)*

8. Indicate the extent to which you have achieved each of the following course objectives:

   a)   **Prepare and lead a group discussion**   1 2 3 4 5 6
   b)   **Prepare and present a short lecture**   1 2 3 4 5 6
   c)   **Etc.**

Comments

   a)   Each objective forms a double question: 'prepare' plus 'lead', 'prepare' plus 'present'. These should be listed as separate items for rating, thus:

EVALUATION TECHNIQUES

    a) Prepare a group discussion   1 2 3 4 5 6
    b) Lead a group discussion   1 2 3 4 5 6
    c) Prepare a short lecture   1 2 3 4 5 6
    d) etc.

b) The rating scales lack 'anchors'. Anchoring a rating scale means labelling the numerical values so that the person using the scale understands clearly what any particular rating value means. At its simplest this requires the two poles (1, 6) to be anchored:

Fully achieved   1 2 3 4 5 6   Completely failed

Sometimes it will be useful to anchor each point on the scale, as in the example below:

The standard reached in the sales presentation to a potential customer was:
6 = Excellent
5 = Good
4 = Satisfactory +
3 = Satisfactory −
2 = Fair
1 = Poor

Each anchor description should be backed up by a paragraph or so which details the different standards of observable behaviour that will justify each particular rating. These descriptions are not usually included in the reactionnaire document itself, but should be available to the person who is administering the instrument to trainees, so that he or she can respond to any questions about the distinctions between scale points.

9. **How useful a technique do you consider discounted cash flow to be in your job?**

   Very useful   6 5 4 3 2 1   Not useful

   Comment

       a) A more fruitful way of posing this question would be to ask 'List situations in which you expect to use discounted cash flow.' The original question allows the respondent to make bland statements of good intent like 'very useful' which may be divorced from any real intention to use the technique.

10. **How much of the course was new information to you?**

    All of it   6 5 4 3 2 1   None of it

Comment

    a) As a quick guide to mismatches of participants and content this scale is better than nothing. However, learners often assess the level of their own knowledge and skills very inaccurately and a self-report scale of this kind is greatly inferior to a pre/post test of learning gain.

11. In how much detail did the trainer cover the topic of strategic planning?

   Excessive detail   1 2 3 4 5 6   Insufficient detail

Comments

a) This scale is different to the other examples provided. The scales shown in questions 1–10 run from 1(low) to 6(high) on a single scale with two poles. This puts all the 'favourable' responses at the higher end of the scale. In the case of Question 11, however, the best response would be a midpoint position (3/4) which represents the 'right level of detail'. This scale would be better presented as a three-item (or possibly a five-item) choice of descriptive anchors:

3 point

Excessive detail/About the right level of detail/Insufficient detail

(*Please circle your preferred response*)

5 point

Excessive detail/A bit too much detail/About the right level of detail/Not quite enough detail/Much too little detail

(*Please circle your preferred response*)

Note: design of questions for use in evaluation interviews and questionnaires is described in detail in the relevant chapters.

ADMINISTRATION OF REACTIONNAIRES

TIMING

Appropriate timing makes a considerable difference to the quality of information collected. Sessional feedback needs to be gathered fairly quickly – either at the end of the session itself or at least on the same day. If you attempt to gather sessional feedback at the end of a course it is likely that some of the sessions and their tutors will have become jumbled in the minds of the trainees.

Information about course expectations should be gathered before the actual course content can influence perceptions – in other words, before the start of the event or at the very beginning, before there has been any introductory discussion of the reasons why participants are attending the event.

Overviews of the training event must obviously follow its conclusion. However, there is often a trade-off here between balanced judgements and high rates of response. If reactionnaires are completed within course time the response rate is high, but responses are frequently distorted by such factors as end of course euphoria (the phenomenon that a trainer in the prison service once described as 'gatefever') and the tendency, where the trainer is liked, to like the training event.

There is a good case for arguing that reactionnaires should be completed about 10 to 14 days after the event finishes. This removes the end of event pressures and also allows some short-term assessment of transfer of learning into the job. If the reactionnaire provides space for comments by the participant's supervisor this gives useful additional reinforcement of the transfer. The disadvantage of deferring reactionnaires is that response rates may drop off.

There are a number of strategies for increasing responses, not all of which will be acceptable in all organizations: provision of addressed reply envelopes; requiring supervisors to oversee completion of the form; follow-up telephone calls to non-respondents (not possible if reactionnaires are made anonymous); and making the payment of expenses claims conditional upon return of completed forms (liable to encourage 'going through the motions'). By far the best way is to persuade participants of the value of what they are being asked to do.

If questions are clearly useful (and not too numerous), do not bias towards favourable answers, and if staff administering the reactionnaire make it clear that action will be taken on the basis of participants' comments, then a much more cooperative climate is established. Experience suggests that participants welcome the opportunity to make constructive comments on a training event, provided they will be listened to. It is the behaviour of some trainers, who collect reactionnaires and then hide them in a filing cabinet, that accounts for much participant cynicism about evaluation of training.

A reactionnaire which is issued for subsequent completion, requires a short covering letter which repeats the key points made in the verbal introduction to the evaluation. Figure 11.11 provides an example of such a letter.

WHO SHOULD ADMINISTER REACTIONNAIRES?

Wherever possible, the reactionnaire should be introduced, collected and analysed by someone other than the trainer who is responsible for presenting the event or the designer who produced the learning materials. It is better that the evaluation is handled by someone who does not have a direct vested interest in the outcome of the inquiry and who is therefore much less likely to try to subvert its purposes, for example by suggesting that participants should not treat the reactionnaire too seriously. Where the reactionnaire is collected by (or posted to) someone other than the course tutor, there is more reality in a promise of anonymity. It also creates the impression that evaluation is sufficiently important to be treated in a careful and systematic manner. Where forms are not anonymous, a third party evaluator is far less likely to discount particular comments or judgements, simply because they know the individual and have arrived at a particular set of expectations about him or her.

REACTIONNAIRES

Boudicca Chariots plc
Training Department
'Marketing strategy, innovation and growth' 12–14 September 199X

To:

Training audit/quality control

We are constantly striving to provide training activities that help managers to achieve their goals. To achieve this aim, we need your help.

Your feedback on the effectiveness of our training events will help us to maintain and improve their quality, their usefulness, and ultimately their contribution to company profitability.

Please help us by completing the attached short questionnaire which will help us to monitor the value of the 'Marketing' seminar to yourself and also provide us with guidance on future events. The information provided will be treated in confidence.

Thank you for your cooperation.

A. Trainer
Head of Manpower Development
Wheeled Vehicles Division

Figure 11.11 Covering letter for a reactionnaire

ANALYSING THE DATA

Reactionnaire data can mostly be dealt with by simple frequency counts of scaled or multiple-choice answers or by a categorization of the written answers to open-ended questions. For example, for a scaled question, a summary of responses might appear as shown in Figure 11.12.

The pattern of responses can be presented in graph form. This makes for an easy visual comparison between one course group and another (Figure 11.13). Alternatively the data may be presented as a histogram (Figure 11.14).

For an open question, the responses must be inspected and then divided into suitable categories. A simplified way of doing this, appropriate to reactionnaires, is to underline key words or phrases in the written answers. These underlined items are then grouped according to the elements that they have in common. For example, they might all be concerned with the extent to which course members had an opportunity to practise certain skills observed on a film, or they all might be concerned with problems about the catering, and so on. Most often the responses to an open question will fairly quickly fall into a pattern and it then becomes a simple matter to draw up a recording sheet for analysing subsequent reactionnaires. The recording sheet will list the key categories of response that have been identified (plus a residual 'other' category to

EVALUATION TECHNIQUES

11. Did you think the clarity of presentation was:

    Unsatisfactory   1   2   3   4   5   6   Satisfactory

Analysis: 115 (96%) completed this item
           5 (4%) gave no rating

Rating	No. of responses	% of total
1	5	4.2
2	10	8.3
3	15	12.5
4	30	25.0
5	45	37.5
6	10	8.3
No rating	5	4.2
Total	120	100

Figure 11.12   Summary of responses to a scaled question

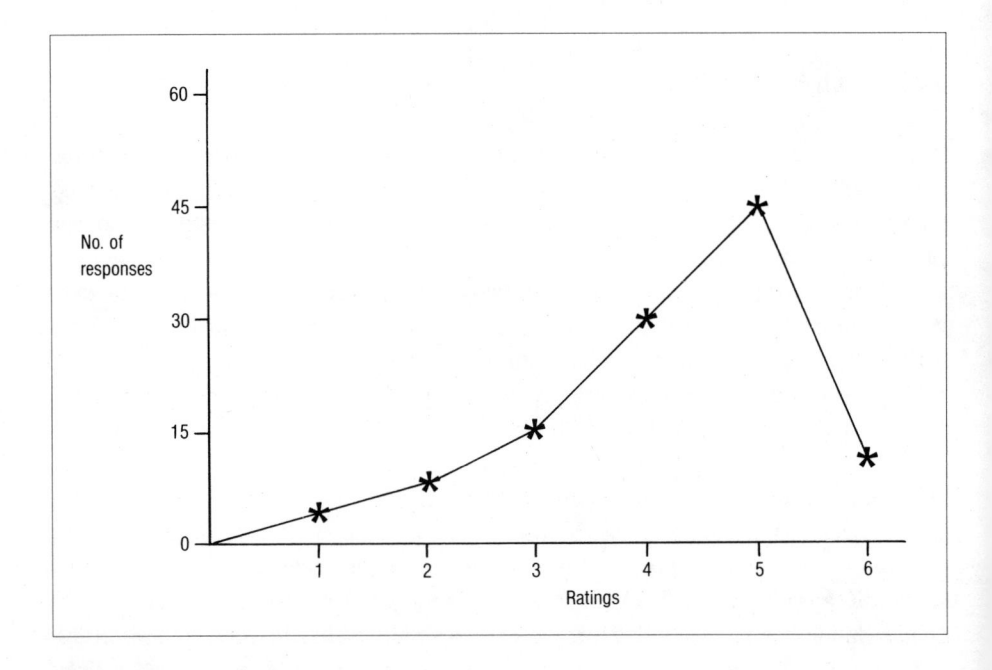

Figure 11.13   Graph showing pattern of responses

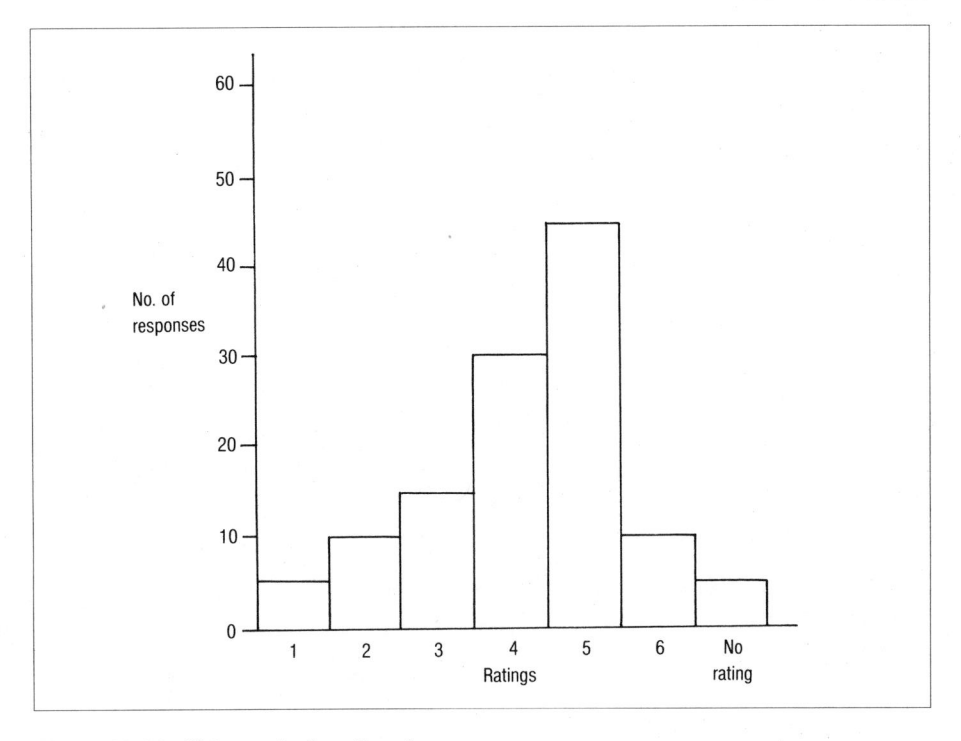

Figure 11.14 Histogram showing pattern of responses

catch the occasional item that does not fit) and frequency of occurrence of each category can be recorded as the reactionnaires are examined. An example of this process is illustrated in Figure 11.15.

It is possible to carry out more complex statistical analyses of reactionnaire data, such as correlating the responses to one question with those to another. Thus, for example, it would be possible to show the relationship between perceived usefulness of a course and the length of relevant work experience possessed by respondents. Appendix II provides guidance on more sophisticated statistical techniques. In general, these are not justified for the sort of data which reactionnaires produce. The strength of reactionnaires is that they are a medium for quick, simple and inexpensive feedback.

CONCLUSION

Reactionnaires sometimes appear to be the trainer's equivalent of family heirlooms – lovingly cherished and handed on from generation to generation. Nobody asks whether grandfather's clock keeps good time or whether the pair of pottery dogs over the fireplace are aesthetically pleasing. So it is with reactionnaires. The same badly worded questions and spurious scales crop up time and again in one organization after

EVALUATION TECHNIQUES

---

16. As a manager, what do you do before a member of your staff attends a training course, so as to prepare them for it?

Likely answers and underling of categories

We discuss her needs at <u>Annual Appraisal</u>.

The <u>Training Department talks</u> to them.

The <u>papers</u> go <u>direct</u> ... <u>I'm not involved</u> at that stage.

We try to find <u>half an hour</u> or so to <u>talk</u> about the course, <u>what it's meant to do</u>, how it relates to <u>Smith's job</u> ...

Possible categories for analysis

Note: This is a brief illustration. In practice it would require many more examples of answers before finalizing which categories will be used.

Categories of response	Frequency of occurrence
Discuss at annual appraisal – general needs	++++ //
Pre-course briefing by manager on aims and job-relevance of course	///
Pre-course briefing by training department	++++ ++++ /
No manager involvement – papers sent to trainee	////
Other*	//

*List items categorized as 'Other':
Discuss with ex-participant of course.
Read a book about the course subject.
Etc.

Figure 11.15 Responses to open questions: categorization and summary

another. Not infrequently the same borrowed or inherited form is encountered in different enterprises, applied to differing kinds of training, and used with at best a fuzzy sense of its purpose, value, or limitations.

It is well worth finding the time to draft locally relevant questionnaires. Only a few hours are needed for a simple but effective design. It will take you no longer to administer a good example than a bad one, and it will be much more favourably received. Furthermore, it is *easier* to analyse a well-designed reactionnaire than one in which the questions are confusing and the responses ambiguous. There is much to gain and nothing to lose.

12 Written tests

Written tests assess the knowledge that trainees possess. Their contribution to training and evaluation includes the following:

- Feedback to trainees during a learning event.
- Measurement of learning gain over time.
- Feedback to trainers on whether or not learning is being assimilated, and thus on whether the learning methods are effective.
- Certification of competence.

In addition to employing written tests in evaluation, they may be undertaken before training, as a diagnostic instrument to determine individual needs. At the beginning of an event they may stimulate discussion and sensitize the participants to the intended learning goals. Following learning inputs, they can provide reinforcement of the topic.

Tests are sometimes objected to on the grounds that learners resent them, perhaps because of negative memories of school examinations. There have been some organizations in which tests of competence post-training are not permitted by the trade union representing the learners. On the other hand, most learners are interested in receiving feedback on how their own knowledge or skill is developing and may welcome the comparatively objective assessment which tests provide. As with most evaluation, much depends on the prevailing climate of the organization and on the quality of the relationships between trainers, trainees and line managers. If tests are seen mainly as punitive then any form of performance assessment is likely to be resisted. Similarly, tests which produce group rankings may also be resisted. Assessment by gain ratios is preferable to raw scores. Conversely, if tests are seen as a legitimate part of quality control in training and as a source of valid and helpful information for the trainee, there is unlikely to be much resistance.

Tests need to be correctly introduced to trainees and they need to be well-designed. Tests which are biased in the choice of items, or which assess only trivial aspects of the subject, help to discredit all testing and evaluation. Tests should comprehensively assess knowledge of all important aspects of the subject and that knowledge should directly relate to training objectives and hence to job tasks.

The credibility of tests is particularly low when a pencil and paper test is used to assess a performance skill. (An exception to this rule is the situation where the trainee is first acquiring the elements of the skill through 'part-whole' sequencing: thus it would be in order to ask a very inexperienced learner driver 'Describe what you should do before pulling away from the kerb'; an experienced learner, however, should be expected to demonstrate the skills under real traffic conditions.) Written tests are *not* a substitute for performance tests (whether concerned with practical skills or inter-personal skills).

Written tests are relatively inexpensive and relatively objective – certainly an improvement on 'general impressions' of tutors or self-reports of learners. Tests are easily administered and can be used on a wide scale to cover large trainee populations. Good tests do require careful thought and design guidelines are given later in this chapter. Two last cautions: first, in multinational or multicultural contexts, tests may contain unnoticed cultural bias and assumptions which are not valid for all test subjects. Second, tests (other than wholly visual items) require a level of literacy which may sometimes be greater than the level required for job competencce or that actually possessed by the trainees.

TYPES OF TEST

There are two categories of test: those employing *recall* items (also known as supply items) and those using *recognition* items.

With recall items the trainee must recall from memory the answer required by the question. The question itself may be of the essay type or short-answer format, or may involve the supply of information in order to complete an answer.

Recognition items require the trainee to identify the correct response when presented with a choice amongst prompting alternative answers. Recognition questions include the true/false type, multiple-choice items and various forms of list matching.

Tests may be of either 'open-book' or 'closed-book' form. Closed-book tests put a premium on memory: this is sometimes appropriate – the learner driver must be able to interpret road signs without reference to the Highway Code. For other subjects, however, it may be more important that trainees can find their way around a reference source (such as a technical manual, or a code of practice) which will be available to them on the job. In such instances, an open-book test will be appropriate.

EVALUATION TECHNIQUES

TEST CONSTRUCTION: AN OVERVIEW

The design of a written test is set out in the seven steps outlined below.

STEP 1

Ensure that you have comprehensive, specific and well-detailed training objectives. Vague objectives make test construction (except perhaps discursive essay items) very difficult: the objectives will require re-writing before test items can be developed.

STEP 2

Draft a large number of test items (whatever the type of test you are using). The purpose is to obtain comprehensive coverage of the training content and also enough items to allow you to select only the best examples.

A balance needs to be struck between the considerable workload (and test administration time) involved in developing a multi-item test, and the problem of a short test being both unrepresentative of the whole subject, and also more likely to become known quickly 'on the grapevine'. One solution is to develop a fairly large number of test items and then to use representative sub-sets of items to give variations of the test to different trainees or trainee groups.

STEP 3

Select test items which are well-designed and which yield adequate coverage of the topic.

STEP 4

Sequence the items in whatever way makes sense. Typically, this would be the order in which elements of knowledge are applied in the job situation to which they relate.

STEP 5

Prepare instructions to the trainees which explain simply and clearly what they have to do during the test (e.g. tick boxes, circle choices, cross out alternatives, etc.).

STEP 6

Prepare a scoring key. It should be designed so that the key can be overlaid on the test paper with key answers positioned next to the trainee's answers. Alternatively, you may be able to design your test paper to permit machine-readable scoring using a computer.

STEP 7

Use the test a number of times and then analyse the scores to assess the reliability of the test and the adequacy of individual items. Revise the test and scoring key as necessary.

QUESTION DESIGN: GENERAL RULES

1. Ensure that you only include questions that cover important or useful aspects of the topic. It is sometimes easier to draft questions on trivial aspects of the topic but it devalues the purpose of testing. Restrict questions to what has been presented explicitly during the learning activity.
2. Match the question type to the sort of knowledge being tested – is recall the issue, or recognition, or more complex problem-analysing skills?
3. Reliability increases with the number of questions. Longer tests can be made more interesting by varying the types of item used, for example mixing short answer, true/false and multiple-choice questions.
4. Questions should be stated in language appropriate to the subject matter and the test subjects. There is no benefit from stating questions in a deliberately obscure way, unless of course this obscurity is typical of conditions prevailing in the work context.
5. Questions should not contain clues to the answer. Exclude any item to which the answer is obvious to a person who does not know the subject area. In particular, avoid leading questions which point the trainee in the direction of a certain answer.
6. The wording of a question should not give clues to the answer to any other question in the same test.
7. It is better to avoid questions phrased as negatives ('What do you not do when ...?'). You may end up simply testing trainees' ability to unravel complicated prose.
8. Questions should aim to be more than just tests of memory. Test the trainee's ability to apply knowledge. In particular, do not simply parrot in question format statements which have appeared as training inputs (whether verbal or in handouts). Use paraphrase. Change the context in which the knowledge element appears.
9. Always avoid putting the correct answer to a multiple choice or true/false item in the same place. Beware of creating patterns unconsciously (e.g. True, False, True, True, False, True, True, and so on). Use dice or random number tables to determine the position of the correct answer.
10. Avoid trick questions. As with obscurely worded questions, you are testing

EVALUATION TECHNIQUES

the trainees' ability to cope with tests rather than their knowledge of the subject.
11. Have as your goal when designing questions the idea that for each question there should be only one correct answer. This will not be true of open-ended essay type questions, but it is a good principle for most test items.
12. Do not make the answer to any question dependent on answering a previous question correctly.

RECALL/SUPPLY ITEMS

ESSAY AND SHORT-ANSWER ITEMS

Essay questions are easily constructed and can test broad areas of knowledge and the ability to structure and analyse information. Essay or short-answer items are used to test knowledge objectives which ask the trainee to do the following:

describe	calculate
state	specify
define	label
determine	list
demonstrate understanding	demonstrate expressive ability
	demonstrate creative thought

An essay is to be preferred where the trainee's ability to explain, compare, argue logically, or build up complex sets of ideas is to be assessed. Essays permit freedom of expression and creativity. However, they take time to write and time to grade. The conventional long essay gives an advantage to the person who writes well even if that person does not know much about the subject. Examples of long essay items are as follows:

> Discuss the influence which the organizational context exerts on whether or not training leads to changes in work behaviour.

> Evaluation of training in organizations is neither simple nor objective. Discuss.

Essay and short-answer questions should specify the target length for the answer.

WRITTEN TESTS

Name the four main types of business unit in UK industry and commerce

For what do the following initials, used in the commercial export business, stand?
FOB
CIF

List in the correct sequence the main documents used in the company's order processing and invoicing system

---

Figure 12.1 **Short-answer items**

Do not ask for too much writing in the time available. An example of a short-answer item is as follows:

Describe (maximum of 50 words) what is meant by a 'SWOT Analysis' when writing a sales proposal.

Short-answer items should encourage trainees to summarize or tabulate their answers rather than write continuous prose. Trainees may be required to give a list of terms, rules, or influencing factors in a situation, or be asked to state the sequence of stages through which an activity proceeds. This is not intended as an English Language test. Figure 12.1 provides examples of short-answer items.

When it is stated in tabulated form, the short-answer item in some ways resembles the multiple-choice item (Figure 12.2).

Essays present particular problems for the grading of trainees' performance. Essay marking is more subjective than other methods of assessment and it often depends on the availability of a subject matter expert to assess and interpret the quality of answers.

Marking schemes

A marking guide should be created simultaneously with the drafting of essay items. This details the key points for which test subjects will gain marks – content, structure, analysis and so on.

The individual marker should work through the test papers assessing the answers to one question, before repeating the process for the next question. This

EVALUATION TECHNIQUES

Indicate (by ticking the box) whether each of the following assets is 'fixed' or 'current'.		
Asset	Fixed	Current
Cash at bank		
Machinery		
Buildings		
Finished products		
Delivery truck		
Trade debtors		
Furniture and fittings		

Figure 12.2 Tabulated short-answer item

helps the marker to keep the same mental perspective on the topic and improves the consistency of marking. Different markers should compare the levels of mark they are giving. Discrepancies should be explored – some people may be marking too harshly or too leniently. As a final precaution, some essays should be re-marked by an independent examiner.

It is common with essay tests to find that markers use a confused mixture of criterion- and norm-referenced elements. Marks will be allocated for subject coverage (more or less precisely criterion-referenced) and also will be adjusted to spread the learners across a distribution curve (i.e. norm referencing). For training purposes a criterion-referenced assessment is usually required and long essays do not easily lend themselves to this.

It is easier to prepare marking keys for short-answer items. Even here, trainees may submit valid answers which the test designers have not anticipated. A question such as that shown in Figure 12.3 will produce many more than four valid answers and in such cases the answer key must contain all possible correct responses, not just the four that are preferred by the test designer.

It is preferable – especially in training tests – to substitute a number of short-answer items for a single long essay item. Short-answer items are especially

WRITTEN TESTS

> Name four areas in which a good salesperson will prepare for selling activities:
>
>
> Possible answers include:
>
>   Personal appearance
>   Planning to reach personal targets
>   Keeping records of contacts with customers and prospects
>   Updating product knowledge
>   Planning sales call content
>   Preparing sales aids
>   Journey planning

Figure 12.3   **Range of valid answers to a short-answer item**

convenient for quick feedback to trainers during a learning activity. However, recall items always carry the risk that they will encourage memorization of the 'right' words, rather than understanding of the sense behind the words or the ability to apply the knowledge in situations that differ from the context in which the knowledge was first acquired.

COMPLETION ITEMS

Completion items provide a test either of recall *or* of the trainee's ability to create an appropriate answer by – typically – calculation. These items can easily become trivial and they may require a subject expert to grade responses. The main application is to test knowledge of simple facts or procedures.

Completion items may consist of an unfinished statement or of a statement with one or two key words omitted, for example:

> The main application of completion items is in the testing of . . .

> A Bill of Loading is a _____ to goods as well as a _____ note which describes goods which are being exported, the ports of embarkation and destination, and the shipping line.

Alternatively, completion items may require an answer to be deduced from the information presented in the question, as illustrated in Figure 12.4.

When drafting incomplete sentence items there are several rules to observe:

173

EVALUATION TECHNIQUES

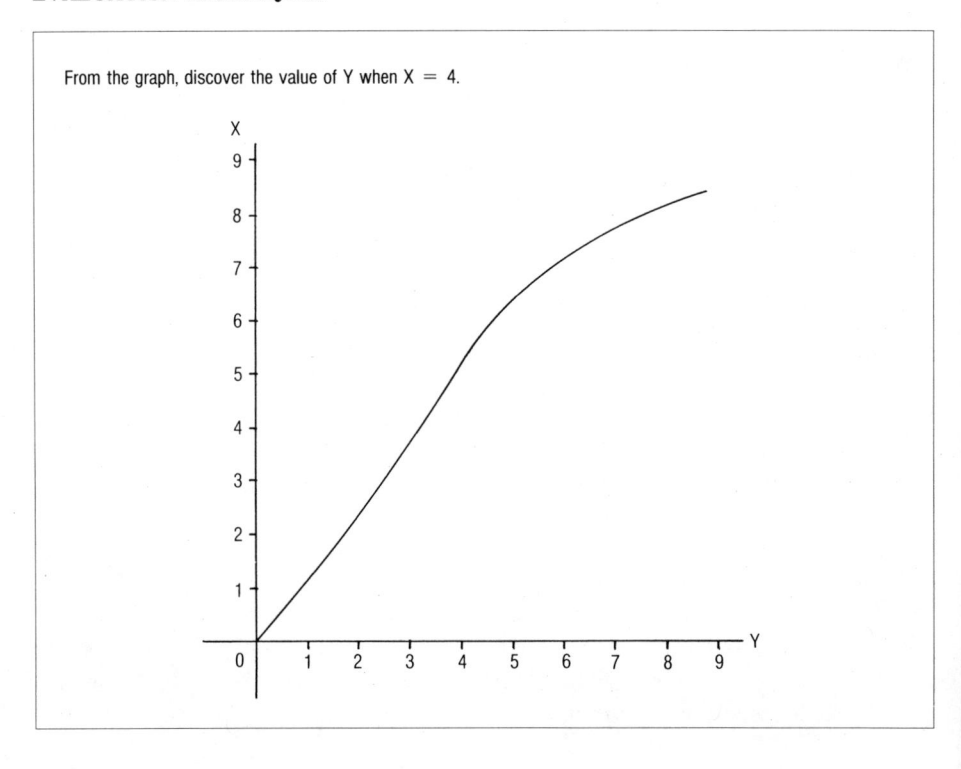

From the graph, discover the value of Y when X = 4.

Figure 12.4 Completion item

- The omitted word should be towards the end rather than the beginning of the sentence (or clause within a sentence).
- Not more than two words should be omitted (three in a long sentence).
- The words left out should be key terms that directly relate to learning objectives.
- There must be only one sensible way to complete the sentence (this is often hard to achieve).
- Sentences should not be repeated verbatim from training objectives or training materials.

RECOGNITION ITEMS

TWO-OPTION ALTERNATIVE ANSWER ITEMS

These items are most often encountered in the form of a statement followed by the options 'true' or 'false'. Sometimes the options 'agree/disagree' are used, but it is more common to find these incorporated into an attitude rating scale with more than two points on it. An example of a two-option item is provided below:

> 'Reserves' indicate how much cash is available to meet contingencies:
> TRUE/FALSE
> (*circle one alternative*)

True/false items are quite easy to design, to administer to trainees and to score. However, it is easy to obtain a good score purely by guessing and/or by relying on memory rather than understanding. True/false items are unsuitable for controversial topics or, indeed, any subject matter which cannot be stated as wholly true or wholly false.

Rules for the design of true/false items follow the general principles of test construction (p. 167) with the addition of the following:

1. Avoid complicated sentences in the statement. The statement need not be brief, but it should be broken up into short sentences that aid comprehension.
2. Only have *one* idea in each item. If there is more than one, the trainee may wish to answer 'true' to one part of the question and 'false' to another part.
3. The statement must be definitely one thing or the other: there is no scope for qualified, ambiguous alternatives.

    Note: few statements are invariably true or invariably false. If you use words like 'every', 'never', 'always', or 'more' these are usually an indication that the statement is unlikely to be true.
4. Beware of giving away the answer by implicit value judgements within the item statement, for example 'The experienced driver does . . .'
5. Establish a rough balance between the number of true and false items in a test. Ensure the sequence of true and false answers is random.

True/false items can have only one correct answer and tests do not need to be marked by subject experts. These items are useful for quick feedback during training activities and to introduce some variety of item design into long tests.

MULTIPLE-CHOICE ITEMS

Multiple-choice items are particularly suitable where training objectives are specified in terms of the following:

EVALUATION TECHNIQUES

select	differentiate
identify	describe
recognize	match
indicate	calculate

Multiple-choice items with four or five plausible answers to choose from greatly reduce the scope for correct guesswork. These items do not require any one answer to be absolutely right – only that one option is appreciably better than the rest. It is also possible for all alternatives to be correct: judgement may be tested as well as knowledge. Multiple-choice questions allow the testing of more complex knowledge areas. Scoring does not require a subject expert and multiple-choice items are quickly administered and scored. However, good multiple-choice items are not easily constructed.

All multiple-choice items consist of a 'stem' and a set of responses to the stem. The responses are made up of the correct response plus three or four 'distractors'. The latter are plausible responses to the stem, which consists either of a question or an unfinished statement. When unfinished statements are used for the stem it is essential that every one of the response options follows grammatically from it as shown in Figure 12.5.

As a rule aim for four or five alternative answers. However, it is more important that the responses all appear to be *plausible* answers. Therefore, where there are only, say, three realistic alternatives it is better to use only these, rather than introduce a fourth distractor which no one is likely to believe. It is bad practice to make up the number of distractors with a phrase such as 'All of the above' or 'None of the above'.

The incomplete sentence format (as shown in the second example in Figure 12.5) usually takes up less space. Sometimes, however, it is harder with this design to obtain grammatically satisfactory sentence conclusions for all the distractors.

What colour or colours of light are displayed by a traffic light, indicating 'prepare to go'?

- Red ☐
- Green ☐
- Green and amber ☐
- Red and amber ☐
- Amber ☐   *(tick one box)*

A malleable substance is one which can be:
- hammered to shape ☐
- stretched to shape ☐
- melted to shape ☐   *(tick one box)*

Figure 12.5 Multiple-choice items

When the stem is a descriptive statement it need not be restricted to one sentence. Sometimes a paragraph of description or a miniature case study will be an appropriate stem in relation to the objective being tested. Of course, long stems do increase test duration and so reduce the number of items that can be assessed. The trade-off is a matter of your purpose and the relative importance of different objectives.

The correct answer and the distractors can be stated in various ways: as words or sentences; as letters or numbers which are keyed to something documented elsewhere (such as a code of practice); as mathematical formulae; as the product of mathematical operations; as drawings or diagrams. In the case of mathematical examples, the distractors should be solutions that would be obtained as a result of the more common errors found with that specific problem (e.g. adding certain figures instead of subtracting).

A guide to the credibility of a set of distractors is that to the trainee who knows the answer only one of the responses stands out; to the person who does not know the answer, all seem equally likely.

There are a number of cues which may reveal which is the correct answer in a multiple-choice test. One kind of cue is to make the correct answer more specific, more detailed, longer, or offering a different point of view to the rest. Grammatical structure can offer cues: avoid ending the stem of an incomplete sentence item with 'a' or 'an'. Rephrase such items as a complete question, or put an indefinite article into each of the distractors. Another grammatical cue occurs with the use of singular and plural nouns in the stem and distractors. Distractors should not repeat words or phrases that appear in the stem:

The best method for training in interpersonal sensitivity is:

an action-centred approach	☐	(*tick*)
role-play	☐	*one*
group discussion	☐	*box*)
sensitivity training	☐	

Lastly, the distractors should not be concepts which overlap each other, nor should they be synonyms of each other.

MATCHING ITEMS

These items consist of two sets or lists of elements. Elements of one list must be matched to elements of the other list. The elements may be proper names and words, as in Figure 12.6. Lists may be compiled from numbers, symbols, pictures and from facts or concepts (see Figure 12.7). Single words may be matched against descriptive sentences.

EVALUATION TECHNIQUES

Match the theorists to the approach with which each is associated by writing the approach number in the appropriate box.

Theorists
a) McClelland ☐
b) McGregor ☐
c) Argyris ☐
d) Schein ☐
e) Mager ☐
f) Beckhard ☐

Approaches
1. Confrontation meeting
2. Theory X and Theory Y
3. Double-loop learning
4. Behavioural objectives
5. Career anchors
6. Achievement motivation
7. Anticipatory socialization
8. Management by objectives

Figure 12.6 Matching items: names and words

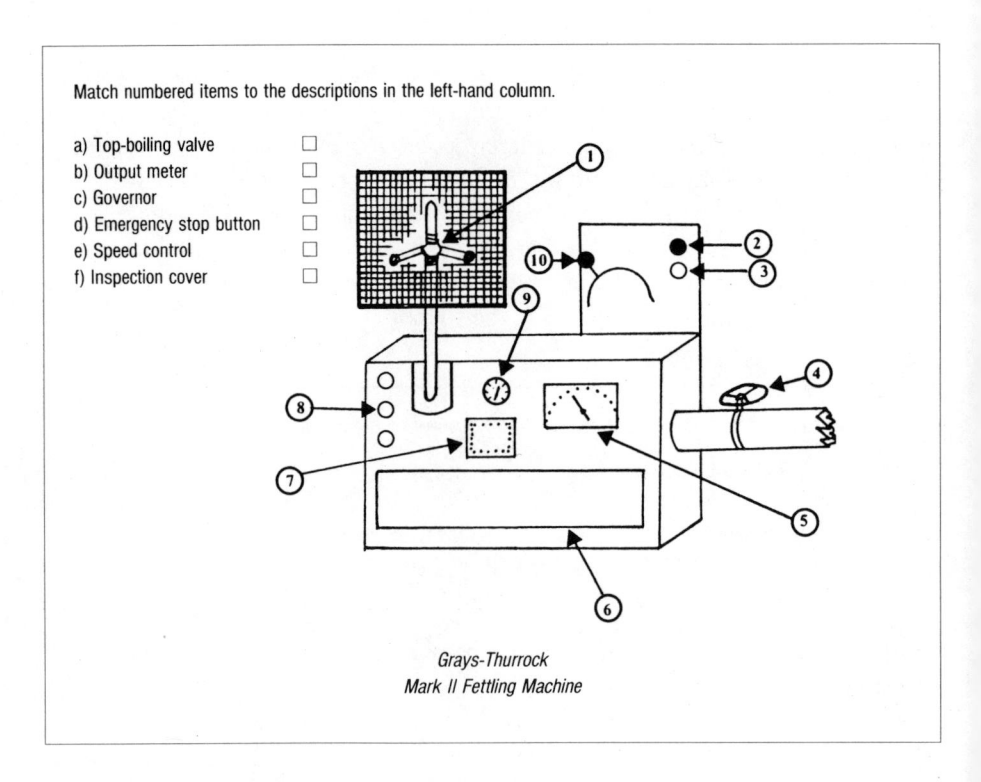

Match numbered items to the descriptions in the left-hand column.

a) Top-boiling valve ☐
b) Output meter ☐
c) Governor ☐
d) Emergency stop button ☐
e) Speed control ☐
f) Inspection cover ☐

*Grays-Thurrock
Mark II Fettling Machine*

Figure 12.7 Matching items: picture and words

Matching items are especially suitable for testing trainees' ability to select or recognize knowledge elements. These items are relatively easy to construct, quick to use and easily scored. Provided matching items are properly constructed, guessing the answers is difficult. The following rules apply to the construction of matching items:

1. Keep the (left-hand) list of items fairly short – in the range 5 to 10. It is difficult to match very long lists and clerical errors become common, lessening the utility of the test as a measure of knowledge.
2. The (right-hand) list of items amongst which the trainee must choose should contain about one-and-a-half times as many items as the list to which it is matched.
3. All items in a list should be related to the same learning topic and all the matching alternatives should be plausible.
4. The items should be placed in alphabetical or numerical order, or in order of chronological occurrence. This lessens the amount of time that the trainee spends searching the lists.
5. The whole of both lists must appear on the same page.
6. There should be clear instructions for boxes to be marked, or for lines to be drawn, from items in one list to items in the other.

13 Practical tests

The applications of practical tests occur almost wholly within the training event – to provide feedback to trainees on their performance or to assess learning gain and terminal competence. Tests can be used as an initial diagnostic aid also. Where a training event consists of a number of distinct self-contained units, pre-testing can identify topics in which the trainee is already competent, thereby saving training time and expense, and increasing trainee motivation. Equally, pre-testing can establish whether trainees possess some minimum level of prerequisite knowledge or skill for entry to the course.

Practical tests are to be used whenever a trainee needs to be able to translate knowledge into application. Tests may measure the quality of a finished task (whether that task is using a lathe to turn a chair-leg, or a word-processor to compose a letter). They may measure accuracy of physical or mental operations, speed of task-completion, completeness of a performance, planning ability, or competence in identifying (say) mechanical components. Written tests (Chapter 12) and practical tests may be used in complementary fashion at successive stages of a trainee's acquisition of new abilities, but written tests alone can never be adequate as a way of assessing performance. Assessment of interpersonal skills is, of course, a form of practical test. However, because of the range of that subject and the different content emphasis, the evaluation of interpersonal skills is treated separately (Chapter 14).

The advantages of practical tests are several:

- They generally have high face validity.
- They reinforce learning by providing additional practice in the skill.
- Practical application of learning encourages transfer into work practice.
- There is rapid feedback to instructors and to trainees about the extent to which skills have been mastered.

There are also some disadvantages:

- Practical tests are time-consuming.
- Realistic simulation may be difficult and/or expensive to achieve.
- Many practical tests require much more supervision during the test period

PRACTICAL TESTS

compared to, say, written tests.
- It may be difficult to prevent trainees observing what each other is doing.
- Scoring reliability can present more difficulties.
- There is the risk of damage to equipment.

TESTING DIFFERENT LEVELS OF OBJECTIVE

Practical tests may be designed to assess several different levels of practical skill. Using P. Harmon's classification[1] the objectives of interest here are those categorized as verbal performance and physical performance objectives.

1. Verbal performance objectives

   Level 1.1: Recall; listing; stating a fact or rule.
   1.2: Explaining a procedure.
   1.3: Responding to questions or statements.
   1.4: Solving a specific problem.
   1.5: Solving a general type of problem.

2. Physical performance objectives

   Level 2.1: Identify physical things.
   2.2: Perform simple physical acts.
   2.3: Perform more complex acts either following instructions or from memory.
   2.4: Perform actions requiring physical skill.
   2.5: Select an appropriate action and perform it.
   2.6: Determine acceptable quality in physical products.

A practical test may be compiled from a number of items each of which relates to one of these levels of objective. As frequently, the test will consist of complex items which require performance of several levels of objective, partly in sequence and partly concurrently. For example, a machine operator must be able to identify all control knobs (etc.) – level 2.1 – as well as carry out from memory a sequence of activities – level 2.3 – and finally examine the product for machining flaws – level 2.6. The test may either assess the quality of the final element of this sequence, or may make a stage-by-stage judgement of each part. The former requires less assessor time; the latter allows corrective feedback (a benefit in terms of learning; a distorting factor in terms of assessing the learning: assisted learners should have a proportion of marks deducted).

Harmon's sets of objectives can in practice be condensed into four groups:

a) Recall/identification tasks (1.1; 1.3; 2.1)
b) Procedure–following tasks (1.2; 2.3; 2.4)
c) Analytical/problem-solving tasks (1.4; 1.5; 2.5; 2.6)

EVALUATION TECHNIQUES

    d)   Tasks requiring manual dexterity (2.2; 2.3; 2.4; 2.5)

Group (a) involves the ability to recall or recognize words, symbols or objects, and to answer simple factual questions, for example:

> 'The telephone operator can state the names of the two overseas exchanges.'
>
> 'The symbol ☂ on a packing case means . . .?'
>
> 'What is this part of the carburettor called?'
>
> 'When asked for directions to a specified department, the reception clerk can provide clear guidance.'

Group (b) requires the trainee to be able to explain a procedure to someone or to follow, either with prompting or from memory, a sequence of actions, for example:

> 'The housing adviser will be able to explain the system for registering as a homeless family.'
>
> 'The trainee carpenter will be able to construct a satisfactory mitred joint.'

Group (c) includes such activities as diagnostic fault-finding; following a decision-tree; preparing for a sales call; dealing with an in-tray; and assessing quality, for example:

> 'The mechanic will be able to identify the reason or reasons why a given motor-car engine will not start.'
>
> 'Using Table 7 in the User's Manual, the evaluator will be able to develop an evaluation strategy for the organization.'
>
> 'The salesperson will analyse available information about the prospect company and prepare a written plan for the interview.'
>
> 'The trainee will establish priorities amongst in-basket items and will deal with each, as appropriate by means of written reply, telephone conversation, or face to face meeting.'
>
> The foreman will be able to state whether or not the quality of a given mitre-joint is satisfactory.'

Group (d) relates to various levels of manual dexterity. At its simplest this may be a specific action to be performed in an appropriate situation, for example to drive a nail. At a higher level, a more complex sequence of activities is involved, for example changing a car wheel; machining a block of metal. The highest skill level combines the analytical/diagnostic skills of Group (c) with practical application skills of a high order, for example to repair a watch.

DESIGN OF PRACTICAL TESTS

The design of practical tests starts from the training objectives. Test methods can be specified to match the four types of objective grouped together in the preceding section. First, there are some general principles of good design to consider.

Step 1

Develop practical tests at the same time as you finalize training objectives, and before you determine the content and methods of the learning activity. It is always good practice to develop objectives in parallel with evaluation – the standards set for objectives and the criteria set for evaluation are obviously closely linked.

In testing, this approach has a further advantage. The test is based upon job-performance standards, reflected in task-based training objectives. This ensures that it is not merely a test of skill performance as it has been demonstrated on a particular training event. If trainees do not attain the criterion standard, that provides an independent check on whether the training has been effective, as well as a more valid indicator of task competence.

Step 2

Base the test activities directly on the training objectives (which in turn should directly reflect job tasks). This may not be straightforward: it is quite common for instructors to train 'by the book' and for trained workers in the field to cut corners. This may be seen partly as a problem of transfer of learning. However, it is mainly an issue about field supervision and disciplinary practice, and especially about the extent to which the organization condones (or even rewards) short-cuts and pays lip-service to the correct methods that are taught.

Step 3

Specify with as much precision as possible the actions to be performed in the test. Neither the trainee nor the assessor should experience any ambiguity over what the test involves. Actions, relevant conditions (such as the availability of tools) and standards of performance should all be specified. There should be no secrets about the way in which judgements will be made.

Step 4

Plan for standardized administration of the test. All trainees should experience the same level of supervision and the same physical situation when performing the test. The same length of time should be made available to each trainee.

EVALUATION TECHNIQUES

Step 5

Make the test environment only as realistic a simulation of workplace conditions as is necessary to ensure that the test is a valid assessment device. It is one thing to be able to solder a joint in a workshop and another to do it in a 'hole in the road'. Environmental realism becomes a particularly important issue when training for emergency situations. It may be necessary to accept a lower level of fidelity in the simulation as a trade-off against unacceptable levels of hazard.

Step 6

As test items are developed, a standard marking scheme should be drawn up concurrently. This must specify exactly what elements of performance will score how many marks. It is the performance and solely the performance that is to be assessed – not the person.

The marking scheme should be test-run and amended where necessary so that any discretionary elements are minimized. If there are to be several assessors, their marking of test performances should be compared and divergent standards investigated.

Step 7

Do not test people for practical skills that they have not been taught. Trainees must have received guidance on the type and standard of performance required, and they must have had opportunities to practise the skill. Skills may be demonstrated 'live' by instructors, or be recorded on video. It is not a satisfactory approach to describe the theory behind a skill and then test its practical application. That fails to maximize learning, and it undermines the credibility of trainers who are seen as preaching but not practising. It is a good principle (assuming that you are using criterion-referenced tests) to assess skill proficiency only when trainees themselves feel ready for it.

Step 8

Test skill development a step at a time until complete mastery is achieved: at that point it may be appropriate to complicate the testing to simulate real life complexities. In general, though, do not test more than a few principles, tasks or skills at any one time. Only trainees who have achieved mastery of a learning stage should be allowed to proceed to the next task. If the learning task is especially important, or particularly complicated, the trainee may be required to demonstrate mastery several times, in different applications, before proceeding further.

Step 9

Use the test results to give feedback to individuals on areas of strength and on matters that need to be improved. Use test results to monitor whether training activities are meeting their aims fully or whether there is a high rate of referrals for additional training. Monitor the trend of test results over time for indicators of rising or falling effectiveness.

Step 10

Ensure that tests are conducted in stringent compliance with safety provisions. Include safe working procedures as part of task specifications and award a proportion of marks for good practice.

Step 11

Determine whether the test is concerned with task process or with the final product, or both. The process concerns the way in which the trainee carries out the task; the product is the end result. For instance, you may wish to assess the accuracy with which a piece of metal has been machined, or whether a weld is free of visible pits or cracks (a product assessment) but you will also be concerned about such factors as use of safety goggles and machine guards, or the handling of gas cylinders (which are process items). Clearly, with process items, the trainee must be observed throughout the test activity whereas with product items you can make the assessment at the end of the test or at a later time. Process tests can be assessed after the event, if the test is recorded on video, but this will be more usual in the practical testing of interpersonal skills.

Step 12

Process items have a number of key design features:
- a) Each item must be observable.
- b) Items should be worded so as to provide a yes/no response, rather than a more subjective scaled response.
- c) Only one process action should be included in each test item – if several actions are combined, you do not know whether a yes/no response relates to some or to all of these actions.
- d) The wording of the item should avoid woolly and subjective terms such as 'satisfactory', 'enough', 'properly', 'well' and similar words.
- e) Items should be listed in the order in which they will be performed and observed.
- f) Where certain items are of critical importance, it may be appropriate to instruct the trainee to pause at that stage so that the instructor can check whether processes have been properly carried out (most obviously, in the case of key safety precautions).

Step 13

Product items too have their own special design elements:

a) Each item must be precisely specifiable, whether this is a matter of engineering tolerances or the quality of the texture of a fresh-baked loaf.
b) Only elements of the product which are critical to the performance of the finished product should be assessed, for example a letter may be relevantly assessed on its Fog Index, but the size of the margins will not normally be critical.

In addition, product items should take account of the guidance under Rule 12, for process items – in particular sub-sections a, c, d and f. For section f, the product equivalent is to instruct the trainee to pause at a stage beyond which physical inspection becomes impossible, for example when jointing cables, to pause before sealing the outer covering of the cable in order that the soldered joints may be inspected.

Step 14

Decide on the level of performance that will be recognized as mastery of the skill. Figures in the range 80 per cent and above are often given for this. However, there is a case for insisting on 100 per cent as the standard of competence. Any lesser percentage implies that there are test items which are not critical.

Would you wish to fly with a pilot who was 90 per cent competent? And if so, which 10 per cent of flying skills would you see as not critical? The penalties of 90 per cent competence (or 10 per cent incompetence) are not always as dramatic as this, but they are still real. If a joint in a water-pipe is soldered with 90 per cent effectiveness, is the steady drip of leaking water acceptable?

Test standards should not be lower than standards expected of experienced workers: the only difference is that trainees should be allowed more time to achieve those levels than that required by experienced workers.

Step 15

Write clear instructions to the trainees, setting out what they are required to do during the test. In some circumstances, it may be more appropriate to give verbal instructions, but these should be read from a standard script to ensure consistency between one test occasion and another. The instructions should state the following:

1. The purpose(s) of the test.
2. The conditions under which the test will occur (e.g. in the workshop; in the field).
3. What the trainee is required to do.
4. Points of particular emphasis:

PRACTICAL TESTS

   a) in terms of process or product assessment, what are critical elements;
   b) safety procedures to which one must adhere.
5. Time limits for test completion.
6. What criteria and standards will be applied to define competent performance.

Step 16

Try it out: first on other instructors, then on a sample of students. Review the instructions and any individual items that appear to cause difficulty. Train the assessors to observe process items and assess product standards in a systematic way. Consistency in marking performance will be increased by asking assessors to rate process ability in parallel (separately if the test activity is on video) and independently to rate test products. Scoring discrepancies can be investigated and acceptable standardization achieved. Monitor the reliability of assessments over time and also between different assessors. The principles of training observers to assess interpersonal skills (Chapter 14, pp. 206–14) are quite relevant here, as are the guidelines on giving feedback to trainees (Chapter 14, pp. 214–16).

EXAMPLES OF TEST ITEMS

GROUP (A) RECALL/IDENTIFICATION ITEMS

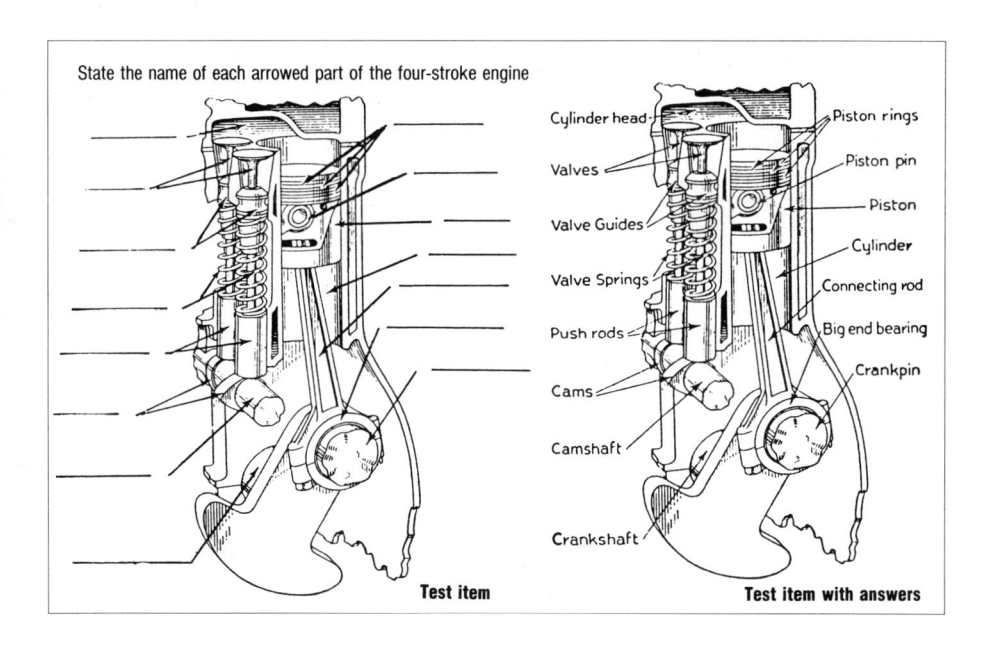

Figure 13.1 Recall/identification item

Source: Hawkes, E. *How it Works and How it's Done*. Odhams Press Ltd., London.

EVALUATION TECHNIQUES

GROUP (B): PROCEDURE ITEMS

Task Check vehicle battery **Student**

Directions Demonstrate proficiency in this task by doing the following:

This test evaluates your ability to check a vehicle battery. You will be allocated a vehicle. Clean and check the battery and slow-charge it to full charge. Write down the temperature and specific gravity each hour.

Safety note: make sure that the instructor checks your connections before turning on the battery charger.

Your performance will be evaluated using the items below; all must be 'yes'.

	Yes	No
1. Detected external defects in the battery during inspection?		
2. Fluid levels in cells checked.		
3. Distilled water added if necessary.		
4. Was the battery cleaned and dried?		
5. Was the battery removed from the vehicle or cable clamps disconnected (earth first) before charging?		
6. Was the charger switch in the OFF position before being connected to the terminals?		
7. Was the charger connected to battery + to + and − to − ?		
8. Was the charger turned on?		
9. Was the charging rate appropriate for the vehicle's battery?		
10. Were the temperature and specific gravity checked every hour?		
11. Was the charger turned off before being disconnected?		
12. Was the battery reinstalled in the vehicle securely?		
13. Were the cables reconnected + to + and − to − ?		
14. Is the battery fully charged?		
15. Will the battery start the vehicle?		

Date: **Test supervised by:**

Figure 13.2   Procedure item

GROUP (C): PROBLEM-SOLVING/ANALYTICAL ITEMS
(i) 'Complaint' sales call

This example consists of three parts – a list of the objectives to be tested (Figure 13.3); two checklists for monitoring preparatory work and the sales call itself (Figures 13.4 and 13.5); and an extract from the master list of behavioural descriptions relating to the checklist items (Table 13.1). (Serial numbers allow cross-referencing between these documents.)

(ii) In-tray assessments

The idea is to simulate in a realistic manner a number of the matters requiring attention which typical job-holders might find in their in-trays. The approach has been used in a somewhat hit-or-miss way as an element of recruitment or promotion selection procedure. It has become incorporated in the more systematic techniques

PRACTICAL TESTS

> The trainee will demonstrate the following:
> a) Reinforce the role of the salesperson as a provider of business solutions.
>
> b) Respond to customer's expressions of dissatisfaction.
>
> c) Use questioning techniques to obtain information.
>
> d) Establish and maintain rapport with the customer.
>
> e) Establish and maintain control of the meeting.
>
> f) Demonstrate active listening.
>
> g) Identify an acceptable solution to the customer's problems and needs.
>
> h) Obtain commitment to a course of action.
>
> i) Recognize and respond to objections.

Figure 13.3 Training objectives to be tested

employed in the assessment centre method, and often is found as part of management or teamwork games within training events.

An in-tray exercise will consist of a number of items – letters, memos, notes of telephone messages – with which the trainee must deal. The exercise may be wholly paper-based, but preferably will include the use of telephones and face-to-face meetings as part of the trainee's response to the in-tray contents.

Scoring will relate to productivity (the number of items dealt with), prioritizing (the extent to which important, urgent items are dealt with first) and quality of response. The quality of response is assessed in various ways, depending on the activity: a telephone call or face-to-face meeting may be judged using purpose-designed behavioural checklists. Written replies to letters and memos can be assessed for the adequacy with which the subject has been covered; for their clarity of communication (using a yardstick such as the Fog Index); for stylistic considerations such as an appropriate degree of formality, a focus on the recipient's interests and needs, or even a rating of the legibility of handwriting where this is appropriate. Problems which require information to be analysed (e.g. a set of accounts for a prospect company, prior to a sales call) may be assessed by comparison with a 'model answer', as to how accurately and completely the analysis is conducted.

There are some problems of scoring and validity to be considered. It is essential that the categories of performance which are to be assessed should be precisely defined, otherwise assessors tend to fall back on 'general impression'. The in-tray items must be a realistic representation of the work task, although even that is not a guarantee that a person will respond in the same way in an assessed training situation as in the workplace. Assessor expectations may distort the scores given to particular individuals (see Appendix II, p. 245).

EVALUATION TECHNIQUES

Assessment checklist		Written preparation for complaint call	Salesperson
Behaviours to be assessed	Behaviour present Y/N	Evidence for the behaviour Comments on the quality of performance of the behaviour	Rating[1] P: F: S−: S+: G: E
27 Sets objectives for the call			
16 Prepares in order to be able to respond to customer dissatisfaction			
1 Plans to establish rapport			
15 Plans to establish control			
10 Prepares in order to be able to recommend specific solutions to customer needs			
29 Anticipates objections			
13 Obtains commitment to a course of action			

Note: [1] P = poor, F = fair, S− = satisfactory minus, S+ = satisfactory plus, G = good, E = excellent

Figure 13.4 **Monitoring of preparatory work**

An in-tray assessment set in a sales-training context might consist of items such as the following:

1. Sales call to new prospect
    1.1 Written preparation.
    1.2 Telephone call to pre-qualify prospect and gain appointment.
    1.3 Initial interview.
    1.4 Follow-up letter.
2. Complaint call concerning existing customer
    2.1 Written preparation.
    2.2 Telephone call to gain information and set meeting.
    2.3 Meeting with customer.
    2.4 Follow-up action.

PRACTICAL TESTS

Assessment checklist		Complaint call	Salesperson
Behaviours to be Assessed	Behaviour present Y/N	Evidence for the behaviour Comments on the quality of performance of the behaviour	Rating P: F: S−: S+: G: E
1 Establishing rapport			
16 Responds to customer dissatisfaction			
15 Establishes control			
2 Use of open questions			
3 Use of closed questions			
4 Demonstrates active listening			
8 Identifies customer problems			
10 Provides a business solution			
13 Obtains commitment to a course of action			
14 Recognizes and responds to objections			

Figure 13.5 Monitoring of sales call

EVALUATION TECHNIQUES

Table 13.1 Extract from master list of behavioural descriptions

Behaviour to be assessed	Positive examples (rated S +; G; E)	Evidence for the behaviour	Negative examples (rates S −; F; P)
(Plans to)			
1. Establish rapport	Easy to talk to. Natural. Relaxed. Supports customer statements. Pleasant sense of humour. Talks customer language. Use of first names.		Awkward. Makes customer feel uncomfortable. Playing at 'being a salesman'. Uptight, starchy, humourless. Too familiar.
(Plans)			
2. Use of open questions	Questions relevant to establishing rapport and gathering information.		Preoccupied with making statements. Open questions used which allow customer to give evasive answer.
(Plans)			
3. Use of closed questions	Questions relevant to getting agreement and commitment.		Closed questions used which close opportunity for customer to explain and expand a statement.
4. Demonstrates active listening	Checks for understanding. Paraphrases customer statements. Responds to conversational leads. Takes notes. Indicates interest in customer's statements.		Inaccurate summaries of customer statements. Silent but inattentive; bored.
8. (Plans to) establish a business purpose/identification of customers' needs & problems	Use of questions. Establishes need for computer application. Establishes business priorities.		Confuses need and interest. Pushes solutions before needs established.
10. Knowledge of products & services demonstrated	Responds to identified customer needs with specific suggestions for products services. Use of aids. Reference sells. Provides 'business solution'.		Uncertain, confused about possibly appropriate products and services.
(Plans to)			
13. Obtain commitment to a course of action	Sale closed. Client agrees follow-up action proposals, e.g. reference visit. Date and purpose of next meeting agreed. All necessary parties are involved.		Unrealistic action plan. Commits to too much action before properly qualifying customer.
14. Recognize and respond to objections	Checks own understanding of objection by questions. Provides satisfactory response – checks response is acceptable. Tactful.		Fails to spot objections. Cannot answer objections. Responds aggressively.
15. Establish control	Asks questions. Guides discussion. Keeps to call structure/objectives. Keeps to subject.		Easily led by consumer. Follows 'red herring' without checking. Allows customer to end call before objectives reached. Gives in too easily on tough questions.
(Plans to)			
16. Respond to customer dissatisfaction	Gives customer space to let off steam. Takes responsibility for the problem. Proposes remedial actions.		Cuts off customer's flow. Blames other departments. Proposes remedies which contravene rules.
27. Set objectives for a sales call/telephone call/meeting	Clear statement of objectives. Are objectives measurable? Are objectives challenging?		Objectives are woolly. Objectives are not related to the current sales situation. Objectives are unambitious/easily achieved.
29. Anticipate objections	Lists likely or possible objections. Lists possible responses to objections.		No planning to handle objections.

PRACTICAL TESTS

3. Meeting of sales team
   3.1 Analysis of information about prospect companies.
   3.2 Preparation for group discussion.
   3.3 Participation in team meeting.
   3.4 Report on planned sales strategy.
4. Specialized information request from a customer
   4.1 Locating the correct information resource.
   4.2 Writing to the customer.

These various elements of the in-tray are assessed by a combination of process and product checklists over the test period (in this example two days). Trainees' performances on different tasks are independently assessed and the results are coordinated by an administrator who is not involved in the assessment process.

GROUP (D): MANUAL DEXTERITY

'Connect plug to cable' exercise

The trainee will connect a three-pin plug to a length of three-core cable. Marks will be awarded for the following:

1. Matching the colour-coded wires to the correct pins (brown: live; blue: neutral; yellow/green: earth). Any wire incorrectly positioned is an automatic fail on the test.

   Score 10 for all correct.

2. Insulation sleeve fits closely to wire-retaining hole in pins (less than 2mm bare wire visible).

   Score 10 for all correct.
   Score 5 for any bare wires with 3–5mm exposed.
   Fail test if any bare wire is greater than 5mm.

3. Core wires are cut to exact length in order to fit the pin positions.

   Score 10 for all correct.
   Score 5 if any wire is 1–5mm in excess of the correct length.
   Score 0 for any excess length greater than 6mm.

4. The cable is held securely by the cable retention bar.

   Score 5 for cable tightly gripped.
   Score 0 if cable can be moved about under the bar.

This test gives a maximum of 35 marks.

There are two items which are automatic 'fails' for safety reasons. For skill mastery, any score less than 35 may be considered unsatisfactory and the test scoring could

EVALUATION TECHNIQUES

therefore be simplified. Each element may be made a pass/fail response, requiring four passes in all for satisfactory performance.

NOTE

1. Harmon, P. (1969), 'A classification of performance objective behaviours in job training programmes', *Educational Technology*, January.

14 Behaviour analysis

Behaviour analysis is a particularly productive technique for the trainer to employ, both in evaluation and as part of the learning process itself, across the diverse range of activities that are labelled 'interpersonal skills.' A far-from-exhaustive list of training topics that benefit from the use of behaviour analysis could include:

- customer service
- supervision
- decision-making
- selling skills
- effective meetings
- performance appraisal
- telephone use
- presentation skills
- equal opportunities
- counselling skills

There are four points in the training cycle at which behaviour analysis can be used to assess interpersonal skills. These are:

- before- and after-training measures of behaviour change
- on-course feedback to trainees about the progress of their own learning (often a useful tool for observers of role plays)
- end of event certification of competence
- post-training follow-up assessments of changes in work behaviour

The core elements of the behaviour analysis technique are that it is unambiguously derived from behavioural training objectives and that it involves the observation of behaviour in a structured and consistent manner. As will become clear from the examples, it is concerned not with the formation of general impressions or intuitive judgements, but with objective judgements about the use of specific skills, or components of skills.

WHEN TO USE BEHAVIOUR ANALYSIS

Interpersonal skills can be examined at four points in the training cycle:

1. On-course feedback to trainees about the progress of their own learning.

2. Pre/post measures of change in behaviour over the period of a training event.
3. End of event assessment of competence.
4. Post-training assessment of changes in work behaviour.

What the four areas have in common is that they involve *observation of behaviour*. The essence of an interpersonal skill is that someone *behaves* in an identifiable way in the presence of one or more other people. Behaviour can be *observed*. A trained person will be able to record relevant behaviours accurately and systematically. The evaluation instrument that makes this possible is the behaviour checklist.

'Interpersonal skills' is not about attitudes nor about the sort of personal constructs that repertory grid yields: attitudes and personal constructs are at most predispositions to behave in a certain way. However, people often do act in ways that conflict with their attitudes or, conversely, hold attitudes which they do not translate into actions.

WHAT IS BEING ASSESSED?

When interpersonal behaviour is examined from a training/evaluation perspective, there are three aspects of potential interest:

1. Content (what kinds of behaviours happened).
2. Task (what activities formed the focus around which interpersonal behaviour occurred, for example a committee meeting).
3. Qualities of the interaction (the presence or absence of behaviours, their duration or frequency, the sequence in which they occurred and their quality).

Each of these aspects may be analysed either by *time* or *unit sampling*. In time sampling the observer collects data on whatever is happening at a series of preset moments in time, for example every thirty seconds, every five minutes, every hour, according to the type of activity. In unit sampling the observer records every occasion that each category of behaviour in which we are interested occurs. If there is a high level of activity – and you can be confident that the level is fairly constant – then time sampling is more economical. In general, though, the trainer is interested in all occurrences of a behaviour and will therefore employ unit sampling.

WHAT IS INVOLVED IN BEHAVIOUR OBSERVATION?

OBSERVERS

There must be one or more persons who have been properly trained to carry out behaviour observation. The number of observers required for any one observation will depend on the number of participants who must be tracked throughout the activity. The more people – and the higher the levels of activity – the more observers are required. It is recommended that one observer should not attempt to keep track of more than about eight different elements of behaviour, for more than about five participants at once.

Training of observers is essential if reliable data is to be collected. This aspect is covered in detail in a later section (p. 206).

The observers may be members of the training staff, or line managers. The latter often exhibit a tendency to make judgements about whether the trainee would fit into the manager's own unit, instead of judging against behavioural categories on the checklist. On the other hand, it is desirable whenever possible to increase manager involvement in training, and with suitable training line managers can perform an effective role as observers.

THE OBSERVED

There must be people who are practising the behaviours which are being analysed. Typically, this will take the form of on-course role-plays and simulation exercises. Role-playing as a technique does involve a degree of artificiality, which is compounded by the presence of an observer. However, many people do learn skills through role-play and commit some part of themselves to the role in spite of the discomforts. Furthermore, on training events, especially those concerned with interpersonal skills, participants become accustomed to looking at their own behaviour and receiving feedback from observers – either fellow participants or trainers. Trainees should, ideally, be assessed only when they have had some opportunities for non-assessed practice of the skill, so that the training experience itself no longer feels too uncomfortable. Similarly, to lessen distortion due to anxiety over the observation, trainees should be assessed on more than one performance of a particular skill area.

Where observation occurs in the workplace, it needs to happen sufficiently often that the person under observation becomes comfortable with the process and acts fairly naturally. It also needs to occur often enough and for long enough to amount to an adequate sampling of the individual's relevant work behaviours.

The idea of systematic behaviour observation in the workplace sometimes causes raised eyebrows, but the practice is quite common in selling – where managers regularly accompany salespersons on visits to customers – and happens extensively (but unsystematically) in most supervisory and management situations. Supervisors do frequently make judgements about their subordinates' work behaviour, although these judgements are often based more on gut reaction than on systematic evidence. However, for some kinds of behaviour it may not be appropriate to ask supervisors to make the assessment: colleagues or subordinates may be better placed for the purpose.

THE METHOD OF OBSERVATION

The main methods of observation are direct analysis of live behaviour, indirect analysis using video recording, and indirect analysis using sound recording. Any indirect recording method increases costs because the analysis time more than doubles the original performance time. It is arguable that a video camera (especially with a cameraman) is even more intrusive than an observer sitting in on the activity. It is also difficult – without an artificial room layout, or multiple cameras – to keep all members of a group activity within the picture frame.

On the positive side, indirect analysis allows 'action replays' of behavioural incidents which may not be easily unravelled 'live'. It allows several observers individually to analyse the data and thereby provide a cross-check on the reliability with which behaviour is being categorized. In the case of interpersonal behaviour on the telephone, analysis of a sound tape is the most realistic method available. An observer who *watches* two people role-playing a telephone call (with or without telephone equipment) will pick up many behavioural cues (gestures, facial expression, posture, etc.) that are not communicated on the phone.

Direct analysis is the least time-consuming method and yields the added benefit of allowing quick feedback to trainees. It does place a premium on observers being thoroughly trained so that they can cope with the rapid flow of behaviours as they arise.

THE OBSERVATION INSTRUMENT

'If everything were a nail, we'd only need a hammer.' It is essential to note that there is no universal checklist which can be applied to every kind of interpersonal behaviour. This warning is necessary because a great many trainers seem to use in indiscriminate fashion the well-known behaviour analysis categories developed by Rackham, Honey and Colbert.[1]

Rackham's work in developing these categories is a model of its kind and it is difficult to think of a more systematically developed tool for analysis of interpersonal behaviour. However, as Rackham *et al.* themselves have written

> we do not have *a* behaviour analysis system: we have an *approach*, which has led us to devise a range of systems for different situations – discussions and meetings, interviews, presentations, selling, counselling, telephone reservations, check-in and so on ... Our general category system is not very appropriate for studying telephone reservations interactions, and the system we devised for the latter would be pretty useless for analysing a meeting.

All of this is by way of saying that you need to design your behaviour observation instrument to match your particular evaluation needs. You do this by basing the categories for observation on the objectives of the training activity. How you do this is described in the next section.

Instruments can be broadly divided into those which concentrate on the behaviour of several people within a group interaction and those which concentrate on individuals. The person being observed may be interacting with another individual, as in an interview or sales call, or with a group, as in a training presentation or when chairing a meeting.

Within these broad categories you might require several kinds of information. At the simplest, it may be enough to know whether or not a particular behaviour was exhibited at all. You may wish to know the frequency with which each of several kinds of behaviour occurs. Alternatively, you may be interested in differences in the frequencies with which individuals contribute, or in the patterns of who talks to whom. You may examine whether rates of behaviour change over the course of an activity.

DESIGNING THE OBSERVATION INSTRUMENT

THE BASIC MATRIX FORMAT

Most observation instruments consist of a list of categories of behaviour, plus space to indicate how often each occurs and/or space to write in specific examples of behaviour which have been observed. Figure 14.1 is a checklist used in a listening skills exercise; Figure 14.2 is a checklist used on a programme for new sales staff.

Where the instrument is used to chart group behaviours, the frequency 'box' will be repeated for each member of the group, as shown in Figure 14.3 (p. 202).

Instead of names, it will sometimes be appropriate to use role-titles (e.g. chairperson, secretary, etc.).

The matrix format may be used to chart names against names (who speaks to whom and how frequently) as illustrated in Figure 14.4 (p. 202).

Another matrix design links names to individual contributions over time (see Figure 14.5, p. 203). This is a useful design for separating training groups into high and low contributors to create more homogenous sub-groups. The benefit of such a division is that low contributors generally contribute more when with similar people and free from the domination of high contributors. Conversely, high contributors tend to reduce their rates of contribution to discussion when in a group of other verbally active people.

SELECTING CATEGORIES FOR BEHAVIOUR OBSERVATION CHECKLISTS

Checklist categories should be derived from the behaviourally stated training objectives of the activity which is being evaluated (and should in turn be an accurate reflection of job or task behaviours). The categories should be a reflection of the most important kinds of behaviour that can occur in the interpersonal skills situation that is being evaluated. These will include positive and negative behaviours and also possible absences of behaviour.

The selection of a useful set of categories should be guided by the following principles.

Rule 1

This is the most important rule. It requires that each category of behaviour is relevant to success in the activity which is being examined. What is relevant depends on the

EVALUATION TECHNIQUES

Listening Skills Exercise: Observer's Checklist	
Trainee	Date ....
Observer	Session No ....
Target behaviours	*Observed behaviours*

1. Body language
    open posture
    relaxed
    mobile
    attentive	

2. Eye contact
    frequency
    staring
    smiling
    facial expression	

3. Listening
    90/10 Division
    Reflective summaries
    Treatment of silences
    Interruptions
    Selective Hearing	

4. Awareness of non-verbal messages	

5. Note-taking
    Making judgements
    Avoiding feelings
    Day-dreaming
    Arguing	

Figure 14.1 Checklist for a listening skills exercise

circumstances. For instance, in Figure 14.1, the whole activity is concerned with different facets of listening skill: thus the categories detail the subject in depth. In Figure 14.2, by contrast, listening skills are only one part of the activity and play a correspondingly smaller part in the list of categories to be observed.

BEHAVIOUR ANALYSIS

Assessment checklist (Sales Development programme)		Second stage sales call/call assessment Salesperson..........	
Behaviours to be assessed	Behaviour present Y/N	Evidence for the behaviour Comments on the quality of performance of the behaviour	Ratings[1] P: F: S−: S+: G: E
1 Establishes rapport			
15 Establishes control			
2 Uses open questions			
3 Uses closed questions			
4 Demonstrates active listening			
7 Establishes credibility			
23 Maintains customer's interest			
24 Establishes basis of customer decision			
10 Describes a computer system to meet customer's needs			
25 Presents an investment appraisal of the computer purchase decision			
14 Recognizes and responds to objections			
13 Obtains commitment to a course of action			

Note: [1] P = poor, F = fair, S− = satisfactory minus, S+ = satisfactory plus, G = good, E = excellent

Figure 14.2 Checklist for analysis of new sales staff

EVALUATION TECHNIQUES

Behaviours	George	Mary	Liz	Participants John	Aziz	Elena	etc.
1. Gives information	||	|	|	⊬⊬⊬ |	|	⊬⊬⊬	
2. Disagrees	|	⊬⊬⊬ ||	|			|	
Etc.							

Figure 14.3 Analysis of individual frequency of contributions

Senders \ Recipients	George	Mary	Liz	John	Aziz	Elena	Totals sent
George		||	|	|		|||	7
Mary	||		|||	|	|	⊬⊬⊬	12
Liz		|		|			2
John	|	|||	⊬⊬⊬		||	||	13
Aziz		|	||	|			4
Elena	|||	|	|	||||	|		10
Totals received	6	8	12	8	4	10	48

Figure 14.4 Matrix showing who speaks to whom and how frequently

BEHAVIOUR ANALYSIS

Participant	\multicolumn{5}{c	}{Elapsed time (minutes)}	Totals of individual contributions	% of all contributions
	0–5	6–10	11–15	16–20	21–25		
George			/	//	/	4	3.2
Mary	/	//	///	//	/	9	7.3
Liz	ℋ	///	ℋℋ	ℋ	ℋ /	29	23.4
John	ℋ	///	//	ℋ////	ℋ //	26	20.9
Aziz	/	///	ℋ /			10	8.1
Elena	ℋ ℋ	ℋ ℋ ℋ ℋ /	ℋ //	////	///	46	37.1
Time period totals	22	32	29	22	19	124	100.0

Figure 14.5 Differential contribution rates over time

Rule 2

Each category must be quite distinct from any other. If categories overlap, there is scope for observers to apply different personal judgements about which category a particular piece of behaviour fits. For example, 'Disagreeing' and 'Unhelpful behaviour' are terms that can be given widely differing meanings by different assessors.

For each category you should prepare a description of actions and statements that are representative of that category. The description should include both positive and negative illustrations of the category. For example, using some of the behaviour categories in Figure 14.2, the descriptions would read as shown in Table 14.1. Note the use of an item serial number. This helps the observer to quickly cross-reference from a specific checklist category to the master list which describes the positive and negative behaviours relating to each category. A blank master page is included for you to develop your own category descriptors (Figure 14.6).

Rule 3

The categories should describe *observable behaviours* and not personality traits. 'Smiles' is a description of behaviour, whereas 'good natured' is an inference about

203

EVALUATION TECHNIQUES

Table 14.1 Behavioural descriptions

Behaviour category	Positive examples	Negative examples
1. Establishes rapport	Easy to talk to – relaxed, natural. Supports customer statements. Acceptable use of humour. Talks customer language. Appropriate use of first names.	Awkward – makes customer ill-at-ease. Playing at 'being a sales person'. Uptight, starchy, humourless. Over-familiar towards customer.
4. Demonstrates active listening	Checks for understanding. Paraphrases customer's statements. Responds to conversational leads. Takes notes. Shows interest (non-verbally) in customer's remarks. 90:10 listening/talking ratio.	No checks. Inaccurate summarizing of customer's statements. Silent, but inattentive posture and eye contact. Looks bored. Talks too much. Interrupts customer.
7. Establishes credibility	Vigorous, positive approach. Speaks with conviction. Uses business language and ideas. Customer accepts salesperson's statements.	Adopts inferior, supplicating position *vis-à-vis* customer. Talks up to the customer. Appears nervous, unconfident or over-confident.
24. Determines basis of customer decision (BOD)	Uses questions to discover BOD. Probes for alternatives. Seeks a BOD favourable to salesperson's own company.	Fails to establish what is BOD. Accepts BOD unfavourable to own company.
14. Recognizes and responds to objections	Checks own understanding of the objection, by use of reflective questions. Provides a satisfactory response. Checks own response is acceptable to the customer. Employs tact.	Fails to notice objections. Unable to answer objections. Responds aggressively.

BEHAVIOUR ANALYSIS

Evidence to be assessed	Evidence for the behaviour	
	Positive examples	*Negative examples*

Figure 14.6 Blank master page of behavioural descriptions

personality. It is critical for success that observers record observable facts and not their intuitions, preconceptions, or wishful thinking.

Rule 4

The categories should be stated in plain English which both observer and trainee can understand and which both can see to be relevant to the analysis. If you use technical terms, jargon, or just complicated language, you are creating unnecessary barriers to understanding. There is a good chance that the people using the checklist will read in different meanings to those you intended. Also, the more opaque your language, the more easily you can evade the task of specifying observable behaviours.

Rule 5

Observers should be trained to separate the *factual recording* of instances of behaviour from the making of *judgements* about the quality of that behaviour. Categories should not, therefore, contain a bias towards recording only good or appropriate behaviours. *All* relevant behaviours should be recorded, for subsequent analysis of their quality.

Rule 6

The number of behaviour categories should be small. An observer can cope with a greater range of behaviour categories when observing an individual – as many as a dozen or more. When observing a group of four or five people a single observer should not attempt to track more than about six categories. In both cases, the experienced observer can cope with a heavier observational load, but the risk inevitably increases that instances of behaviour will be missed in the rush of events. A large group will require several observers. One variant approach is to adopt the fishbowl method: trainees are divided into two equal groups; one group observes the other, tracking behaviours on a one-to-one basis.

Rule 7

If behaviours normally occur in a particular sequence then they should be listed in that sequence. Alternatively, behaviours which usually occur most frequently should be listed first. In either case, the intention is to make completion of the checklist easier.

AN EXAMPLE OF CATEGORY DEVELOPMENT

This example consists of three elements: the training objectives for the particular session to which an assessed role-play relates (Figure 14.7); the assessment checklist derived from the objectives (Figure 14.8); and the master list of behavioural descriptions which underlie the categories (Table 14.2). The example concerns initial training of inexperienced salespersons. The role-play in which the trainees are assessed concerns a first approach to a possible new client. All trainees receive the same briefing. The staff member playing the potential customer aims to act the role at a consistent level of difficulty so that all trainees are treated equally.

BEHAVIOUR ANALYSIS

		Checklist item
a)	Demonstrate adaptation of personal style to the specific selling situation.	10
b)	Establish rapport with customer.	1, 5
c)	Establish a business purpose with the customer.	8
d)	Obtain commitment to a course of action.	11
e)	Recognize objections and scepticism and respond appropriately.	12
f)	Demonstrate use of open and closed questions.	2, 3
g)	Demonstrate positive non-verbal signals.	6
h)	Establish and maintain credibility.	7
i)	Demonstrate active listening.	4
j)	Show appropriate knowledge of company products and services.	9

Figure 14.7 Training objectives of session

DEVELOPING OBSERVER SKILLS

The task of acquiring skills of behaviour observation is greatly eased if you can work with one or more colleagues. Two or more people can work together on transcripts of real or imaginary situations that resemble the situation to be measured; each can make an independent assessment. You can then discuss any variances in your data that emerge. Similarly, you may conduct a parallel observation of the same interaction, either using a 'live' situation (e.g. a role-play) or a video recording of such a situation. If you create a small collection of videos which illustrate the skills you are training people to use, these can provide a standard against which new observers can practise and themselves be assessed. Standard videos are particularly useful for the observer who is being trained alone, as is the test/retest method by which the individual compares his or her own ratings of a particular set of behaviours at different points in time, with a view to identifying inconsistencies and inaccuracies.

For the individual trainer who lacks any opportunity for 'safe' practice of behaviour observation, one possible strategy is to use film and television as practice media. Draw up behaviour checklists for two or three common TV formats – the one-to-one interview, the group discussion, 'set-piece' scenes in plays or serials. Try out your category lists and refine them in the light of experience. An interesting and useful alternative, which involves tracking up to twelve characters (with only one or two active at any one time) is to use the first twenty minutes of the Henry Fonda film *Twelve Angry Men*, which is set in a jury room.

EVALUATION TECHNIQUES

Assessment checklist: Initial approach sales call   Date   Salesperson

Behaviours to be assessed	Behaviour present Y/N	Evidence for the behaviour Comments on the quality of performance of the behaviour
1 Establishing rapport		
2 Use of open questions		
3 Use of closed questions		
4 Demonstration of active listening		
5 Choice of language		
6 Use of non-verbal behaviour		
7 Credibility established		
8 Business purpose established		
9 Demonstration of knowledge of products/services		
10 Salesperson's adaptability to the situation		
11 Commitment to a course of action obtained		
12 Objections recognized and responded to.		

Figure 14.8 Assessment checklist

Table 14.2 Behavioural descriptions

Behaviours to be assessed	Positive examples	Evidence for the behaviour Negative examples
1. Establishes rapport	Easy to talk to. Natural. Relaxed. Supports customer statements. Pleasant sense of humour. Talks customer language. Appropriate use of first names.	Awkward. Makes customer feel uncomfortable. Playing at 'being a salesperson'. Uptight, starchy, humourless. Too familiar in use of first names.
2. Use of open questions	Questions do not invite short yes/no answers. Questions encourage customer to talk freely about needs, interests, etc. Questions build rapport with customer.	No appropriate use made of open questions. Salesperson preoccupied with making statements. Uses open questions which allow customer to avoid giving direct answer. Questions are irrelevant to purposes of the meeting.
3. Use of closed questions	Questions invite a clear, brief response. Questions seek customer's agreement to statements. Questions gather detailed information on factual matters. Questions gain commitment to action.	No appropriate use made of closed questions. Questions block off opportunities for customer to explain or expand statements. Questions produce short, uninformative yes/no answers. Questioning sounds like interrogation.
4. Demonstrates active listening	Checks for understanding. Paraphrases customer statements. Responds to conversational leads. Takes notes. Indicates interest in customer's statements.	Inaccurate summaries of customer statements. Silent but inattentive – body language and eye contact indicate lack of attention. Bored.
5. Choice of language	Jargon-free. Clear. 'Needs', not 'Problems'. Customer (business) language. Simple without talking down. Tactful. Avoids abbreviations and technical terms. Uses customer's jargon.	Emphasizes technicalities. Uses company jargon. Patronizing. Preaching. Tactless. Talks 'down' or 'up'.
6. Non-verbal behaviour	Looks alert, interested. Sits forward.	Looks bored. Overdoes the 'keen and eager' look.
7. Establish credibility	Positive approach. Projects a mature personality. Uses business language and ideas. Speaks with conviction. Customer accepts salesperson's statements.	Adopts inferior status. Talks up to the client. Nervous, unconfident, over-confident.
8. Establish a business purpose	Use of questions. Discovers what need exists for salesperson's products and services. Ascertains customer's business priorities.	Confuses interests with needs. Pushes solutions forward before needs have been established.
9. Demonstrate knowledge of own company's products and services	Responds to identified customer needs with specific suggestions for own company's products. Uses reference sells. Uses visual aids. Provides a business solution for customer's situation.	Uncertain or confused about what would be the appropriate products and services to match the customer's needs.
10. Adaptability to the situation	Responds to change of direction by the customer. Modifies tactics to respond to new opportunities. Turns objections to advantage. Retrieves misunderstandings.	Sticks to predetermined script regardless. Persists in selling what is not wanted. Thrown off-balance by the unexpected. Awkward silences.
11. Obtain commitment to a course of action	Sales closed. Client agrees follow-up action proposals, e.g. reference visit. Date and purpose of next meeting agreed. All necessary parties are involved.	Unrealistic action plan. Commits to too much action before properly qualifying customer.
12. Recognize and respond to objections	Checks own understanding of objection by questions. Provides satisfactory response – checks response is acceptable. Tactful.	Fails to spot objections. Cannot answer objections. Responds aggressively.

EVALUATION TECHNIQUES

If you are training a number of observers the following steps provide guidelines. They can be fairly easily adapted for the needs of the solo trainer/evaluator.

Step 1

Describe and explain the particular skills which the training event is designed to develop. Skills should be specified in precise and behavioural ways – exactly what you could see someone doing – rather than in terms of personality characteristics which you could only infer.

Step 2

Describe and discuss the categories of behaviour that will be analysed by the observers. Make it clear what connection exists between each behaviour category and one of the objectives set for the training activity. Make it clear that the primary task of observers is to record instances of particular behaviours, not to make immediate judgements about them.

Step 3

Practise applying each category to examples of behaviour. This may start with transcripts of simple verbal statements, for example 'That's all very well, but . . .', 'I'd like to add to that suggestion . . .'.

Trainee observers should categorize these statements according to the checklist they are learning to use. The results should then be compared with a list of standard answers for these examples. Any incorrect categorizations must be discussed thoroughly to discover how the error is arising.

Practice may then continue with more complex applications, using sound or video recordings of role-play situations. At intervals the tape should be stopped so that the category of behaviours being observed can be discussed and errors of categorization corrected. Repeat this exercise to develop speed and accuracy amongst the observers. By using particular tapes as standard items, comparison levels of observer performance can be established over time.

Step 4

New observers then work in parallel with experienced observers to record behaviour during a variety of live training events. The reliability of recording is assessed (see the next section) and, if necessary, further training provided for the new observer.

Step 5

The observer is employed in training events. Reliability over time for the individual, as well as reliability between observers of the same activity, should be monitored. Occasional 'refresher' training sessions are useful. The more experienced observer can become involved in the training of new observers.

RELIABILITY OF OBSERVATIONS

There are three elements to reliability:

- Consistency between one observer and another when assessing the same piece of behaviour ('inter-rater reliability').
- Consistency of a checklist as a measure of behaviour between one occasion of use and another ('test/retest reliability').
- Adequate coverage of the *range* of behaviours that may occur during a particular interaction ('sampling reliability') (see earlier comments on choice of time or unit sampling).

A measure of reliability is provided by calculation of the rank-order correlation between two sets of observations. For example, two observers may use a checklist to record the frequency with which specified behaviour categories arise as they watch the same interaction. The behaviour categories are then ranked in order of their frequency of occurrence. This ranking is applied to each observer's checklist. The two rank orders are then correlated (using the Pearson formula, discussed in detail in Appendix II).

The correlation coefficient provides a measure of the extent to which the observers differed or agreed. A correlation coefficient of $+1$ means that there is perfect agreement; -1 implies total disagreement; and 0 means that any agreement between the observers is the product of chance.

The following correlation coefficients are provided by Rackham *et al.* as a guide to acceptable levels of reliability for different purposes.

$+0.7$ Complex categories of non-verbal behaviour
$+0.75$ Simple categories of non-verbal behaviour; complex sequences of behaviours
$+0.85$ Verbal (interactive) behaviour
$+0.95$ Activity categories; clearly defined content categories

Observers should be reliable not only with regard to putting a particular observed behaviour into the right checklist category but also in attributing the behaviour to the right individual (obviously a more difficult task in group interactions than one-to-one events). A measure of overall reliability is obtained by multiplying the correlation coefficient for the behaviour categories dimension with the coefficient for the 'Who is behaving' dimension. For example, if the former is $+0.9$ (a satisfactory level for, say, verbal interactions) and the latter is $+0.8$ (suggesting errors in attributing behaviours to participants) then the overall reliability is $0.9 \times 0.8 = 0.72$ which is a poor level of reliability for this type of behaviour. Reliability can be increased in two ways: by careful design of checklists and by thorough training of observers.

RATING OBSERVED BEHAVIOURS

Up to now, the emphasis has been on accurate factual observation – recording the presence or absence of behaviours, without making judgements about the quality of

EVALUATION TECHNIQUES

performance of the behaviour. The governing principle here is that observers should follow the sequence below:

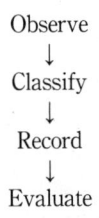

Observe
↓
Classify
↓
Record
↓
Evaluate

The logic of this procedure is to ensure that full attention is paid to actual behaviour, rather than leaping to judgements based on 'general impression' or intuition. The factual content of the behaviour is the most important question to determine. The checklist shown as Figure 14.8 (p. 208) does not contain any provision for ratings, precisely in order to encourage observers to concentrate on the nature of the behaviours observed.

Assessments of individual performance need to be based on more than one observed activity and here too an emphasis on factual recording is helpful. The records of behaviour from several observed activities can be consolidated and will then provide a basis for observers to discuss the quality of performance exhibited by the individual trainee. This will be discussed further in the following section.

Judgements of quality based on observed behaviours, which reflect training objectives and hence job tasks, enable you more readily to operate with criterion-referenced standards of judgement. What this means is that participants are assessed against a preset criterion of satisfactory performance for people engaged in that type of activity, rather than ranked in order of ability across the group who happen to be assembled on any particular training event. The criterion used should be the 'standards' element of a well-drafted, three-part training objective (*viz.* behaviour–standard–conditions).

One method of rating is to use a 3–5 or 4–6 point scale such as: Excellent/Good/Satisfactory+/Satisfactory−/Fair/Poor. The argument against scales with odd numbers of intervals is that they allow an exact midpoint position and raters will tend to play safe by opting for this position. However, the same central tendency will operate with S+/S− middle ratings. It is debatable whether for this kind of activity a finely graduated scale is worthwhile.

Whatever the scale, it is essential that everybody who makes ratings on the basis of observed behaviour has the same understanding of what each point on the rating scale means. This makes it necessary to divide up master lists (such as that on p. 209) so that there are separate descriptors of the specific behaviours that are associated with each point on the rating scale. (It may be that you will come to share my own view that rating of observed behaviours is in fact an irrelevance: if trainees exhibit the right – or the wrong – behaviours, that is all you need to know. If you add a rating on top of that data, all you are probably doing is saying whether or not you like the individual. Should you need further persuasion, a list of common sources of error in rating people follows.)

COMMON SOURCES OF INACCURATE RATING

Halo effect

When an assessor rates a person on more than one aspect of that person's behaviour, it is common to carry over a general impression of the person's competence from one rating to the next, or to try to make the ratings appear consistent with each other. In reality, most people are more competent at some aspects of a task than others. Provided observers concentrate initially on accurately recording the relevant behaviour which is being exhibited, and make a positive effort to base *each* rating independently on its *specific* behavioural evidence, the bias created by the halo effect can in principle be reduced.

Generosity error

There is a tendency for raters to overestimate the desirable qualities and level of performance of trainees whom the rater likes. Observers need to consider the extent to which their rating assessments may rationalize personal likes and dislikes rather than reflect the behavioural evidence.

Moderation error

Raters are inclined to avoid making extreme ratings and tend to assign individuals to the more moderate categories.

Contrast error

This arises from a tendency on the part of raters to see the trainee as being opposite to themselves in characteristics and behaviour.

Frame of reference errors

Where different raters, making assessments of the same piece of behaviour by the same individual, arrive at different scale positions, this is often due to the raters holding differing views of the nature of what is being observed. Clear definitions of the behaviour being observed and specification of the various positions on the rating scale help to reduce this unreliability. Concrete illustrations help, as does extensive discussion amongst the raters, prior to their use of a new instrument.

Individual rating skill

Some general conclusions from research into differences in individual ability to make accurate ratings are given below:

- Individuals may differ in their ability to make ratings of different characteristics – some are sensitive to one thing, some to another.
- Personal acquaintance with the person being rated does not lead to increased accuracy.
- The rater's confidence in his or her own judgement is not necessarily an indicator of its validity.

EVALUATION TECHNIQUES

- Raters who would themselves be judged 'high' on a characteristic which is generally considered to be undesirable or unfavourable are poor judges of that characteristic in other people as well as in themselves.

Team ratings are one way of increasing the reliability of individual ratings. Several raters make independent judgements. They then compare their results and discuss any discrepancies between raters. Each then makes a second set of independent judgements which in turn are averaged to yield a final score. This approach has the limitation that it requires more than one assessor to observe each trainee's performance.

USING THE DATA

Behaviour observation data is important to the evaluator to the extent that it shows whether or not people can perform skills which a training event has tried to impart. That information will usually serve a second purpose of providing feedback to the learners on the development of their competence. A third area of application is to use behaviour observation as a pre-training diagnostic aid.

Without a pre-training assessment, you can never claim that change in interpersonal skills has occurred. The most that an end of course (or post-course workplace) assessment yields is a test of competence. Without a pre-test, you cannot know whether or not the trainee already possessed some of the skill before training took place.

During a training event, a number of observations should be collected for each participant. Checklists may be fed back to an administrator session-by-session. The administrator transfers behavioural descriptions onto a master summary for each individual. In this way, feedback and assessment can be tied to each individual's behaviour during the training event, without explicit comparison being made between one person and another. When this summarizing process is complete, the observers should discuss their recorded examples of behaviour, rather than ratings. When the behavioural basis of individuals' performance has been examined, observers may then consider making ratings or ranking the individuals, if they feel it is necessary. However, the main value of the assessment lies in the factual evidence of skill utilization. An example of an individual summary document for assessment of learning and/or feedback is shown in Figure 14.9.

When the aggregated data are used to give feedback to trainees, this should be done in a structured fashion, based on the main themes that have been assessed. Some general principles for giving feedback are listed below.

Feedback skills

1. The purpose of giving feedback is to help the learner. It should not be used to vent irritation or to punish the recipient.
2. In order to be useful, feedback must be understandable and acceptable. It needs

BEHAVIOUR ANALYSIS

Test {	Name of salesperson: Written test score: % Comments on test:	

	Assessment themes	Comments	Ratings[1] P: F: S−: S+: G: E
Telephone performances {	Telephone: potential customer		
	Telephone: complaint call		
	Telephone: locating company resource		
Letter writing tasks {	Follow-up to telephone call to potential customer		
	Follow-up to approach sales call		
	Follow-up to telephone call to complaining customer		
	Locating company resource – letter to customer		
Interpersonal skills {	Approach sales call		
	Second stage sales call		
	Complaint call		
	Area sales meeting		

Note: [1] P = poor, F = fair, S− = satisfactory minus, S+ = satisfactory plus, G = good, E = excellent

Figure 14.9 Individual feedback summary form

to be specific, concrete and in language compatible with the learner's point of view.
3. If you express opinions or judgements, do not present these as facts.

EVALUATION TECHNIQUES

4. Refer to the learner's task performance, not to his or her personality.
5. Stick to observable specifics – avoid inferences about what you believe is going on inside the person's head.
6. Evaluate performance only against criteria previously agreed for the task.
7. Present feedback in close proximity to the performance.
8. Invite the learner to suggest ways in which he or she might improve the task performance.
9. Remember that reinforcement of good performance through praise is even more important than correction of errors.

NOTE

1. Rackham, N. *et al.*, (1971). *Developing Interactive Skills*, Wellens Publishing.

15 Cost-benefit analysis

WHO PAYS FOR TRAINING

This chapter describes the opportunities that exist to attach monetary values to training activities. It starts with an overview of costing systems. The more frequently-encountered costing of training inputs is then extended to include the pricing of training outputs. Cost-benefit analysis is distinguished from cost-effectiveness analysis and methods for implementing monetary-value evaluations are discussed, as is the use of performance ratios.

There are two means by which organizations fund training: overhead systems and recharging systems. Overhead systems make the training budget an indirect cost for the whole organization. Sometimes this overhead will be apportioned amongst departments on an arbitrary 'equal shares' basis; sometimes it will be apportioned roughly in line with a department's level of use of training facilities. Recharging systems operate on a different principle. In effect, the training unit functions as a self-contained business (a 'profit centre') within the organization. The training unit sells its services to the departments and its success in doing this determines its survival.

Each approach has advantages and drawbacks. Overhead systems allow a longer term view of organizational training needs and perhaps lessen the emphasis on fire-fighting activities. However, overhead systems also tend to create inertia in the training system: it is far easier for trainers to run standard menus of courses from year to year with little or no review of organizational needs, and to put their main energies into the training activities which they most enjoy, rather than those the organization most needs.

Recharging systems have the virtue of increasing line management interest in the process of selecting people for training. This alone is enough to justify this approach compared with overhead costing, where in practice nominating managers are largely indifferent to the costs of training.

There is a potential risk with recharging systems that the direction of training will be 'hijacked' by managers who are interested only in the latest training novelty. However, there is also a valuable opportunity to educate line managers in the basic concepts of systematic training, especially those concerning accurate identification of needs, setting of specific objectives for changing behaviour, and management reinforcement of the learning process.

Some organizations have in recent years retained an overhead funding system coupled with zero-base budgeting. In this approach, each budget calculation begins from the position that any expenditure has to be justified on its own merits. This certainly provides a check against a quite common approach found in overhead systems. That is the approach which takes last year's budget and adds to it a percentage big enough to allow for 'concessions' in the subsequent budget negotiations.

To conclude: it is worth stating that 'who pays for training' has a very noticeable effect on how seriously training is treated in an organization. When training comes 'free' to the user, there is usually less concern for its relevance and its job application, and less management involvement, along with lower expectations of learning and performance change. In the extreme, this leads to training which is seen as 'rest, reward and recreation'. Time and again, I have encountered large organizations which retain elaborate management development programmes which originated in the late 1960s and early 1970s during a time of expansion and frequent promotion opportunities. Yet these programmes survive even though these same organizations now face an urgent need to shed redundant middle managers (a trend which information technology will inevitably hasten).

COSTING METHODS

The trainer will usually be working within an existing system of financial records. The training department's costing system will need to be compatible with the system employed for the rest of the organization's transactions. Clearly, the trainer should discuss his or her needs with the appropriate accounting specialist. However, the trainer should also be prepared to argue for a cost classification system that matches the information and cost control needs of the training unit. The section on costable inputs of training (p. 223) provides a checklist of categories from which you can draw those items most relevant to your particular information needs. A useful guideline for where to concentrate your effort is that you should devote attention to any particular cost category in proportion to its share of the total costs. Some guidance notes on different costing terms follow.

ABSORPTION COSTING

In this approach all the costs of an activity are accounted for by allocating them to a cost centre. A cost centre may be a particular functional unit (e.g. the training department), a particular location (e.g. the Northern Regional Staff Training College), a person (e.g. the internal OD consultant) or a piece of equipment (e.g. the 747 flight simulator).

Costs are divided into two broad categories: direct costs and overheads. Direct (or prime) costs comprise labour, materials and other expenses which directly relate to a particular activity. Examples of direct costs are as follows:

- Trainers' salaries for time spent on design and tuition of specific programmes.
- Film-hire.
- Printing of materials for specific courses.
- Hire of a hotel suite in which to run a training event.
- Fees for external courses.

Indirect or overhead costs are all those costs which are allocated to a cost centre on an apportionment basis. Examples of indirect costs would include the following:

- Salaries of administrative and clerical staff.
- Costs incurred for maintenance and day-to-day running of a training centre.
- Provision and depreciation of general training equipment (e.g. overhead projectors) which is not specific to a particular course.

Once both direct and indirect costs have been allocated to a cost centre the total costs can be re-allocated to 'cost units'. These are units of training output such as a course or an individual (e.g. a graduate trainee). This process allows training services to be priced for recharging to end-users as well as yielding cost control information over time. An important question to address when planning a costing system is to ask how comprehensive it should be. There are a number of costs which do not always (or often) find their way into training accounts. Salaries of participants (and salary overheads) are commonly not included whereas wages of weekly paid employees may be. Sometimes even training premises are 'lost' in general overheads, as may various routine administrative expenses such as stationery and photocopying. What is included is probably as much a matter of convention and organizational politics in the particular enterprise as it is a matter of accounting principle. The case for full-cost treatment of training expenditure is that it concentrates attention on the true level of spending on training. This can have the salutary effect of encouraging more explicit consideration of cost-benefit equations when making training decisions.

MARGINAL COSTING

Trainers will be interested in marginal costing when faced with decisions about whether or not to run an extra session of an established course, or whether or not to allow an extra person to attend a fully subscribed event.

Marginal costing records the *extra* costs incurred by a change in the level of activity, compared with a baseline position. For example, if all development costs have been absorbed in the costings for the first ten occasions that a sales training course is run, then the eleventh run of it will incur only those (marginal) costs which directly vary with the number of courses, for example:

- Hire of hotel suite.
- Travelling expenses of participants.
- Trainer salaries for tuition time.
- Duplication of handouts.

EVALUATION TECHNIQUES

For marginal costing purposes, costs are divided into fixed and variable costs. Fixed costs do not vary in the short run. Examples would include the following:

- Programme development costs (salaries etc.).
- Printing a stock of course handbooks.
- Making a video.
- Purchase of a car engine for apprentice training.

Variable costs are incurred each time a training activity is run. Examples of variable costs are as follows:

- Fees to visiting speakers.
- Short-term hire of films.
- Hire of training premises.
- Accommodation and meals.
- Travelling expenses.

Given the total fixed costs and the variable cost per unit of output the trainer can calculate alternative selling (recharging) prices at which the training service will break even. Break-even selling price will need to take account of the size of the potential market. If the target course group is 15 and there are 150 potential users it is obviously a mistake to spread fixed costs over fifteen courses (though eleven or twelve may be realistic, if there is high staff turnover which would bring new users into the available pool). An example of break-even analysis is given in Figure 15.1.

HISTORICAL AND STANDARD COSTS

Historical costs are simply those costs which have already been incurred and recorded. They may be analysed as direct or indirect and also according to the type of cost (salaries, materials, etc.).

Standard costs are based on an analysis of historical costs. They represent 'typical' or 'average' costs for particular activities and can be used to compile budgets and to provide a yardstick against which current expenditure trends can be measured.

OPPORTUNITY COST

Opportunity cost is the value of the best available alternative use of funds. It is the value which inevitably is lost when a different use of funds is chosen. Thus opportunity cost gives the trainer and investment decision-maker a yardstick of value foregone, against which to measure the value that will be contributed if the funds are invested in a training project. Two examples follow.

Organizational opportunity cost

The training department has identified a training need which requires an increase in the existing training budget. The training manager needs not only to make a case in terms of

COST-BENEFIT ANALYSIS

Total fixed costs	£48,000
Variable costs per course	5,600
Target number of participants per course	8

Assumption A: 20 courses will run

Fixed costs $\dfrac{£48,000}{(20 \times 8)} =$ £300

Variable costs $\dfrac{£5,600}{8} =$ £700

Total cost per person per course   £1000   = Break-even recharging fee

Assumption B: 5 courses will run

Fixed costs $\dfrac{£48,000}{(5 \times 8)} =$ £1,200

Variable costs $\dfrac{£5,600}{8} =$ £700

Total cost per person per course   £1,900   = Break-even recharging fee

Figure 15.1 A five-day supervisory skills programme: break-even analysis

the benefits the training will produce, but also in terms of why the extra funding for training is the best use of resources (as opposed to applying it to some other department's needs). In short, the case for the money going to training must be stronger than the competing claims.

Opportunity costs within a training department

It is not uncommon for a training department to be faced with a fixed budget and a number of proposed new projects that look worthwhile. Sometimes, existing projects are simply given priority for funding and new ideas are deferred. It is better, however, to carry out a comparative analysis of costs and benefits attributable to both existing and proposed projects, in order to identify which provide the greatest return. Where one project offers clearly defined pay offs, that will provide an opportunity cost yardstick against which alternatives can be weighed.

Two other applications of the principle of opportunity costing are the use of the Pareto principle and the technique of Risk Analysis.

The Pareto principle

The Pareto principle suggests that in general 20 per cent of the effort or activity put into any task generates 80 per cent of the benefits. For example, 20 per cent of a salesperson's clients produce 80 per cent of business; 20 per cent of files account for 80 per cent of information-handling in an office; even (a subversive thought) 20 per cent of a training course accounts for 80 per cent of the learning achieved. The practical problem, of course, is that of knowing which is the fruitful 20 per cent. In some kinds of activity, the fruitful 20 per cent may only be achieved after the less fruitful 80 per cent of effort has created a necessary foundation. Nevertheless, the principle is a useful reminder that activities are often pursued in a quest for perfection that produces rapidly diminishing returns on the effort expended. The use of appropriate ratios (e.g. expenditure per trainee/day), combined with indicators of learning gain within the training event, provide rapid indicators of trends of this kind.

Risk analysis

Risk analysis is the study of the statistical probability of an undesired event occurring. It provides an assessment of its cost in financial and human terms, as well as the costs and methods of preventing the occurrence. Perhaps the most obvious area of training application is in preventative safety training. Accidents may occur because of human error or because of inadequate training. The costs of providing adequate training can be balanced against the potential costs of accidents occurring, although in the case of safety training, humanitarian and legal considerations may outweigh the purely financial.

An example of risk analysis can be made by considering customer service. The customer complaints section in a firm has the responsibility for investigating and responding to dissatisfied clients. The risks of a bad decision in this area are potentially very serious for the business. The risks include loss of customer goodwill, loss of sales, and loss of potential new customers. If a business has a turnover of £20 million from 1 000 customers and loses one customer due to a bad decision within the customer complaints section, there is a potential loss of (on average) £20 000 turnover. Given a gross profit margin of 25 per cent, that loss of turnover represents a £5 000 loss of profits. This loss does not include possible knock-on losses amongst other existing customers or potential clients, nor any redundancy costs that may arise from reduced production.

COSTABLE INPUTS AND PRICEABLE OUTPUTS OF TRAINING SYSTEMS

It is often suggested that it is relatively easy to identify the costs that are incurred in setting up and running a training activity, but it is harder or even impossible to identify the value of outputs from that training. There are various measures available to assess the changes achieved by different kinds of training and those measures enable a value or price to be put upon that training. In my experience, the obstacles to measuring training output are usually 'political' – managers will not cooperate by reviewing on-job performance, trainers resist from a fear that they will be shown to be failing to make any difference.

The checklists that follow provide you with a summary of training inputs and training outputs, to which cost and value can be attached. Some inputs may not be included within the conventions of your organization's accounting system, thereby reducing visible training costs; some outputs may already be monitored whilst others will require a specific effort to collect data. It is surprising how often when helping trainers to put evaluation projects together, it turns out that – unknown to the training department – someone, somewhere is collecting information that could be used to measure and value the outputs of training.

It is worth restating a basic principle in training design: if you cannot specify what will be different as a result of training (i.e. measure the outcome) you are basing the decision to invest in training solely upon wishful thinking.

COSTABLE INPUTS

Fixed capital

- Buildings and training rooms.
- Fixtures and fittings – chairs, tables, wall-boards, carpets.
- Fixed services (e.g. aerial sockets, wired CCTV and computer links).
- Equipment – audio-visual equipment, typewriters, word-processors, demonstration machinery, tools.
- Provision of a training resource centre and/or library.
- Motor vehicles.

In the short-to-medium term these costs do not vary. Provision must be made for the depreciation of equipment which may wear out, break, or become obsolescent. The appropriate period and rate of depreciation is a matter to be decided in association with your own organization's accountants, taking into account your judgement of the life-cycle of that particular training need.

Working capital

- Consumable supplies (e.g. stationery).
- Maintenance of equipment and premises (routine maintenance plus breakages).
- Materials used during training (e.g. in metalwork, catering, assembly tasks).

These costs vary with the level of training activity.

Administrative and personnel costs of the training function

- Cost of employment for the training manager and administrative and clerical staff.
- Apportioned costs of rates, rent, heating, lighting, cleaning, etc. for training rooms or premises.
- Salaries (etc.) of instructors/trainers when not engaged in development of training programmes or in giving instruction.

Where the manager holds a dual role, such as personnel and training manager, salary (etc.) should be apportioned between the different functions. Administrative and personnel

EVALUATION TECHNIQUES

costs are largely fixed overheads which can be apportioned between cost units such as individual courses.

Costs of providing instructors/tutors

This cost is that incurred in training trainers whether these are line managers, experienced workers, or externally-recruited training officers. These costs include the following:

- Fees for external training of trainers courses.
- Marginal costs of attendance at existing internal courses.
- Recruitment and selection costs.
- Refresher and developmental training for established trainers.
- Salaries and salary overheads, plus expenses during the training of trainers.

These are largely variable costs which reflect the overall level of internal training provision. Increases in training provision lead to the need for more instructors and in turn to higher training-of-trainers' expenditure.

Costs of training development

- Salaries (etc.) of trainers whilst carrying out analyses of training needs, development of objectives and content for training activities, and evaluation of programmes.
- Fees to consultants for similar purposes.
- Expenses incurred on visual aids, printing of course materials, etc.
- Computer time charges (for development of CBT).

These are fixed costs which can be allocated over the life-span of the particular training activity, or over the anticipated number of trainees who would experience the activity.

Costs of giving instruction

These are the costs incurred in the employment of trainers subsequent to their initial training. These exclude that part of trainers' time spent on developing new training activities. They may include the following:

- Cost of trainers' employment.
- Travel and accommodation expenses.
- Membership fees for professional associations.
- Subscriptions to training journals.
- Fees for external consultants.
- Licence fees for use of copyright materials.
- Guest speakers' expenses and fees or (if internal) a proportion of salary.
- External course fees and expenses.

These costs will vary with the number of courses run and some items with the number of participants in each course.

COST-BENEFIT ANALYSIS

Costs arising from participants' attendance at training events

- Apportionment of salary or wages and employee overheads during attendance on course.
- Travel and accommodation costs.
- Costs of temporary replacement staff.
- Costs (where quantifiable) of lost 'output' due to attendance on course.

These are variable costs.

By allocating a serial number to each cost category, each training event, and to the stages from identification of needs through to evaluation, it becomes a simple matter to assemble cost data for any particular stage of a given programme, for example 0093705 is composed of Trainer salary (009) Apprentice Module FM13 (370) Evaluation (5).

PRICEABLE OUTPUTS

1. Reduced training time to master task skills:
   - reduced training costs;
   - reduced wastage;
   - higher output.

2. Improved quality of output:
   - reduced quality control costs;
   - less wastage.

3. Sales volume increases:
   - overall;
   - in more profitable lines;
   - in preferred market sectors.

4. Lower accident rates:
   - lost production;
   - compensation payments;
   - avoidance of penalties.

5. Reduced turnover of employees:
   - improved output;
   - reduced recruitment and selection costs;
   - increased public and customer confidence leading to more sales.

6. Reduced absenteeism, industrial conflict, etc.:
   - improved output;
   - less supervision.

7. Increases in output of goods and services:
   - higher returns on existing investment or lower resource requirements for a given output.
8. Greater resource utilization:
   - less machine downtime;
   - fewer 'idle time' payments;
   - lower stock levels of raw materials, work in progress, and finished goods;
   - shorter invoicing and debt collection periods.

THE COST IDENTIFICATION MATRIX

The matrix shown in Figure 15.2 provides a convenient framework within which the trainer can analyse the resource requirements and anticipated costs of a planned training activity, stage-by-stage through the training cycle. The appropriate resource needs and cost estimates are entered into each box and then summed both vertically and horizontally. The target date column will be used when a cash-flow analysis is being compiled (see the following section on cash-flow budgets).

CASH-FLOW BUDGETS

Cash-flow analysis of training expenses and revenue is sometimes needed. This analysis may be required for an individual project (e.g. 'the middle manager programme') over its life-span or for a complete cost centre (e.g. the training department) over a fixed budgeting period, typically one to five years.

Cash-flow analysis applied to a single project can usefully start from the information collected in the cost identification matrix. The trainer can make informed guesses about the time-scale for each part of the programme and add dates to the five stages listed in the matrix. In this way the expenditure element of the cash flow can be predicted.

Income can be predicted from the anticipated throughput of trainees once the training is implemented. The pattern of throughput will vary: some training runs at a steady rate year in, year out, following the initial start-up. Other programmes require an intense initial 'blitz' to achieve maximum early throughput, followed by a low level of continuing provision. The first pattern is typical of routine training required for skills and knowledge that are in fairly regular use. The second is often found in sales training, where a new product line is being introduced, and also with crisis-driven training, for example, where a serious accident triggers intensive remedial safety training.

The time dimension in cash-flow analysis may be clarified by looking at income and expenditure in terms of the typical life-cycle of a training event: initial research and development; piloting and full-scale implementation; and a final stage of declining need and transition of resources to other newer areas. This is illustrated in Figures 15.3, 15.4 and 15.5.

COST-BENEFIT ANALYSIS

Target date	Training proposal	Personnel	Equipment	Premises	Materials	Totals
	Identification of needs					
	Objectives setting					
	Design of training activity					
	Implementation					
	Evaluation					
	Totals					

Figure 15.2 The cost identification matrix

EVALUATION TECHNIQUES

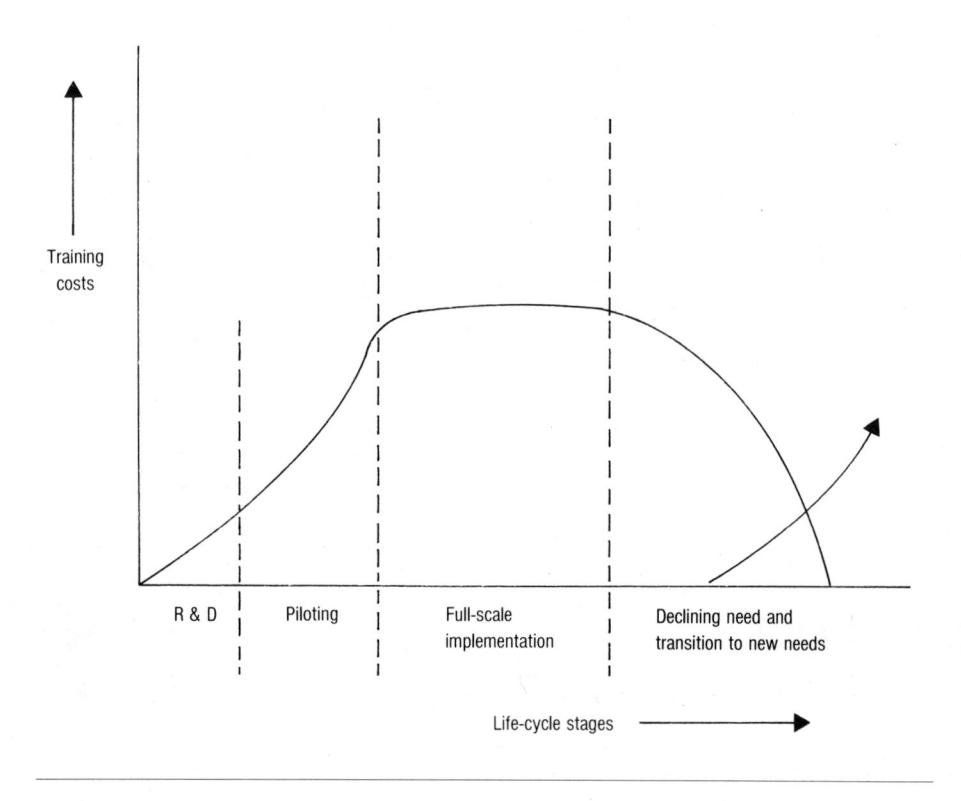

Figure 15.3 Conventional training programme with steady throughput

Budgeted costs are entered on the graph. Subsequently actual expenditure can also be plotted to give a quick visual indicator of under- or over-spending.

Cash-flow analysis applied to an ongoing cost centre, such as a department, starts with the cash-on-hand at the beginning of the budget period, adds sources of cash that arise during the period, and deducts cash expended, in order to arrive at a figure for cash-on-hand at the end of the period.

A cash-flow analysis which is used as a retrospective record of the directions in which money has flowed, can be prepared from an analysis of changes in balance sheet items from year to year. A cash-flow analysis which is used as an aid to financial planning will start from the balance sheet position and build on to that base month by month predictions of anticipated revenue and expenditure. It is the convention that depreciation is charged to profits *after* calculating cash flows. Cash flow consists of the funds provided by the operations of the business which are made up of retained profits plus depreciation.

Does cash flow matter? Yes! Many business analysts would argue that a healthy cash-flow position is far more important than profitability. A company may have a backlog of orders for its goods or services and may expect in the long-term to show a substantial

COST-BENEFIT ANALYSIS

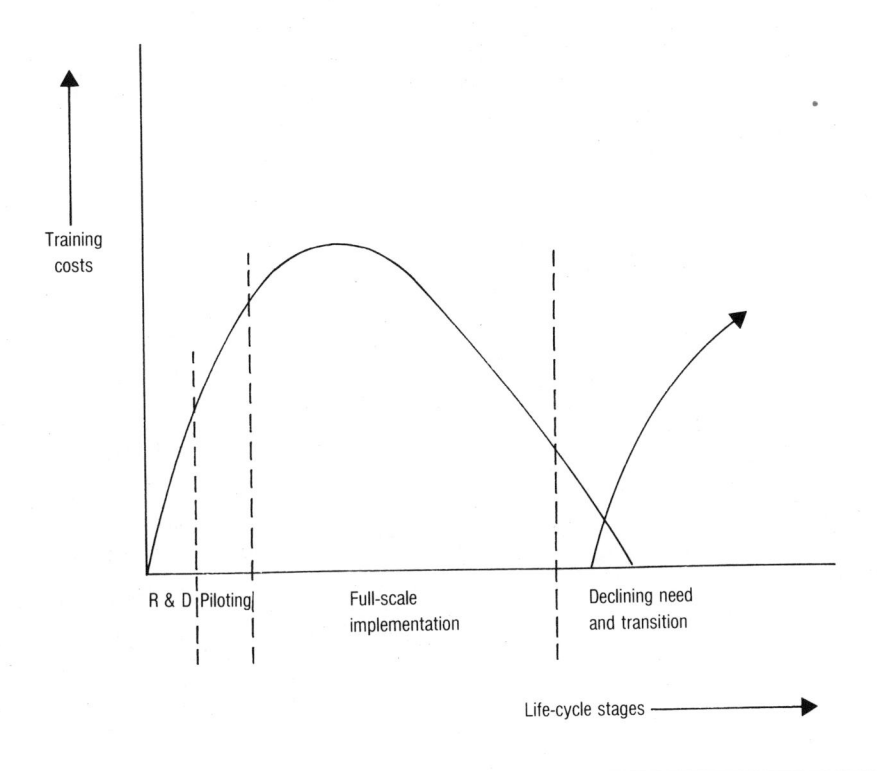

Figure 15.4 Conventional training programme with high short-term throughput

profit, but if in the short-term it cannot meet its wages bill or the rent on its premises, it will not survive into that prosperous future.

COST-BENEFIT AND COST-EFFECTIVENESS ANALYSIS

The distinction between cost-benefit analysis (CBA) and cost-effectiveness analysis (CEA) is only one of convention. Different writers on the subject use these terms in ways that blur their distinctions. To simplify this area of confusion, the practice adopted here will be to use CBA for any analysis where both costs and benefits of training can be expressed in monetary terms. Cost-effectiveness analysis will be employed for analyses where the costs can be specified but the training outcomes, though identifiable, may not be readily priceable. In principle a price can be put on the output but in practice the costs of collecting that data far outweigh the benefits. Both CBA and CEA have their part to play as evaluation techniques. Wherever practicable they should be used in conjunction with control measures which help to eliminate spurious connections of apparent cause and effect. The use of control groups is discussed in detail in Appendix I, p. 237.

EVALUATION TECHNIQUES

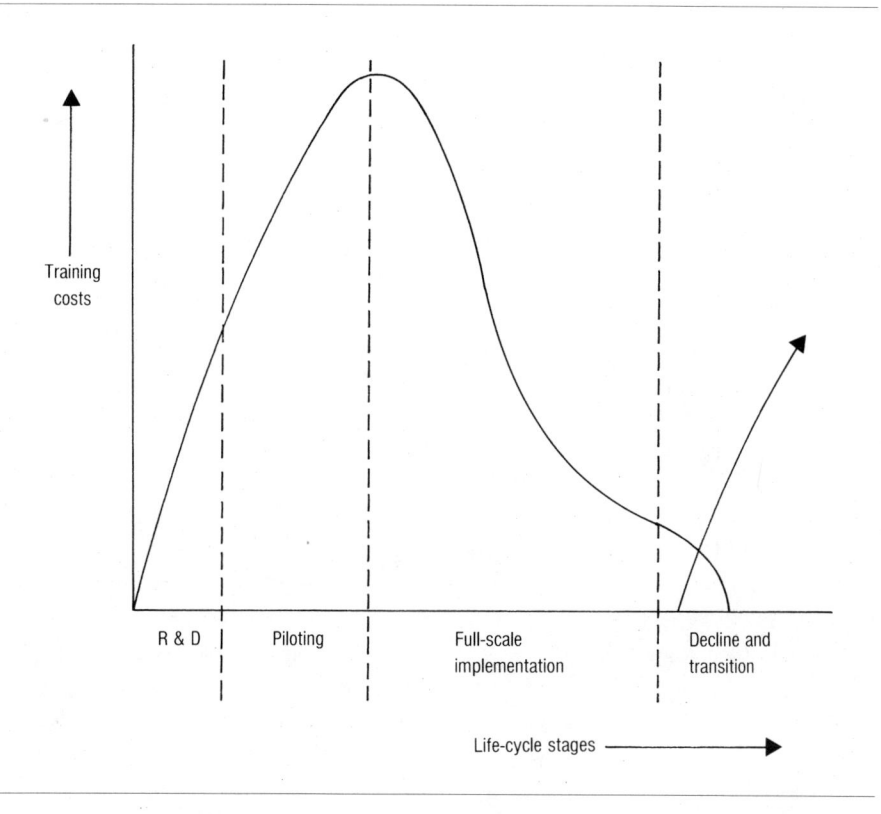

Figure 15.5 CBT programme with high initial development costs

COST-BENEFIT ANALYSIS

CBA is a matter of identifying anticipated costs (using the cost identification matrix) and weighing them against the monetary value of anticipated outcomes.

Outcomes can be identified most directly by examining the training objectives. The objectives will specify the changes in performance behaviours that trained persons should display. These changes will sometimes have an unambiguous and predictable value.

For example, improved quality control by assembly workers reduces the costs of testing, repairing defective items, shipping defective stock, and making refunds to dissatisfied customers. Appropriate sales training should lead to quantifiable changes in sales volume, or sales mix, or territory penetration, all of which have clear bottom-line impact. In management training, trained persons may undertake special projects based upon what has been learned and the costs and benefits of such projects can be assessed. Implementation of action plans may be monitored and changes in work practices priced – whether the outcome is increased physical production (value measured by extra profit, or fuller utilization of capital equipment) or, say, a reduction of staff turnover arising from team-building training (where value may be measured by recruitment costs and, so far as

Table 15.1 Development times for different training methods

Type of training	Preparation hours per each tuition hour
Formal technical courses	5–15
Self-contained packages for instructor use	50–100
Management development	20–30
Programmed instruction	80–120
On-site technical training	1–3
Computer-based learning	c.350 (or more)

practicable, by the losses of productivity due to friction and the losses of production due to employees leaving).

Second-order outcomes are less directly obvious than those linked to training objectives. These outcomes require a little creative thinking (brainstorming is a useful technique here) to identify such priceable results as a reduction in training time due to the use of a particular method. Second-order outcomes are discussed further in the section on CEA.

The cost-benefit analyst has to make decisions on a number of issues before the analysis begins. One is to determine the criterion of effectiveness that will be applied. Different meanings of effectiveness are analysed in the following section. In addition, there are several technical decisions which are best made in association with your accounting department: first, the time span over which costs and benefits are to be calculated; second, the probability weightings that should prudently be attached to the costs and – especially – to the anticipated benefits; and, third, the discount factor which is to be employed in order that you can calculate the present value of future expenditure and revenue.

Present value is calculated by the formula

$$P = S_n \frac{1}{(1 + r)^n}$$

Where P is present value
S_n is total sum at the end of n years
n is number of years
r is rate of interest assumed for discounting purposes

A fourth factor to consider when using CBA in a predictive mode is the ratio between development time and time spent on learning. Assumptions made here have a considerable impact on the cost side of the analysis. Table 15.1 shows ratios of development time to tuition time for estimating training development costs of different types of training.

Using performance indicators in CBA

In every organization records will exist that monitor some aspects of performance. It is an obvious economy of effort if these records can be used to supply the data for the 'benefit'

EVALUATION TECHNIQUES

element of CBA. Where suitable records do not exist, or existing records cannot be adapted for evaluation purposes, then new recording systems will need to be created.

Sometimes a particular activity will be routinely measured in a number of ways. For example, in a manufacturing context, the efficiency of a unit may be assessed by the following:

- Quantity of output per hour.
- Proportion of output failing quality standards.
- Proportion of output produced to time deadlines.
- Percentage utilization of equipment.
- Cost of overtime per unit of output.
- Average labour cost per unit of output.

In similar fashion, there may be more than one indicator of labour turnover, for instance:

$$\text{crude wastage \%} = \frac{\text{No. of learners}}{\text{Average total employed}} \times 100$$

$$\text{stability index \%} = \frac{\text{No. of employees with 1 or more years' service}}{\text{Total employees one year ago}} \times 100$$

Which particular measurement record (or records) is adopted will depend on which most closely matches the objectives of the training activity to which the evaluation relates.

Where new records have to be created, several questions need to be answered: Who will develop the system and design any necessary documentation? Who will collect, record, and analyse the data? What can be done to encourage the people who hold the information – and who may not be committed to the evaluation – to contribute to the information-gathering system?

Once record systems have been identified or created a routine data-collection system can be instituted. This is a task ideally suited to integrated information technology systems which can automate the collection and analysis of data and the presentation of results. In some instances where a large throughput of trained personnel are involved, it will be appropriate to sample records on a random basis.

Table 15.2 shows some examples of performance records.

The advantages of using performance records in CBA are several:

- Existing records are cheap to use.
- The data is usually objective and reliable.
- The data is highly job-related and has substantial credibility for evaluation purposes.
- There is little or no effect on the subjects whose performance is assessed because the assessment is routine rather than a high-profile, special purpose evaluation.

The use of performance ratios

Comparisons between one enterprise and another are often made on the basis of key indicators of profitability and performance: the 'quick ratio' for calculating liquidity, or the return on capital employed, for example. Within an organization, the performance of a

COST-BENEFIT ANALYSIS

Table 15.2 Performance records: some examples

Operational measures	Personnel measures	Financial measures
Accident rates/costs	Absenteeism	Budget to actual comparison
Customer complaints	Induction time	Overhead/direct costs ratio and trend
Equipment downtime	Employee grievances	Return on investmment
Percentage utilization of equipment	Promotion rates	Cost per unit of output
Proportion of quality control failures	Time keeping	Inventory/turnover ratio
On-time delivery	Dismissals	Overtime cost per unit
Percentage achievement of targets	Industrial disputes	Bonus payments
Wastage and breakage	Training time	Costs per sale
Sales volume	Stability/voluntary severance rates	
Backlog of orders		
Quantity of output (goods, services)		
Market share		

particular function may be compared against the same function in other organizations within the same industry. In the very large organization, one training unit may be compared against another.

Ratios are useful as quick indicators of matters that may need closer investigation. What ratios do not do is indicate the reasons for divergences from the industry norm. Ratios are also useful when examined over a period of time. In this application they provide trend data that may highlight declining efficiency in the training function or in particular aspects of it. On the other hand, a trend of rising costs may reflect the situation where a training department has been engaged in extensive development work on new programmes, or where there has been a shift from standard courses to client-tailored provision.

There are several notes of caution to be struck: ratios taken in isolation can be very misleading. One training unit may produce a lower cost per trainee/day than another, either because it is more efficient in its use of resources, *or* because it provides training which is less costly because it is less effective. Equal effectiveness cannot be assumed. A measure of costs per trainee/day is a crude index unless the units being compared face similar demands, constraints and opportunities. This ratio is made even more unreliable where a significant proportion of training contact time is not accounted for as on-course trainee/days, for example where the training department is actively involved in a coaching or an internal consultancy role.

Ratios used in training applications include the following:

1. $\dfrac{\text{Actual training costs}}{\text{Turnover}} \times 100 = \%$

2. $\dfrac{\text{Actual costs}}{\text{Budgeted costs}} \times 100 = \%$

EVALUATION TECHNIQUES

3. $\dfrac{\text{Cost of sales training}}{\text{No. of salespersons}}$ = Cost of training per relevant employee

4. $\dfrac{\text{Actual training costs}}{\text{No. of employees}}$ = Cost of training per employee

5. $\dfrac{\text{Actual training costs}}{\text{No. of trainee/days per annum}}$ = cost per trainee/day

6. $\dfrac{\text{£ Benefits} \times 100}{\text{£ Costs}}$ = % Return on investment

There is a strong political case to be made for referring to 'training investment' in preference to 'training spend' or 'training cost'. It creates a more positive orientation towards training and an expectation that a return on investment can and should be identified.

COST-EFFECTIVENESS ANALYSIS

CEA is a useful technique to employ for several purposes:

- Comparison of the relative costs of two (or more) programme designs which are intended to produce the same learning outcomes.
- Comparison of the levels of learning achieved by programmes or techniques with equal cost limitations.
- The monitoring over time of any changes in costs and effectiveness of a specific training activity. It is a waste of resources to continue training beyond the point at which learning has been established to the standard required.

Nothing further needs to be said about the cost element of the equation. The effectiveness aspect raises the question of what precisely this term means, and the distinctions between priceable, quantifiable and identifiable outcomes of training.

What is meant by 'effectiveness'?

The usual distinction made between efficiency and effectiveness is that efficiency involves undertaking tasks in the way that is most economical in the use of resources; effectiveness involves undertaking the correct tasks.

The first step in CEA, as with all evaluation, is to define the audience for the findings and to specify the criteria that will be applied. 'Organizational effectiveness' is never an adequate criterion on its own. That and similar phrases such as 'meeting organizational needs' have to be clarified and made specific to the particular situation within which evaluation is taking place. This is because the meaning of job effectiveness varies between individuals, across job functions and at different levels within an organization. It is also the case that 'effectiveness of training' will have a different meaning to trainers, to participants and to nominating managers. A useful framework for thinking about effectiveness is that provided by Cameron.[1]

It is the criterion of effectiveness held by the client for the evaluation study which must take precedence over any abstract concept of 'effectiveness' divorced from time, place, or particular purpose.

It seems to be the case in larger organizations that lower levels of manager and supervisor think of effectiveness primarily in terms of their own work group or functional specialization. The effectiveness of internal processes and the ways in which other functions value their contribution are the two main considerations. More senior managers are inclined to think in terms of policy goals and time-defined targets. Two groups are particularly interested in satisfying constituents. One is the top tier of policy-makers who work on the boundary between the organization and its socio-economic environment. The other is any specialist function within the organization that has an advisory (staff) relationship with other functions and in some sense and to varying degrees must 'sell' its services to potential users if it is to survive.

Priceable, quantifiable and identifiable outcomes

Priceable outcomes of training are the kind of financially measurable performance changes that were listed in the section on CBA. Quantifiable outcomes can be measured, but may be difficult to value in monetary terms. They are nevertheless useful indicators of the impact of a training event. For example, the finding that 70 per cent of participants in a course on time management subsequently made a daily 'things to do' list is a useful indicator of effectiveness. Conversely, the finding that only a small percentage of participants in an industrial relations course ever played a role in industrial relations activities is an important quantification of a mismatch of training provision to participants.

The third category is that of identifiable benefits which are not readily measurable or priceable. Some of these outcomes may be only tenuously connected with training objectives. An example would be perceived improvements in the tone of internal communications in an organization, or long-term improvements in an employee's domestic relationships as a result of an in-company counselling skills programme. These identifiable but non-quantifiable outcomes are important for some cost-effectiveness evaluations, where they may represent the only evidence on which to base judgements about the effects of the training.

Implementing CEA

The initial step is to compile cost data for the alternatives which are to be compared (or for the same programme at different points in time). The cost identification matrix provides a convenient framework for this.

The second step is to brainstorm lists of actual and potential outcomes from the programmes being compared. Some outcomes will relate directly to training objectives. Others will be second-order consequences of the alternative designs, such as staffing requirements in a tutor-led programme and computer facility requirements in a CBT alternative. Further second-order outcomes include the time required by trainees to master the learning topics; the differential costs incurred for accommodation and travel (as between a centralized training college and decentralized terminals for self-tuition); and the benefits to workplace efficiency where staff can be trained in short intervals and slack periods on a computer-based distance learning pack, as compared to the need to be away from work for one or several days on a conventional course.

Some of the outcomes generated by the brainstorming process will in fact be priceable, bringing the analysis closer to a cost-benefit calculation. Others will be quantifiable or, at the least, identifiable. At that stage, an element of judgement and value preferences enters the process. The evaluator has the task of weighing one set of outcomes against another of equal cost, or of balancing a cheaper but less effective design against a more effective but more expensive programme.

There may be several different outcomes to be balanced against cost, but no common denominator (such as price), in which case the evaluator may allocate arbitrary weightings to each output. The weighted values may then be aggregated. This method obviously involves subjective value judgements about the weights, and it is a good policy to use more than one weighting system so as to reflect different points of view (there may be several different clients for an evaluation).

As a general rule, more weight should be given to the outcomes that are priceable and quantifiable and only then, or by default, to outcomes that can be identified but not measured.

SUBJECTIVE CBA

This chapter has focused upon finding objective financial measures for the worth of training. However, there is a useful, comparatively simple but more subjective form of CBA. This consists of simply asking the client (manager, trainee, etc.) what he or she feels the benefits of the proposed training are worth in cash terms. It is a question best put at the initial diagnostic stage of needs analysis: 'If training can solve this problem for you, how much would that be worth to your department?'.

NOTE

1. Cameron, K. (1980), 'Critical Questions in Assessing Organizational Effectiveness', *Organizational Dynamics*, Autumn, pp. 66–80.

Appendix I: Scientific method and evaluation

It is always desirable to use as rigorous a methodology as circumstances permit, but of course evaluation of an organization's training is of necessity carried out in working organizations rather than in the experimentally controlled conditions of a laboratory. Very often, in evaluation studies, we simply cannot claim that our conclusions are unarguably valid – the samples may be too small; there may be no control groups excluding non-training influences on the outcome; there may be reliance on self-reports which, in practice if not in theory, may be unverifiable.

However, there is a world of difference between merely *asserting* that you believe training to be working and being in the position to present *evidence* for the effects and value of training – evidence which has been collected as systematically as circumstances allow and which offers usable, useful and authentic information on which decision-makers can act. Evaluation provides a practical tool for making choices about training in organizations, in such a way that the influence of 'gut feeling' or preconceived judgements is minimized, and the influence of carefully collected evidence is maximized. More information, collected with care, is better than less; and information collected carelessly, naively, or cynically is dangerously misleading. Evaluation judgements are more like judicial judgements based upon a balance of evidence and probability than deterministic scientific statements of the 'If x occurs, then y follows' type.

It is, then, essential that the methods we use are as good as we can make them. This calls for some understanding of the use of control groups and sampling so that when the opportunity does present itself, the most thorough methods can be used.

CONTROL GROUPS

The most convincing evidence for the effectiveness of a training activity is that which shows changes in the trained group which are absent in similar groups that have not been trained. A control group is a group of people who are as similar as possible to the people in the trained group. Ideally the *only* difference between the groups is that the control group does not experience the training activity which the trained group undergoes. The groups should be equivalent in their job situation, experience, skill levels, abilities and demographic characteristics (age, sex, etc.). The control group should, if possible, be formed by random selection and the identity of its members should not be revealed.

In work situations, genuine control groups are rarely practicable. It is very difficult to prevent contamination of a control group's existing levels of knowledge or skill through leakage of information on the 'grapevine' by persons in the trainee group. If the control group is located at a different site to the trainees, then there is the problem that the group is unlikely to be identical in character to the trained group.

Control groups may also be unacceptable on policy or ethical grounds, for example it is not acceptable to have a control group which is prevented from receiving training in safety procedures. Control groups may also be inappropriate where learning relates to totally new subject areas and no meaningful comparison can be made with untrained subjects. What is sometimes possible is a comparison between formally trained persons and control groups who have informally 'picked up' skills on the job.

Figure AI.1 shows in diagram form the options open to the evaluator when seeking to control for non-training variables. The terms 'pre-assessment' and 'post-assessment' refer to any measurement, observation, or written or practical test applied to the people receiving training. The pre-test occurs before the training starts and the post-test after the training is completed.

Designs A, B and C, as shown in the figure, may be used where no comparison between groups is feasible. Designs D and E offer increasingly sophisticated controls which increase the certainty with which changes in work behaviour can be attributed to the training. If control groups can be established, and the training is important enough to justify the effort, it is certainly desirable to use the more rigorous methodology. However, in many situations what trainers need is a quicker, simpler method such as A, B or C, which does not control for variables outside the training. If there is clear evidence of changed performance following training, for most practical purposes that will provide convincing evidence of the success of the training.

A   SINGLE GROUP, POST-ASSESSMENT

This method is satisfactory where trainees have no knowledge or skill that can be assessed prior to training. A post-test will yield a measure of learning gained during the training. If trainees already possess some relevant knowledge or skill, then post-assessment offers only a measure of their competence after the event – the training itself may have increased, decreased, or had no effect on their competence. Such certification of competence has its uses, but not for evaluation.

```
A.  Single group with post-training assessment

    training                  > assessment

B.  Single group with pre/post assessment

    pre-assessment            > training              > post-assessment

C.  Single group with time series assessment

    pre-assessment 1          > pre-assessment 2      > training
                              > post-assessment 1     > post-assessment 2

D.  Two groups with pre/post assessment

    Group A (control):  pre-assessment                > post-assessment
    Group B (trainees): pre-assessment    > training  > post-assessment

E.  Two groups with post-assessment

    Group A (control):                                > post-assessment
    Group B (trainees):        training               > post-assessment

F.  Solomon four-group design

    Group A             pre-assessment                > post-assessment
    Group B             pre-assessment    > training  > post-assessment
    Group C                                           > post-assessment
    Group D                               > training  > post-assessment
```

Figure AI.1 Control group designs

B SINGLE GROUP, PRE/POST ASSESSMENT

This provides a measure of the learning gain within a training activity. However, there is always the possibility that the pre-test may have a 'sensitizing' effect on participants, for whom it may have highlighted the key learning tasks. This design also fails to control for possible effects external to training, such as changes in the organization, the environment, the workplace and so on. Nevertheless, it would represent a major leap forward in evaluation technology for a great many organizations.

C SINGLE GROUP, TIME SERIES

In this design, the trainee group serves as its own control group. A series of measures are taken before and after the training event (preferably starting and finishing several months distant from the training event). This design provides some control for external factors and is valuable in illuminating the long-term pattern of how learners make use of what they have learned.

For all their limitations, assessments of types A, B and C are of vital importance to all evaluation efforts. The reason is this: the trainer might evaluate, say, changes in performance indices, or differences in workplace behaviour, and find no significant changes. The trainer would then have no way of knowing whether people had learned what they were meant to learn within the training event, unless there was some measure of their competence at the end of that event. Thus, without a post-assessment, the trainer cannot know whether the lack of workplace change was due to a failure to learn or to factors in the workplace which prevented application of acquired skills or knowledge.

D SINGLE CONTROL GROUP DESIGN WITH PRE/POST ASSESSMENT

In this design, two matched groups are used, one of which receives training. This controls for all threats to validity except for the effects of the evaluative testing itself. A pre-test of knowledge or skills may affect the performance of both groups in a way that cannot be determined in this two-group situation.

E SINGLE CONTROL GROUP DESIGN WITH POST-ASSESSMENT

An alternative to design D is to use a post-test only, with a control group. This design eliminates the possible effects of a pre-test as well as most threats to validity. However, it does not allow measurement of learning gain attributable to the training programme itself and is therefore only appropriate where the subject of the training is wholly new and unknown to the trainees.

F SOLOMON FOUR-GROUP DESIGN

This design offers the greatest control of non-training variables. It requires four matched groups and this makes it very difficult to achieve in non-laboratory conditions. It controls for the effects of pre-testing on the untrained groups and for the effects of the training programme isolated from any external effects such as operational changes, work experience, individual maturation and the like.

SAMPLING

The object of sampling is to economize the effort necessary to gather data, whilst remaining confident that the findings from the sample are representative of the population from which the sample has been drawn. Most of the theory of sampling within human populations is derived from social science research or market research, both concentrated upon opinion data and in most instances drawing their samples from numerically large populations. The training evaluator usually faces a much smaller total population (which, other things being equal, implies a proportionately larger number of people in the sample), coupled with practical pressures to keep the sample size 'manageable' (i.e. smaller) in terms of the workload that it will impose on both evaluator and respondents.

Some basic concepts of sampling are as follows:

- 'Population' – the total group of individuals whose characteristics are to be investigated.
- 'Sample' – the sub-group selected from the total population for the purposes of the survey.
- 'Random or probability sample' – a sample, compiled by random selection of individuals from the population, in which the probability that an individual will be included can be known and is not zero. The probability that an individual will be drawn in a simple random sample is given by n/N, where n is the number drawn in the sample and N is the number of individuals in the population.
- 'Precision or sampling error' – the extent to which the sample precisely mirrors the whole population (also called 'reliability' of the sample result). Precision can be specified provided that we know the probability that the sample estimate will lie within various distances from the result that would be obtained from a survey of the total population. The measure of the extent to which the sample results differ from the population value being estimated is determined using the standard deviation formula.

Most sampling is *random* (in other words, every member of the population has an equal chance of being selected for the sample) in order to obtain findings that can be generalized to the whole population from which the sample is drawn. However, where the quality of the ideas that respondents give is the main consideration, then a *purposive* sample, with deliberate, careful selection of who is to be included, may be appropriate.

In generating samples, the evaluator is faced with a choice between trying to apply one of the various statistical textbook formulae for calculating sample size, or adopting a more pragmatic basis of sampling, relying on sampling indicators outlined in published evaluation studies. M. E. Smith[1] provides a useful survey of the sample sizes employed in a number of different evaluation projects and what follows is indebted to his analysis.

Sample size varies with a number of factors, first, population size. The larger the population, the larger the total number required in the sample, but the smaller the sample needs to be as a proportion of the population. Table AI.1 shows sample size relative to population size (assuming that every member of the population is identical in all relevant respects and, of course, that every member of the sample is selected

EVALUATION TECHNIQUES

Table AI.1 Sample size and population size

Numbers in population	Numbers in sample
1 500	285
1 400	280
1 300	273
1 200	276
1 100	275
1 000	280
900	270
800	264
700	245
600	231
500	205
400	194
300	165
200	148
100	78
50	48

Source: derived from Krijcie and Morgan[2]

randomly). The table provides a practical basis for planning evaluation projects using questionnaires.

The second factor affecting sample size is the variability within the population, measured in terms of standard deviation (SD). SD can be estimated on the basis of previous studies or a pilot project, or from knowledge of the work operations under study. Where the range of possible scores is already known, SD can be estimated adequately by dividing the range by six (for a normal distribution, six SDs will account for more than 99 per cent of the range).

A third factor is the presence or absence of control groups. Smith suggests that the difference between a controlled experiment and a less rigorous opinion survey without control groups is such that the sample size for the former may need to be no more than 20 or 30 whereas for the latter the numbers may range from 300 upwards.

A fourth consideration is the extent to which the training itself makes large or small differences to the trained population. If the training is expected to make large differences, then a small sample will be sufficient to show statistically significant differences between trained and untrained groups.

The number of possible responses ('values') for each evaluation question also has a bearing on sample size. For example, a question which offers a simple 'good/bad' or 'agree/disagree' choice represents a variable with two values. A question which requires a response on a five-point scale offers five values. The sample size also needs to be larger, the greater the number of variables that the evaluator wishes to analyse simultaneously (as, for example, when seeking correlations between the responses to

APPENDIX I: SCIENTIFIC METHOD AND EVALUATION

Table AI.2 Sample sizes

No. of variables for simultaneous analysis	No. of values per variable		
	1	2	3
1	40	60	80
2	80	180	320
3	160	540	1 280
4	320	1 620	5 120

different items in a questionnaire). Table AI.2 shows ideal sample sizes for several combinations of the number of variables and number of values per variable to be analysed simultaneously.

In summary, the more variability there is within the population, the absence of control groups, and the use of training activities that produce only small measurable differences all point towards a need for larger samples. Conversely, stratification of the population (on some criterion relevant to performance on the measured dimension) into sub-populations which can be individually sampled helps to reduce sample size. Such stratification might be made, for example, on the basis of length of service, prior qualifications, age, full-time versus part-time employment and so forth.

Yet another factor affecting sample size is the degree of precision required: larger samples increase the accuracy of the data. Precision will also be determined, when using sampling formulae, by the level of statistical significance chosen: for Type I errors, this is the probability that an apparent difference between, say, one training method and another is due not to it being a better method but to chance fluctuations in the performance of trainees; for Type II errors it is the probability that a real difference between methods is concealed by the random element in the data. Preliminary questions for the evaluator are: How large a statistical error is tolerable before the conclusions drawn from the survey will lead to the wrong action being taken? and What level of risk is acceptable, that the results of the survey may be in error by more than that level? Perhaps the biggest practical contribution to precision, however, is to ensure that your *population is correctly defined* and that its *key features are thoroughly understood*, so that the sample can accurately reflect them.

Experience (rather than statistical theory) suggests that certain evaluation techniques lend themselves to much smaller sample sizes than others, irrespective of the population size. For example, when using interview or behaviour observation a sample of around 20 to 30 subjects is usually quite adequate – persistence with larger numbers yields repetition of information which may be reassuring to the evaluator, but adds nothing new to what has been learned already. The following sample sizes (Table AI.3) are recommended for the data collection techniques listed.

EVALUATION TECHNIQUES

Table AI.3 Evaluation techniques and sample sizes

Technique	No. in sample
Behaviour observation (trained observer)	15
Behaviour observation (line supervisor)	50
Test of knowledge or practical skills	30
Critical incident method	50
Action plan review	50
Interview	30
Cost-benefit analysis from work records	50
Reactionnaire	50

Source: adapted from Smith[1]

NOTES

1. Smith, M. E. (1980), 'How big a sample do I need for my evaluation?', *Performance Instruction*, 11,10: 3–10.
2. Krijcie, R. V. and Morgan, D. W. (1970), 'Determining sample size for research activities', *Educational and Psychological Measurement*, 30: 607–10.

Appendix II: Statistical issues in testing

This appendix surveys the main statistical questions that can arise during evaluation projects. The reason for using any particular statistical technique is described and it is then presented in step-by-step fashion so that it can be applied by a person with little formal knowledge of statistical methods. Note that the descriptions of various kinds of 'average', of measures of dispersion (such as standard deviation), and of the comparison of frequencies using the chi-squared test are all located on pp. 112–16 where they form part of the discussion of interview design and analysis.

There are two reasons for including this survey of statistical issues. One reason is that there are certain kinds of evaluative conclusion that simply cannot be reached unless statistical techniques are employed, for example to compare the scores of several groups or to assess the predictive value of any one question within a test battery. These are not matters for an intuitive assessment.

A second reason is that trainers sometimes criticize the whole notion of evaluation on the grounds that it lacks 'rigour'. More often than not, the criticism is actually a covert attempt to avoid the evaluation process, using the spurious argument that if you cannot have perfectly controlled conditions, any information you obtain will be valueless. The appropriate use of the statistical techniques outlined here is one (amongst several) measures which the evaluator can take in order to increase the methodological rigour of the study.

SCORING TESTS: RAW SCORES, CRITERION REFERENCING, NORM REFERENCING

The simple numerical total which a person obtains in a test is known as the raw score. The difference between the raw scores achieved by different people is not an absolute or fixed amount: if A scores 80 and B scores 40 that does not mean that A knows twice as much about the subject area – only that A knows twice as much about the *sample* of the subject area which the test represents.

EVALUATION TECHNIQUES

There are two ways to make better sense of raw scores: by criterion referencing or norm referencing and by use of gain ratios (p. 249). In norm referencing, the scores of individuals are ranked in order so that any one score can be translated into a position relative to the tested population. Thus, one might say that somebody performed better than 75 per cent of the trainees who were tested during a given period. This approach has been characteristic of many examinations in schools or higher education. Norm-referenced criteria often creep into assessments of interpersonal behaviour: instead of judging performance against the required standard of behaviour, the assessor may consciously or unconsciously compare the performance of one person against another.

Trainers will usually wish to adopt a criterion-referenced approach. This judges the trainee's ability to perform to a satisfactory standard which, in a training context, is generally of more relevance to organizational effectiveness than is the competitive ranking of individuals. (Here, we are not concerned with the motivational role played by competitive ranking, although I recognize that some training, particularly in sales and in management team leadership, does encourage rivalry amongst trainees.)

Ideally, in a criterion-referenced system, everybody would score higher than a pre-set standard which represents the minimum acceptable level of achievement for the learner to be considered competent in the subject. There are two kinds of criterion referencing and, again, one is more common in training applications. 'Content referencing' is where the criterion requires trainees to demonstrate directly their attainment of training objectives. By and large, it is towards this that trainers are working. 'Predictive referencing' occurs where a test is used to predict performance in a situation different to that of the test. For example, a test which assessed how well trainees had assimilated certain skills of numeracy and logical analysis might be used to predict ability as a computer programmer. This sort of application arises most commonly in hybrid training events which combine elements of training for a future job (or potential job) with elements of assessment centre methodology.

An example of this approach occurred in a local government setting where potential foremen in the building works department were given a three-week training course in supervisory skills, combined with assessment of learning achieved. Successful candidates were then placed on a short list to fill vacant supervisory jobs as these became available.

COMPARING GROUPS

The trainer may wish to compare scores and rankings achieved on a test by different groups (or by the same group at different times).

PERCENTILE SCORES

Percentile scores convert rank positions to a percentage basis. An individual trainee's percentile rank shows the proportion of the group that scored below that person. For

APPENDIX II: STATISTICAL ISSUES IN TESTING

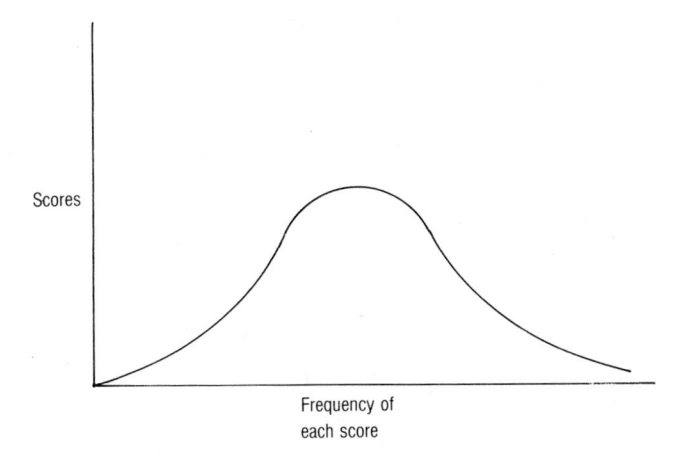

Figure AII.1 **Norm-referenced scores**

example, if a person is ranked 28th out of 39 trainees, the calculation would be as follows.

Step 1
There are (28–1) people scoring higher and (39–28) scoring lower, that is, 27 and 11.

Step 2
The individual who scores 28th (and anyone whose score ties with this) is arbitrarily divided between the upper and lower groups, which become 27.5 and 11.5.

Step 3
The percentile rank is calculated by the formula:

$$\frac{11.5}{39} \times 100 = 29.48\%$$

Thus 29.48 per cent of the group score less than this individual. The correct measure of central tendency of scores amongst the trainee population is the median, not the arithmetic mean. The median is that score which has an equal number of scores above and below it. In the example here, the median score is that represented by the $39/2 = 19$th trainee's score.

Norm-referenced scores plotted in graph format typically show a normal distribution curve, as shown in Figure AII.1.

Criterion-referenced scores will usually show a skewed distribution, as in Figure AII.2.

Percentile scores, in contrast, provide a distribution that approximates to the rectangular, more perfectly so the larger the sample of scores. Where the percentile

EVALUATION TECHNIQUES

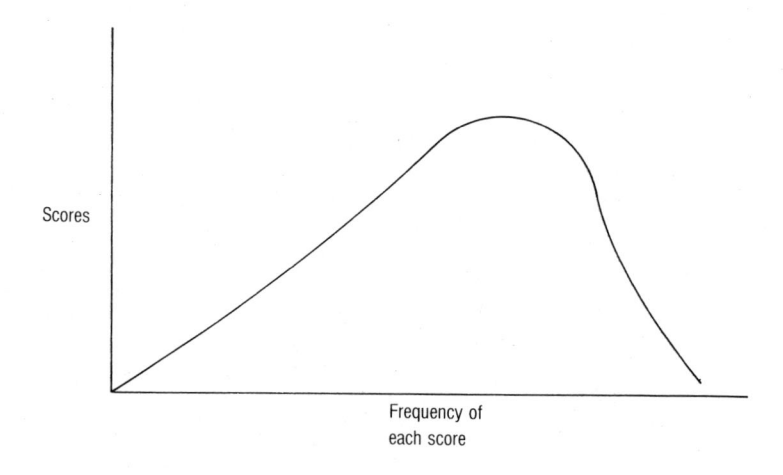

Figure AII.2 Criterion-referenced scores

value of the median is higher in one group than another, that group can be considered the more competent in the subject tested.

MEAN AND STANDARD DEVIATION

The *mean* is the arithmetical average of a group of scores. As such, it is not in itself very informative since the same mean can be produced by very different patterns of individual scores. The *standard deviation* yields a measure of the spread of scores within a group. It is a measure of the average of the differences between individual scores and the group mean.

The formula for standard deviation is as follows:

$$S.D. = \sqrt{\frac{\text{Sum of squares of individual deviations from arithmetic mean}}{\text{Number of items}}}$$

for example:

Scores	Deviations from arithmetic mean (AM)	Squares of deviations
4	−1	1
7	+2	4
3	−2	4
5	0	0
8	+3	9
2	−3	9
6	+1	1
Total 35		28

AM = 35/7 = 5
No. of Scores = 7

$$SD = \sqrt{\frac{28}{7}} = 2.0$$

APPENDIX II: STATISTICAL ISSUES IN TESTING

STANDARD SCORES

Sometimes the trainer will need to compare the results that trainees achieve on several different tests which may be of different lengths and not directly comparable. The recommended method to employ is the Z-score conversion, amended to eliminate negative scores. This amendment sets the mean as 50 and each standard deviation as equal to 10 points. The formula is as follows:

$$\text{Amended Z-score} = 50 + \frac{10 \ (\text{raw score} - \text{mean})}{\text{standard deviation}}$$

Example A

Suppose the mean is 41.6 and standard deviation is 8.3. A raw score of 60 converts to an amended Z-score as below:

$$50 + \frac{10 \ (60 - 41.6)}{8.3} = 50 + 22.17$$
$$= 72.17$$

Example B

Suppose the mean is 31.9 and standard deviation is 4.8. A raw score of 27 converts to an amended Z-score as follows:

$$50 + \frac{10 \ (27 - 31.9)}{4.8} = 50 + \frac{-49}{4.8}$$
$$= 50 - 10.2$$
$$= 39.8$$

GAIN RATIOS

With written and practical tests the interest is sometimes focused on the levels of attainment over time for a given course or tutor ('Are results consistent?') and sometimes on the amount of learning achieved by each trainee during the learning event (pre/post testing). Pre/post data can, of course, also be used to contribute to analysis of long-term trends.

It is difficult to compare learning gains using the raw scores of trainees and *gain ratios* provide a convenient and simple technique. They provide a measure of the learning achieved by a trainee, expressed as a percentage of how much that person could potentially have learned, given his or her initial level of knowledge.

Gain ratios are calculated by the following formula:

$$\% \text{ gain ratio} = \frac{(\text{post-score}) - (\text{pre-score})}{(\text{maximum score}) - (\text{pre-score})} \times 100$$

Table AII.1 shows gain ratio calculations for 12 trainees. Note that trainees E, F and J each scored a different raw increase pre/post (37, 53 and 15 respectively) but all three achieved a gain ratio of 100 per cent. This is because each achieved the maximum possible gain from their initial pre-test level of performance.

249

EVALUATION TECHNIQUES

Table AII.1 Gain ratios

Maximum score possible = 130

Trainee	Pre-score	Post-score	Post less pre (a)	Maximum less pre (b)	Gain ratio % (a ÷ b × 100)
A	25	75	50	105	47.6
B	48	96	48	82	58.5
C	80	103	23	50	46.0
D	110	125	15	20	75.0
E	93	130	37	37	100.0
F	77	130	53	53	100.0
G	10	50	40	120	33.3
H	56	83	27	74	36.5
I	90	102	12	40	30.0
J	115	130	15	15	100.0
K	42	71	29	88	32.9
L	97	126	29	33	87.9
				Total	747.7

$$\text{Mean gain ratio} = \frac{747.7}{12} = 62.3\%$$

As well as yielding a comparison of trainees' performance, the average gain ratio for a group can provide an indication of whether a satisfactory level of learning is being achieved. In interpersonal skills training, quite low levels of gain ratio are not unusual and scores of 50 or 60 per cent would be quite good. For training activities with well-defined objectives and good feedback to trainees on the progress of their learning, as in CBT systems, very high gain ratios would be expected (90 per cent or more, depending on the performance standard set).

A gain ratios calculation form is given in Figure AII.3.

COMPARING FREQUENCIES

There may be occasions when the trainer will wish to compare two groups in terms of the frequency with which some aspect of testing occurs rather than in terms of the levels of scores, for example, different rates for passing, failing, or being required to resit a particular test.

This analysis might be used to compare two trainee populations which have experienced different learning activities based on the same set of learning objectives (traditional instruction versus CBT, for example). It might be used to monitor success and failure rates over time, for a single course. The sort of data that might be obtained would resemble the table on p. 252:

APPENDIX II: STATISTICAL ISSUES IN TESTING

Trainee	Pre-score (a)	Post-score (b)	(b) less (a) (c)	Maximum score less (a) (d)	Gain ratio (c) ÷ (d) × 100 = %
				Total	
				Mean	

Figure AII.3 Gain ratios calculation form

EVALUATION TECHNIQUES

	Passed	Failed	Required to resit
Instructor-led training	189	47	39
Computer-based training	51	5	3

The technique for analysing this frequency data is the chi-square test. This is discussed at some length in Chapter 7 (see p.113).

THE GUESSING CORRECTION

Both true/false and multiple-choice test items contain the risk that trainees will guess the correct answer and thus be credited for knowledge which they do not in fact possess. This is a controversial issue within the literature on educational technology and various writers make distinctions between informed, intuitive, pure random and illogical guesses.

There are a number of techniques by which raw scores from multiple-choice items can be adjusted to make allowance for the effects of guessing (though no guessing correction can distinguish between a genuine mistake and an incorrect guess). Michael Akeroyd[1] suggests that the most efficient system for making guessing corrections is as follows.

Marks are allocated:

1 mark: correct answer only.
½ mark: 2 answers indicated, one of which is correct.
¼ mark: No answer given.
0 mark: Incorrect answer or combination of answers.

(These marks assume a four-option multiple-choice item; for a five-option item the 'no answer given' mark would be one-fifth.)

In the case of true/false items where there is a 50/50 chance of guessing correctly, a simpler formula can be applied:

$$\text{Corrected score} = \begin{bmatrix} \text{no. of correct} \\ \text{answers} \end{bmatrix} - \begin{bmatrix} \text{no. of wrong} \\ \text{answers} \end{bmatrix}$$

This is a version of the formula:

$$\text{Corrected score} = \begin{bmatrix} \text{no. of correct} \\ \text{answers} \end{bmatrix} - \begin{bmatrix} \dfrac{\text{no. of wrong answers}}{\text{no. of options in each item less 1}} \end{bmatrix}$$

APPENDIX II: STATISTICAL ISSUES IN TESTING

This formula can be applied to multiple-choice items but it has the disadvantage that all incorrect responses are classified as if they were failed random guesses and trainees' marks are reduced unfairly. Note also that the formula can only be applied to groups of multiple-choice questions where all questions within the group offer the same number of answer options (e.g. all 4, or all 5).

RELIABILITY

Reliability in testing refers to the idea that tests should be consistent in the way that they measure performance. Reliability refers to the consistency of the test items themselves and to the consistency of the assessors' judgements (particularly important when applied to behaviour observation). The central idea is that a given test should produce the same score results when administered to the same group of people on different occasions. (There is an implicit assumption here that these people's knowledge has not changed in the intervening period.)

Test reliability indicates the extent to which differences in an individual's test scores are attributable to real factors and how far to chance errors. A measure of reliability can only be correctly applied to a test which is being administered under standardized conditions to subjects who are like the people with whom the measure was developed.

There are several quite simple steps which will increase test reliability:

- Increasing the length of the test so that the range of training objectives is more thoroughly reflected in the test items used.
- Creating explicit, unambiguous instructions to guide the trainees in how to complete the test (and pre-testing the instructions to ensure they really are fool-proof).
- Standardizing the use of the test (the duration, physical conditions, amount of guidance provided).
- Standardizing the scoring (including where necessary training the scorers) so as to minimize or eliminate subjective marking judgements.

All reliability measures are concerned with the degree of consistency between two sets of scores and can be calculated as a *correlation coefficient* (written in formulae as 'r'). All correlation coefficients fall within the range $+1$ to -1. A perfect positive correlation is indicated by $r = +1.00$. Here one set of scores on a test is a perfect predictor of a second set and the test is a totally consistent measure. A perfect negative correlation is shown by $r = -1.00$. In this case, the best scoring individual on the first use of the test will be the worst scoring on the second; the worst will become best and so on. Where $r = 0$ there is no relationship between the scores: changes in scores achieved by individuals on the two occasions of test use are random – some may be better and some worse. In practice r usually is a value greater than zero and less than $+1.00$.

It is useful to know *how* reliable your tests actually are. There are several methods of calculating reliability coefficients, for example test-retest, alternate form and split-half. Each suffers from error variances (due to time sampling or content sampling

EVALUATION TECHNIQUES

Table AII.2 Split-half method

maximum test score = 100

Trainees	Odd no. scores (x)	Even no. scores (y)	x^2	y^2	xy
A	39	38	1 521	1 444	1 482
B	45	42	2 025	1 764	1 890
C	18	21	324	441	378
D	14	15	196	225	210
E	26	25	676	625	650
F	10	12	100	144	120
G	33	35	1 089	1 225	1 155
H	38	39	1 444	1 521	1 482
I	41	39	1 681	1 521	1 599
J	23	24	529	576	552
n = 10	$\sum x = 287$	$\sum y = 290$	$\sum x^2 = 9585$	$\sum y^2 = 9486$	$\sum xy = 9518$

inadequacies) which distort the calculation of true variance attributable to the test itself.

SPLIT-HALF METHOD

In practice, the method most convenient for the trainer is the split-half method. In this approach a test is administered only once to a group of trainees and the answers to test items are then divided into two sets. Typically, the division will be into odd- and even-numbered items. The two sets (halves of the test) are then treated as if they were two independent applications of the test. The scores of the split halves are correlated to arrive at the correlation coefficient.

The calculation of **r** illustrated here makes use of the Pearson product moment correlation coefficient. The formula for this is as follows:

$$r = \frac{n \sum XY - \sum X . \sum Y}{\sqrt{[n \sum X^2 - (\sum X)^2][n \sum Y^2 - (\sum Y)^2]}}$$

where n = number of trainees
      X = odd number scores
      Y = even number scores

Table AII.2 shows the application of the split-half method to the scores of 10 trainees. Using the data from Table AII.2:

APPENDIX II: STATISTICAL ISSUES IN TESTING

$$r = \frac{10(9518) - (287)(290)}{\sqrt{[10(9585) - (287)^2][10(9486) - (290)^2]}}$$

$$= \frac{95180 - 83230}{\sqrt{(95850 - 82369)(94860 - 84100)}}$$

$$= \frac{11950}{\sqrt{(13481)(10760)}}$$

$$= \frac{11950}{(\sqrt{13481})(\sqrt{10760})}$$

$$= \frac{11950}{(116.10)(103.73)}$$

$$= \frac{11950}{12043.05}$$

$\underline{r = 0.99}$

Note the effect of splitting the test is that each half constitutes a shortened form of the test and shorter tests produce lower **r** values. It is therefore necessary to adjust the value of **r** arrived at above, using the Spearman Brown correction.

$$r^1 = \frac{2r}{1+r}$$

$$r^1 = \frac{2 \times 0.992}{1 + 0.992} = \frac{1.98}{1.99} = 0.99$$

In this example there is a very high level of correlation already and the rounded-off **r** does not show any change. (Actually, **r** = 0.992 becomes **r¹** = 0.995). Larger shifts are seen when the value of **r** is lower, for example:

where **r** = 0.82
then **r¹** = 0.90.

There is one further test to apply to **r**. If **r** is calculated from a fairly small sample of scores there may be results due to chance. A precaution against a false **r** value is to calculate the *probable error* value, using the following formula:

$$\text{Probable error} = \frac{0.67[1-(r)^2]}{\sqrt{\text{No. of items}}}$$

In the previous example, this formula becomes

$$\text{Probable error} = \frac{0.67[1-(0.99)^2]}{\sqrt{10}}$$

$$= \frac{0.67 \times 0.02}{3.162} = \frac{0.0134}{3.162}$$

$$= 0.004238$$

If **r** is less than the probable error then there is no evidence of correlation. If **r** is more than 6 times the size of the probable error then the existence of the correlation is

EVALUATION TECHNIQUES

virtually certain. In this example, probable error × 6 = 0.025. There is thus virtually no likelihood that the correlation is false. **r** can be stated as 0.99 ± 0.025.

It may be thought that the amount of calculation involved makes this a cumbersome and unattractive procedure. However, **r** is a valuable indicator to the trainer of the proportion of students who are being incorrectly assessed by the test. As **r** gets smaller so the proportion increases whose test marks do not reflect their actual knowledge (whether positively or negatively distorting the individual's results). As a guide:

r =	% incorrectly scored
0.5	50%
0.7	40%
0.8	33%
0.9	23%

VALIDITY

The validity of a test concerns whether or not it provides an assessment of that for which it is designed. Validity can be determined only by reference to the particular application of the test. There are a number of different forms of validity to be considered.

CONTENT VALIDITY

This is probably the most important kind of validity. It concerns the extent to which the test is representative of the content of the training event on which the assessment is being based. The test material must give balanced coverage of training content and no important elements should be omitted. Test coverage of training content should be more or less proportional to the amount of time spent on that content during the learning activity.

You should guard against including a disproportionate number of test items just because they lend themselves easily to writing test items. The test must adequately reflect the training objectives and not merely the content. A method for this is to draw up a planning matrix such as that shown in Table AII.3. This enables you to keep track of the balance of items and the completeness of your coverage.

Content validity requires the involvement of subject matter experts as well as a technical analysis of the individual questions using item analysis (discussed on p. 258).

FACE VALIDITY

This concerns the *perceived* validity of the test to the trainees who take it. The issue is one of presentation and 'public relations' rather than of technical design and content. Face validity does matter: if a test is seen as irrelevant, or an insult to the subject's intelligence, or as being unfair (for instance, because it requires greater literacy than is usual in the tested population), then the test itself may be rejected. The whole principle of using tests in the organization may become a matter of controversy which will be

Table AII.3 Examples of planning matrix

Content areas	Recall of knowledge	Training objectives Classifying knowledge	Application of knowledge	Problem-solving and analysis	Total
A. Company safety policy	5	2	4	2	13
B. Emergency shut-down procedure	3	0	6	5	14
C. Site evacuation procedure	3	1	4	6	14

fought on political and industrial relations grounds that have little directly to do with training aims. Face validity can often be increased quite simply by rewriting test items to place them in situations and language with which the test subjects will readily identify.

CONSTRUCT VALIDITY

A construct is an abstraction – a mental concept – which we use to describe some feature of the subject area. Examples include the following:

- Ability to read a scale.
- Skill in conducting an appraisal interview.
- Attitude towards the employing organization.

The test designer's task is to show that a test item is a valid measure of the construct to which it relates. The first step is to define in detail what the construct represents. This definition is then employed to review validity, using one of several techniques: expert opinion; factor analysis of correlations; logical deduction; or examination of test results when the test is administered to a group who are known to possess either an abundance or a deficiency of the particular criterion.

PREDICTIVE VALIDITY

This concerns the extent to which the test can predict the future performance of test subjects (as in the example of a training and assessment centre). This requires a systematic method of collecting data on future performance (e.g. criterion-based workplace checklists) with which test results can be correlated. A high value for r, maintained consistently over time and retesting of workplace performance, indicates high predictive validity. Note the weak predictive link, already commented upon, between attitudes and behaviour.

EVALUATION TECHNIQUES

A multiple-choice question with five alternative answers is administered to 45 trainees. The correct answer is D. The distribution of answers amongst the five alternatives is shown below:

No. of trainees	Alternative answer selected
5	A
7	B
7	C
18	D
8	E
45	

$$\text{Facility value} = \frac{\text{No. answering D}}{\text{Total no. tested}} = \frac{18}{45} = 0.40$$

(FV should be calculated to two decimal places.)

Figure AII.4   Facility values

ITEM ANALYSIS

There are two main areas of interest in item analysis: facility values and the index of discrimination.

FACILITY VALUES (FV)

FV provides a measure of how difficult it is to answer any test item. Difficulty is expressed in terms of the proportion of trainees who correctly answer the test item. This degree of difficulty is called the facility value. Figure AII.4 illustrates the application of FV.

Items which are very easy will be correctly answered by most trainees, giving high FVs. Conversely, items which are very difficult produce low FVs. If the FV is low, then it becomes possible to score as well by guessing as by trying to answer the question: in the example in Figure AII.4 random answers should produce 20 per cent correct responses, equal to an FV of 0.20. The question is not much more effective than random guessing as a way of distinguishing good and bad trainees.

In a criterion-referenced test, where the expectation is that a large proportion of trainees will attain a specified standard, the FV ought to be high: 0.70 or greater. In a norm-referenced test, where the intention is to spread trainees across a range of scores for ranking purposes, then FVs in the mid-range are more useful (0.30 to 0.70).

APPENDIX II: STATISTICAL ISSUES IN TESTING

Table AII.4 Index of discrimination

Trainee scores distribution	A	B	Alternative answers C	D	E	Total
Trainees within top 12 on test	0	1	2	9	3	15
Middle 21	2	3	2	5	3	15
Trainees within bottom 12 on test	3	3	3	4	2	15
Totals	5	7	7	18	8	45

INDEX OF DISCRIMINATION (ID)

ID gives the trainer a measure of how well a particular item can be used to discriminate between good and bad trainees. The calculation requires the test group to be divided up into the top 27 per cent, bottom 27 per cent, and middle 46 per cent on *overall performance* in the test.

Using Figure AII.4, the group comprises 45 people. Twenty-seven per cent of 45 is 12.15, rounded to 12. By inspecting overall test scores for each of the 45 trainees, the top 12 can be identified as can the bottom 12. The responses made on the individual item are then tabulated (Table AII.4).

ID is calculated as the proportion of the top 27 per cent who get the answer correct (i.e. D) minus the proportion of the bottom 27 per cent who get the answer correct.

$$ID = \frac{9}{18} - \frac{4}{18} = 0.50 - 0.22 = 0.28$$

An ID of this level is low. What it implies is that the top group was not much better than the bottom group in answering this question. Note that a negative ID means that poor trainees score better on the item than good trainees. Also note that a high FV makes it inevitable that the ID will be low – if everyone has scored high, then the item is not discriminating amongst the population. As a guideline, the levels of FV and ID should not fall below the paired indices in the table below:

FV	ID
0.9	0.1
0.8	0.2
0.7	0.3
0.6	0.4
0.5	0.5
0.4	0.6
0.3	0.7

EVALUATION TECHNIQUES

Items that have satisfactory levels of FV and ID should be filed for re-use, creating an item bank of tested questions.

NOTE

1. Akeroyd, M. (1982), 'Progress in Multiple Choice Scoring Methods 1977–81', *Journal of Further and Higher Education*, 6(3), pp. 86–90.

Part III
CASE STUDIES

Introduction to Part III

This section describes a number of applications of evaluation. The main substantive findings of each study are usually stated, to demonstrate the kinds of information the studies can yield, but the primary purpose is to illustrate how the methods of evaluation can be used in a wide variety of organizations and different training contexts. The amount of detail in each case varies but the aim has been to keep to the minimum necessary for understanding the particular example. Details which would identify the organizations in which the evaluation studies were made have been suppressed. A summary table of the case studies follows.

CASE STUDIES

Chapter	Type of training	Evaluation technique	Sector	Subjects of study
16	Personal development	Interview	Computer engineering	Electronics graduates
17	Training of trainers	Behaviour observation	Retail (stores)	Instructors
18	Job procedures	Interview and psychometrics	Retail (food)	Till operators and others
19	Customer service skills	Written test	Financial (life/pensions)	Clerical and junior management
20	Job knowledge and procedures	Questionnaire	Government department	Clerical new entrants
21	Outdoor development	Interview	Retail (stores)	Graduate high-flyer middle managers
22	Pre-training preparation	Interview	Computer sales	Sales managers

SUMMARY OF MINI-CASE STUDIES

Chapter	Type of training	Evaluation technique	Sector	Subjects of study
23	Technical up-date training	Practical testing	Utility	Maintenance engineers
23	Sales training	Reactionnaire	Retail (white goods)	Sales assistants
23	Industrial relations for managers	Questionnaire	Service industry	Middle managers
23	Technical	Test reliability	Training centre	n/a
23	Clerical procedures	Cost-benefit analysis	Utility	Clerical
23	Supervisory skills	Critical incident	Local government	Supervisors

16 Personal development of computer engineers

This evaluation was carried out for a computer manufacturer at a time when various aspects of the business, including training, were undergoing re-appraisal. The survey was carried out over a period of three months. The analysis and comments were positively received by the client and a number of the recommendations were implemented. However, some months after the survey, the client took early retirement as part of a wider restructuring and the opportunity for longer term follow-up was lost. The study remains interesting for the issues it raises concerning the application of evaluation to 'developmental' training (see also Chapter 21).

EVALUATION – THE KEY QUESTIONS

1. For whom is the evaluation being undertaken? ('the client')

The training manager responsible for providing technical skills training and personal/professional development for the subjects of the survey.

2. Which particular training activity will provide the subject for the evaluation project? ('the course')

A developmental programme with elements of counselling skills for professional engineering staff, run by external consultants, referred to here as the 'EngDev' course.

3. What is it about the training process that the client wants you to assess? ('the criterion of worth')

To review the usefulness of the course and to demonstrate the application of formal evaluation methods to interpersonal skills training.

4. Who is likely to have answers to your assessment questions? ('the subjects')

This data was sought from the participants on the course. Initially, a random sample was drawn from the total population of former participants. Following the first three interviews, it became apparent that earlier attendees had great difficulty in dis-

CASE STUDIES

Introduction: Purpose
        Confidentiality – interviewer's independence of the company
        Time available for interview
        Options for recording answers

1. When did you go on the course?
2. Can you think back to before the course and remember what you expected from it.
3. Did it meet or differ from your expectations?
   (Probe for specifics)
4. How relevant to your job did you see the course as being?
5. What, if anything, have you done differently in your job as a result of that course?
6. Is there anything about that course that you would like to be different?
7. Given what the course was intended to do, would you have preferred some other way of doing it?
8. What did you find the least easy parts of the course to cope with?
9. How do you feel about this interview as a way of evaluating your experience of the course?

Figure 16.1   **Interview schedule – participants**

tinguishing between effects of the course itself and effects of other courses attended subsequently. The sample was redrawn to include only people who had attended the course during the last eighteen months (population = 107; sample = 20; 18.7 per cent). In addition, one in two of the managers of participants was sampled.

The total population was not large enough to justify stratifying the sample on the basis of geographical location; however, the random sample in fact threw up a range of locations that covered most of the UK.

Interviewing unfortunately coincided with a busy, end of year period in the company and in consequence the actual numbers interviewed were 17 participants (15.9 per cent of the population) and 8 managers.

5.   What will be the appropriate evaluation technique for use to use? ('the technique') Interview was selected as the technique most suited to probing the participants' experiences of developmental training and the benefits that they perceived to have derived from the training. Experience shows that written answers to such questions are virtually always guarded and uninformative.

Interviews were tape-recorded (with one exception) and full transcripts (totalling 150 pages of single-spaced text) were made before analysis and selection of edited extracts.

A standardized interview schedule was employed, plus supplementary (improvised) questions where appropriate. The interview questions asked are shown in Figures 16.1 and 16.2.

PERSONAL DEVELOPMENT OF COMPUTER ENGINEERS

Introduction: Purpose
　　　　　　Confidentiality – interviewer's independence of the company
　　　　　　Time available for interview
　　　　　　Options for recording answers

1. Were you the manager of ... (*named participant*) at the time he/she attended the 'EngDev' course?
   　　IF 'YES' CONTINUE WITH SEQUENCE A
   　　IF 'NO' CONTINUE WITH SEQUENCE B.

Sequence A
2. What did you hope he/she would gain from the course?

3. Do you think the course delivered what you were hoping for?

4. Can you identify any specific examples of changes in job behaviour that you could attribute to that course?

5. For what ... (*named participant*) got out of it, do you yourself feel that the course was a justifiable investment of time and money?
   　(Probe: how?)

6. Are there any changes to that course that you feel might be useful?

Sequence B
7. Do you know anything about the purpose of that course? (If 'no', describe purposes briefly)

8. From your own knowledge of ... (*named participant*), do these seem useful learning goals?

9. Are you aware of any need to improve his/her performance in that respect?

Figure 16.2 Interview schedule – managers

6. What will be the best time to carry out the evaluation? ('the timing')
See comments under 4 above (the subjects).

SELECTIVE SUMMARY OF FINDINGS AND IMPLICATIONS

QUALITY OF THE DATA

Qualitative interview data may be reviewed against criteria of grounding, consistency and utility. Grounding of data refers to whether or not the person interviewed is able to make explicit links between particular judgements and the situations or events on which the judgement is based ('This is how I made use of that element of learning' statements). Grounding the data provides a check against 'wish-fulfilment' statements. Absence of grounding data gives early warning that participants in training have experienced difficulty or lack of interest in transferring learning into practice. In respect of this study, grounding of judgements was poor.

Consistency applies within individual interviews (are people avoiding self-contradiction?) and between interviewees (are people saying the same things?). Certain patterns in the data were consistent and these are discussed in detail in the main analysis. Note: it is sometimes useful to include as an appendix to the evaluation report substantial verbatim extracts from recorded interviews; this allows the readers to form their own judgements on the nature and consistency of responses, and can lend immediacy to dry analytical conclusions.

1. What participants expected from 'EngDev'

Findings: Most had a very imprecise idea of what the course was intended to achieve. Many apparently attended on trust that it would be worthwhile on the basis of the course title or an unspecific recommendation. Examples of expectations included the following:

- Marketing skills.
- Helping people to make their own plans.
- Influencing skills.
- Solving a specific problem with a customer.
- Helping people to change the company.
- Speed up career progress.
- Attended with an open mind.
- Didn't really know why attending.
- Sent as a guinea pig.

Implications: Learning is increased where learners have a clear idea of where they are heading. It is also easier to determine whether progress is being made. If the 'EngDev' course is intended to change job behaviour, then a much sharper focus is required. If, however, it is seen as a developmental experience which is justified solely by the opportunities that it presents for personal exploration, then none of these comments matter, although further questions are then raised about the ethics of allowing participants to enter a psychologically stressful training situation without adequate pre-briefing or subsequent counselling support.

2. What managers expected participants to gain from the course

The quality of managerial responses was poor: managers did not appear able to make assessments of changed work performance attributable to the course. This reflected their very imprecise knowledge of the course and a vague perception that 'development' was a 'good thing'.

3. Information available to participants

Personal recommendations by colleagues or managers were taken as sufficient in themselves, however, most managers were surprised by the difference between what they thought the course to be about and what it actually comprised, when this was described by the interviewer.

Where the course brochure was consulted, the information was (with hindsight) considered inadequate; the course title was felt to be misleading. One inference might be that the company does not encourage its employees to question the reasons for attending training events; trainers apparently collude in this by neither expecting nor insisting on proper pre-course briefing of participants. This can lead to mismatch of needs and content, resistance to learning, and – in some instances – psychological distress.

4. Application of learning back at work

There was only a little evidence of transfer of learning into work practices. Much of the interviewees' comments were at the level of generalized statements about increasing their confidence and responsiveness when dealing with other people. Whilst there is no reason to doubt this, only two respondents could ground that judgement in specific examples.

Most of the interviewed managers reacted to this question with embarrassment and the implications are obvious. An integrated relationship between managers and trainers can do much to reinforce learning transfer; post-course evaluation by managers is quite feasible when the managers know what the training is about, but is futile when they do not.

5. Should the course be different?

There were a number of concerns stated about the risks of counselling on personal problems; a recurring theme (or fantasy) that it had been better in other small groups within the course; and demands for both theory and more practical application.

Comments show the usual pattern of tinkering with detail. However dissatisfied, respondents very rarely present radical alternatives to the existing product. In any case, revision of the course needs to be based upon a thorough re-examination of the organizational needs which it is intended to meet.

6. Other comments emerging from interviews – the psychological contract

Much of the dissatisfaction and discomfort generated in the course may be traced back to the psychological contract between trainers and participants. There simply cannot be a freely achieved agreement about learning processes when the information on which to base a decision to take part only becomes available on the course itself. And if participants then commit themselves to a contract about learning and confidentiality which they do not fully understand or which they go along with cynically, then it can be no surprise if it comes unstitched later and rebounds against the reputation of the course.

7. Use of the evaluation interview

Most respondents said that an interview was necessary to gather their thoughts about the course; most would either not respond at all, or respond in a limited way, to a written questionnaire. Two people suggested that the experience of the course was inherently not communicable to non-participants which raises a question about their

CASE STUDIES

powers of expression and about whether the company should be in the business of providing inscrutable training experiences.

There was comment on the desirability of discussing the course with an independent outsider and a consensus that about six months post-course was the optimal time for conducting the interviews. Several people saw the interview itself as having a review and reinforcement role in relation to what had been learned on the course.

GENERAL CONCLUSIONS

Many people learned new skills from the course and some of them valued those skills highly. A revised version of the course should be developed which incorporates the key elements identified by the evaluation study:

1. A thorough diagnostic review of the learning needs which the course is meant to address.
2. Comprehensive pre-course information to managers and potential participants.
3. Attention to learning methods employed, including an analysis of preferred learning styles of participants.
4. A substantial enhancement of the job-relevant content of the course and a greater emphasis on preparing for application of new skills.
5. On the basis of the interview data, there is no value in proceeding to a proposed second stage of evaluation using postal questionnaires.

17 Training trainers

The context in this case was a series of evaluation workshops for central and functional trainers, together with their training manager, as part of which each participant undertook an evaluation project. Such projects related either to the trainer's own field of activity or to training carried out by local (departmental) trainers. The project described here focused on the training provided by a central trainer to enable a departmental trainer to carry out keyboard/VDU training for operators of a new computerized stock control system. The departmental trainer had a grounding in basic instructional techniques and had spent some time running youth training activities.

EVALUATION – THE KEY QUESTIONS

1. For whom is the evaluation being undertaken? ('the client')

The main client was the central trainer who wished to know whether or not the training programme was effective in upgrading the skills of the departmental trainer. The training manager had a similar interest in the study.

2. Which particular training activity will provide the subject for the evaluation project? ('the course')

The training provided by the departmental trainer to keyboard operators.

3. What is it about the training process that the client wants you to assess? ('the criterion of worth')

Whether or not the departmental trainer has learned to analyse tasks, develop appropriate training, and deliver the training in an effective manner.

4. Who is likely to have answers to your assessment questions? ('the subjects')
The departmental trainer.

5. What will be the appropriate evaluation technique for you to use? ('the technique')

A combination of behaviour observation, used whilst the departmental trainer was

CASE STUDIES

Table 17.1 Behaviour checklist

Behaviour to be assessed	Evidence for the behaviour	
	Positive examples	Negative examples
1. Puts trainee at ease	Builds confidence	Undermines confidence
	Encourages	Critical
	Informative	Uninformative
	Empathises	Threatening
2. Explains and demonstrates task	Clear	Confusing
	Shows how	Does not check understanding
	Ensures trainee can see & hear	Talks about, rather than shows
	Gives opportunity for questions	Does not check with trainee
		Does not encourage questions
3. Possesses knowledge of task	Has thorough knowledge	Incomplete knowledge
	Able to answer questions	Unsure of some answers
	Confident	Anxious or flustered
4. Uses appropriate language	Clear	Muddled
	Jargon free	Uses jargon without defining terms
	Does not 'talk down'	Patronizing
	Does not use value judgements	Prejudiced
	Gives feedback in a helpful manner	Tactless
5. Non-verbal behaviour	Correctly positions trainee	Trainee unable to see or hear clearly
	Looks interested	Looks bored
	Sits or stands, as appropriate to task	Slouches; stands or sits in defensive posture
6. Responds to trainee	Shows has listened (e.g. reflective summary)	Inattentive
		Mis-hears
	Responds to questions, comments, movements	Ignores signals from trainee
7. Uses open questions	Checks understanding, gathers information	Allows trainee to talk about irrelevancies
8. Uses closed questions	To obtain precise answers	To block trainee's responses
	To get facts or commitment	Used in interrogatory manner
9. Checks understanding	Asks trainee to explain	Tells trainee
	Clarifies any misunderstandings	Asks if trainee understands
		Allows misunderstandings to go uncorrected
10. Summarizes	Recaps key points	Fails to draw learning points together
	Explains next stage	
	Gets trainee's commitment to planned actions	

training keyboard operators, and individual interview with the trainer. Agreement to the evaluation processes was obtained from the departmental trainer and the trainer's direct supervisor. The departmental trainer explained the presence of an observer to the trainees.

The observation checklist is reproduced as Table 17.1 and the interview schedule in Figure 17.1.

1. What were your expectations before being trained?
    1.1 Were these expectations met?
        If yes, how?
        If no, why do you think this was so?

2. Has the training equipped you to train the keyboard operators?
        If yes, how?
        If no, why not?
    (Probe: What do you do now that you would not have done prior to training?)

3. Are there any areas which you feel:
    a) should have been covered?
    b) should have been covered in more depth?
    (Probe: How would that make a difference to the way that you train?)

4. Were there any areas that you found unnecessary to cover?
    (Probe: Why?)

5. What are your views on the methods used for the training?
    (Probe for examples)

6. What are your views on the timing and duration of the training?
    (Probe: Too long/short; too hurried/drawn out?)

7. Is there anything else on which you would like to comment?

Figure 17.1   Training trainers interview schedule

6. What will be the best time to carry out the evaluation? ('the timing')

The observations were conducted during the early sessions of the new training for operators, with the interviews almost immediately afterwards, in order that any necessary corrections to the training could be introduced rapidly.

CONCLUSIONS AND COMMENTARY

The project demonstrates some excellent design work on behaviour observation. The study found that the trainer was performing in the way that the training had intended. However, methodologically, the study suffers from the absence of a baseline against which progress as a result of the training could have been measured; this post-training design yields a measure of performance competence which itself may be very useful, but it does not allow the effects of the training of trainers course to be distinguished from the effects of earlier learning and experience. Observations pre-training would have strengthened the study greatly.

CASE STUDIES

It is sometimes argued that people are likely to be on their 'best behaviour' when they know that behaviour observation is taking place. This is very likely. However, whilst the observed person may be able to suppress their worst behaviour characteristics for the duration of the evaluation, they are not usually capable of simulating skills that they do not possess.

It is also sometimes argued that the observed person will lapse into unsatisfactory behaviour as soon as the observation period is ended. Again, this may happen with some people, but this represents a problem of motivation and supervision, not a critique of evaluation itself. Where such lapses are suspected, the proper evaluation response should be a follow-up survey, using less visible means if possible, to check whether or not correct behaviours persist and to assess whether or not managerial reinforcement is playing its part in the behaviour patterns observed.

18 Job procedures

This project was one of a number undertaken for a particular client over a period of several years. In this instance, the evaluation was of training that the company which commissioned the study was providing to its clients, rather than upon internal training. The project evolved through the usual steps of discussing frameworks for effective training and the ways in which practical evaluation techniques could be incorporated, through to formal proposals, agreed objectives and a timetable for implementation. The anticipated benefits from the evaluation were seen in terms of the following:

1. Systematic data on which to base training methods and content in the future, with a potentially very large number of employees, not only those of the current client group but also within other retail companies who might purchase the till system.
2. Credibility when selling training to customers, based upon the more rigorous approach that had been achieved through evaluation.
3. A basis for building in quality control and learning reinforcement tests as an integral part of the total training package, including training client personnel to design and use evaluation techniques themselves in the future.
4. Data that might help shape the future marketing directions of the training function.

EVALUATION – THE KEY QUESTIONS

1. For whom is the evaluation being undertaken? ('the client')

The direct client was the training function of a company which supplied till systems to supermarkets and department stores. The supermarket chain in which the survey was conducted also constituted a client, both in terms of the need to manage access to subjects with minimal disruption to work routines, and in terms of its interest in the findings which could have wider implications for the supermarket group's own internal training.

2. Which particular training activity will provide the subject for the evaluation project? ('the course')

There were two centres of attention: the training provided directly to managers and cash office staff who operated the till system control equipment and records; and the training of trainers provided for supervisory staff to enable them to carry out direct training of till operators. At the time of the study, training had been delivered in four large stores and was scheduled to roll-out nationally over the following 12–18 months.

3. What is it about the training process that the client wants you to assess? ('the criterion of worth')

What had worked and what needed improvement in terms of the training materials and the way that training was delivered.

4. Who is likely to have answers to your assessment questions? ('the subjects')

A cross-section of employees was included in the study, including store managers, supervisors and till operators.

5. What will be the appropriate evaluation technique for you to use? ('the technique')

Interview was chosen for a number of reasons: it is the best medium for exploring people's experiences of a learning process; it is invaluable wherever self-analytical introspection and fluency in writing cannot be taken for granted – careful questioning yields answers that would never be committed to writing; and it greatly increases the response rate, especially in cultures where there is antipathy to paperwork. However, interview was supplemented by two paper-based instruments which were administered at the time of interview, thereby ensuring a virtually 100 per cent response rate. These were (a) a tick-box type checklist which documented the involvement of each interviewee with the till system; and (b) the Honey–Mumford[1] learning styles questionnaire.

The sample of interviewees was selected to provide satisfactory coverage of the key occupational areas to which the training related. For cash office staff, the sample was typically 80 per cent of employees in each of the four stores visited. For till staff, the percentage sample was much lower (especially in stores predominantly staffed by part-timers) but the cumulative numbers were adequate in terms of quality of data obtained. It is always worth remembering that interview, as a technique, tends to yield rapidly diminishing returns of fresh information. The sample sizes were managers and assistant managers, 10 from 21 (4 female, 6 male); till supervisors, 11 from 20 (female); cash office supervisors, 5 from 7 (female); cash office staff, 8 from 10 (female); till operators 19 from 65 (female).

Confidence in the data was increased by their consistency both between individuals and between different geographical locations (which included Tyneside, Lancashire, Dorset and the West Midlands). Data were generally well-grounded in specific, concrete examples, rather than in general statements of abstract principle or wishful thinking.

The interview schedules are reproduced in Figures 18.1 and 18.2.

JOB PROCEDURES

Introduction: Confidentiality
　　　　　　　Anonymity
　　　　　　　Use of tape recorder
　　　　　　　Purpose of survey

1. Here is a list of tasks connected with operation of the till system.* Would you please put a tick in Column A against each task that you have carried out at some time or other.

2. Will you please go down the list again and put a tick in Column B for any task that has caused you diffficulty at any time.

3. For each item that you've ticked in Column B, what was it that made it difficult for you?

    3.1 Are any of these items still causing you any difficulty?

    3.2 What do new till operators/cash office staff find most difficult to learn?

4. Could I now ask you about any training you've received to help you operate the till system?

    4.1 Did you receive any training?

    4.2 Who delivered your training?

    4.3 How was the training delivered?

    4.4 How did you feel about the training?

    4.5 What might have helped you to learn about these topics more easily?

    4.6 Have you any suggestions for improving the training?

5. Is there anything that you currently use to jog your memory about how you should use the system?

6. Last, would you please complete this questionnaire which will give us some information about the ways in which people like yourself prefer to learn new skills (such as the till equipment).

Note: *Separate checklists were provided for supervisors, for till operators and for cash office staff; these are not reproduced here for reasons of commercial confidentiality.

Figure 18.1 Interview schedule – supervisors, till operators, cash office staff

6. What will be the best time to carry out the evaluation? ('the timing').

The study was carried out in a fairly tight 'window' between completion of training in the first four stores and the installation of the new till systems in the next batch of outlets. In a perfect world, the survey might have been usefully conducted immediately after the training had occurred, but overall the interval between training and interview was rarely more than two or three months at the longest and only occasionally gave rise to problems of recall.

CASE STUDIES

Introduction: Confidentiality
Anonymity
Use of tape recorder
Purpose of survey

1. Would you tell me, please, what is your own involvement with the till system?

2.1 What, if any, training did you yourself receive to prepare you for that involvement?

    2.1.1 Who delivered the training?

    2.1.2 How do you feel about that training?

    2.1.3 What might have helped you to learn about those topics more easily?

2.2 (If no training received) How did you learn to do those tasks?

3. Have any of those areas of involvement caused you difficulty at any time?

4. Is there anything you currently use to help you remember how you should use the system?

5. Are there any aspects of the till system with which the staff you supervise seem to have particular difficulty?

6. What do you think are the causes of that difficulty?

7. Last, would you please complete this questionnaire which will give us some information about the ways in which people like yourself prefer to learn new skills (such as the till equipment).

Figure 18.2 Interview schedule – store managers, departmental managers

SELECTIVE SUMMARY OF FINDINGS AND IMPLICATIONS

TILL TRAINING

Findings: There were several problems created by training on tills under the gaze of customers. The structure for training was inflexible, not allowing for individual differences in speed of learning. Training was itself subverted, on occasion, by pressure to put new operatives into a customer-serving role very quickly. Procedure-learning (especially more complex sequences) needed to be built up on a parts-to-whole basis. Product knowledge training tended to be skimped, with negative effects on till performance. Role plays with 'awkward customers' were universally detested and also inappropriate, since complaints were actually handled by supervisors. A range of 'home-made' aids to memory were encountered and most of these could usefully be formalized as reminder cards beside the till.

Comment: There is a case for a full-time trainer in-store to handle all induction and basic training and to maintain performance standards over time. Training of till operators needs restructuring and a more individual approach.

CASH OFFICE TRAINING

Findings: The operator comments were largely repeated: in addition, there was a need to see an already operating system, for example at another store, and a need for simulations of system failures. The training provided had been too rushed and too theoretical.

MANAGERS' TRAINING

Findings: Within a very small sample of managers, there was wide variation in the extent of hands-on experience of the system as against general understanding coupled with delegated operational responsibility.

OTHER COMMENTS

There were a number of comments relating to the design of the equipment, particularly ergonomic problems, and to software. The manual supplied with the equipment was widely commented upon as being too complicated and full of jargon.

LEARNING STYLE PREFERENCES

The Honey–Mumford[1] learning styles questionnaire was administered to all subjects at the end of the interview. The LSQ authors were contacted but at the time no norms existed for comparable occupational groups and the data therefore had to be interpreted in isolation. In summary, the findings were as follows:

Till supervisors: no dominant style; virtually equal preference for all four styles.
Till operators: strongest preference was reflector style. This was at odds with the activist style of till training provided.
Cash office supervisors: pattern very similar to till operators.
Cash office staff: pattern similar to till operators but with even weaker preference for the activist mode.
Male managers: profile very similar to cash office staff (and markedly less activist in pattern than existing UK norms for managers).
Female managers: an equal preference for reflector, theorist and pragmatist learning styles, with a lesser preference for the activist (and lower than male managers' activist preference).

The implication of the findings was that most people would learn more or less equally well from theorist and pragmatist methods – and least well from activist. However, where one style can be seen to dominate, it is always the reflector style.

GENERAL CONCLUSIONS

There was a fair level of satisfaction with the training provided to the stores, but qualified by a number of detailed criticisms and learning shortfalls. Whilst the client very evidently put much effort into the training it was delivering, that training was shaped too much by the technical content and too little by consideration of learners' needs. The problems were mainly problems of how the content was delivered rather than of what the content needed to be.

The low level of training for managers reflected both pressures of time where new stores were opening and also an expectation that they did not need any depth of knowledge of the operations or the till system.

A number of business opportunities for the client company's training function were identified but are not listed here for obvious reasons of commercial confidentiality.

The other significant outcome of the evaluation project was a seminar run by the manufacturer for the supermarket group, to present and explain the findings of the survey and to suggest how in-store training could be enhanced.

NOTE

1. Honey, P. and Mumford, A. (1982), *The Manual of Learning Styles*, Honey Publishing.

19 Customer service

The evaluation described here centred upon one module within a customer service/total quality/culture change project extending over two years and for all levels of employee in a large life insurance and pensions company. The requirement was for a workable system to assess whether or not staff who were undergoing training had attained an acceptable standard in the various topics covered. The intention was to provide further remedial training for those who failed to achieve the required level of competence when tested. The particular challenge and interest in this case study arises from the requirement to assess learning through written test rather than behaviour observation. This requirement was a response to the sheer volume of other changes going on within the company at the time, such that the involvement of line management in the assessment process, though desirable in principle, was impracticable on this occasion.

EVALUATION – THE KEY QUESTIONS

1. For whom is the evaluation being undertaken? ('the client')

The ultimate client in this case was the top management team of the company, which wanted to know whether or not the investment in training was producing the results it wanted. A second group, with a similar interest, was the company's quality council which had oversight of the whole culture change project. The direct client was the line manager who chaired the working party responsible for production of the particular module to which this evaluation relates.

2. Which particular training activity will provide the subject for the evaluation project? ('the course')

The subject was a training module on customer service skills (towards both external and internal customers) delivered by in-house trainers and comprising elements of video, text-based material and trainer-led exercises and discussions. Both the training material and the test material were developed by me.

CASE STUDIES

3. What is it about the training process that the client wants you to assess? ('the criterion of worth')

The long-term goal was to assess use of skills in the job and a behavioural observation checklist (not discussed in this case study) was developed for this purpose. The short-term objective was to find out whether or not each participant in the course had learned enough, at a cognitive level, to be in a position to use the skills back in the workplace.

4. Who is likely to have answers to your assessment questions? ('the subjects')

The subjects comprised approximately 2 500 clerical, supervisory and specialist grades – everybody who underwent the training was tested.

5. What will be the appropriate evaluation technique for you to use? ('the technique')

The technique adopted was written test. A test bank using questions in multiple choice formats was prepared together with a fully developed marking scheme to eliminate discretionary elements in the assessments. The test bank made it possible to vary the questions that different groups would have to answer, thereby reducing the risk of people learning the answers in advance. Examples of test questions and answers are given in the next section.

6. What will be the best time to carry out the evaluation? ('the timing').

The tests were conducted at the end of each training course and were subsequently marked and the results fed back to participants and their line managers.

EXAMPLES OF TEST QUESTIONS AND ANSWERS

All questions on a given topic carry equal marks and the total of marks available in each test is 20. Questions within the test bank on the same topic were drafted so as to offer equal difficulty. Different topics were, however, given weightings to reflect their relative importance within 'customer service' as a whole.

The breakdown of potential marks by topic is as follows:

What is good customer service   3
Customer complaints   4
Standards of work performance in customer service   1
Passing On Work   1
Listening   2
Assertiveness   3 + 2
Clear English   4

Examples of questions drawn from the test bank are given below.

TOPIC: WHAT IS GOOD CUSTOMER SERVICE ABOUT?

1. Why is it that many people who are dissatisfied with customer service do not complain to the company about it?

CUSTOMER SERVICE

Only a minority of people ever complain to the company (1); many more people simply stop doing business with the company (1); and most of those who do not complain to the company, still complain to all their friends and relations (1).

2. Who is responsible for preventing customer complaints? (*tick the boxes which apply*):

the Board	☐
the Managing Director	☐
Senior managers	☐
professional specialists (e.g. actuaries)	☐
section supervisors	☐
clerical staff	☐

All of these apply. 3 points for all ticked; deduct 1 point from 3 for each one not ticked, down to zero.

7. The company and its customers don't exist in a vacuum: what does this mean in terms of how customer expectations are set?

Customer expectations are set outside of the company's control (1) and outside the financial services industry (1). The intrinsic properties of goods and services are no longer the major factor in consumer choices (1) – it's the way they are supplied that determines customers' choices (1).

TOPIC: RESPONDING TO COMPLAINTS

2. List four common causes of customer complaints.

Award 1 point for each correct answer, up to a maximum of 4.

- *Unmet expectations in quality of products or service.*
- *Limited choices within product and service ranges.*
- *Frustration from errors or from unclear communications.*
- *Delays in deliveries or response to enquiries.*
- *Unprofessional behaviour (e.g. indifference, rudeness).*
- *Difficulties getting in touch with the company.*

5. In handling a complaint, list four kinds of verbal behaviour that you should avoid.

Award 1 point for each correct answer, up to a maximum of 4.

- *Retaliation.*
- *Argument.*
- *Becoming defensive.*
- *Jumping to conclusions.*
- *Blaming other departments, the computer, or yourself.*
- *Hiding in jargon, or unexplained statements about 'company policy'.*

CASE STUDIES

TOPIC: PERFORMANCE STANDARDS AND CUSTOMER SERVICE

1. What is meant by the standard 'Right First Time'?

It contains no errors which require work to be redone or completed by someone else (1).

2. One of your internal customers may need to deal with your work if you are away – what does the relevant standard say about this?

The files and papers for any work in process must always be in a state such as would enable the work to be taken on easily and immediately by someone else (1).

TOPIC: PASSING WORK TO COLLEAGUES ... HELPFULLY

3. Apart from meeting the 'Right First Time' standard, state one other thing that makes the difference when you are passing work on to colleagues.

Award 1 point maximum for any one of the following:

- Correct recipient.
- Promptness.
- Clear statement of priority.
- Realistic promises.
- Basic information is checked (e.g. names, policy numbers, etc.).
- Previous errors are corrected.

TOPIC: EFFECTIVE LISTENING

2. What are two things that you can do to check out your understanding of what has been said?

Award 1 point for each of the following, up to a maximum of 2.

- Ask clarifying questions.
- Give 'reflective summaries'.
- Hear even the things you don't want to hear.

6. When transferring telephone calls or putting a caller on hold, specify two very important things you should *not* do if you want to keep the customer contented.

Award 1 point for each of the following, up to a maximum of 2.

- Play 'pass the parcel' with the caller.
- Abandon the customer while searching for information.
- Make promises you can't keep.

TOPIC: ASSERTIVENESS

(Question 1 counts for 3 points; question 6 for 2 points; the topic of assertiveness was covered by two sub-sets of questions, with one example being drawn from each group for any on-course test.)

CUSTOMER SERVICE

1. The key distinction between assertive, aggressive and passive behaviour lies in how you feel about yourself and how you feel about the other person with whom you are in contact. In respect of *assertive* behaviour, describe the following in a few words:

   a) How assertive people feel about themselves.
   b) How assertive people feel about other people.
   c) The characteristic behaviour pattern of assertive people.

Award 0.5 points for each correct answer within each of the three sub-sections (a, b, c) up to a maximum of 1 point per section (3 for the whole of question 1).

   a)
   - My self-esteem is mine and is defined by me.
   - I accept myself and other people, flaws and all.
   - The things that I can't do or don't know about do not cause me to have low self-esteem.

   b)
   - They are more or less the same as me; overall, we come out about equal.
   - I can do some things they can't but they can do things I can't.
   - Your self-esteem is yours and defined by you.

   c)
   - *comfortable and self-confident.*
   - *Competent to deal with situations; in control.*
   - *Thinking behaviour.*
   - *Effective problem-solving.*
   - *Knowing what you want and asking for it in a way that does not damage either your own self-esteem or that of the other person.*
   - *Able to decide which of the three behavioural styles is appropriate to any particular moment.*

6. Angry customers are an unfortunate but sometimes unavoidable fact of life. List two things you can do to defuse the situation constructively.

Award 1 point for each correct answer, up to a maximum of 2.

- *If possible avoid transferring or putting on hold – get someone to call them back promptly.*
- *Let them blow off steam before you get into the details.*
- *Take notes and check these back with the customer to show you're listening seriously.*
- *Politely steer customer to relevant matters.*
- *Try to keep a calm tone of voice.*

TOPIC: USE OF CLEAR ENGLISH

3. Briefly describe four things that you can do to improve the presentation of your written documents.

CASE STUDIES

Award 1 point for each correct answer, up to a maximum of 4.

- *Give it a heading so that the subject is clear.*
- *Ensure that your writing is spaced evenly in the available space.*
- *Use a new paragraph for each major point or theme.*
- *Number the paragraphs.*
- *Check the spelling of any word about which you are unsure.*

GENERAL CONCLUSIONS

The evaluation task was made much easier by the fact that it was integrated from the start with the design and development of the training materials to be assessed. Once again, the value of clear training objectives is demonstrated by the comparative ease with which valid test questions could be drafted.

The issue of test-marking expertise and consistency was met most effectively by the temporary recruitment of two graduates to the task. This also resolved the common concern in evaluation studies that training departments may sit in judgement on matters in which they have an interest.

The testing itself has worked well at a practical level, with little resistance to the principle of testing, and the questions have been regarded by most subjects as having face validity. A small number of people have felt that they ought not be tested, and some that their own failure on the test was evidence that it was invalid. The failure rate has run at about 7.5 per cent and includes a small but significant number of people who possess quite substantial experience with the company and are amongst the higher grades who went through the training programme.

For the future, it would be desirable that the index of discrimination and facility value measures be applied to the test battery; it would also be useful if an on-job assessment of improved customer service were to be carried out, using the behavioural observation checklist. Results from that could fruitfully be correlated with the data from the end of course tests.

20 New entrants

The survey was carried out by an in-house trainer as part of a series of evaluation workshops for the national training group of a government department.

The context was one in which new clerical level entrants were issued with a considerable amount of paper-based material – 'training aids' in the form of notes, algorithms, pictorial explanations and so forth. This material was intended to serve both as an initial training medium and subsequently as a reference source. A substantial training package was about to be prepared in response to new legislation and the evaluation exercise therefore offered an opportunity to gather data on the effectiveness of the existing system of training aids before replicating that approach with the new material.

EVALUATION – THE KEY QUESTIONS

1. For whom is the evaluation being undertaken? ('the client')
The principal audiences for the evaluation were, first, the writers of self-instruction material in general, and, second, the team with specialist subject matter responsibility for the newly legislated topics.

2. Which particular training activity will provide the subject for the evaluation project? ('the course')
Existing self-instruction material for new entrants.

3. What is it about the training process that the client wants you to assess? ('the criterion of worth')
    a) Whether or not the training aids proved useful to new entrants, and
    b) Whether or not these continued to be used on the job.

4. Who is likely to have answers to your assessment questions? ('the subjects')

A number of evaluation projects was being launched simultaneously, and therefore a decision was taken to limit the survey to a particular group of offices within the department. Within these, the target population consisted of all employees who within the previous three months had completed new entrant training in knowledge and procedures. Initially, a postal questionnaire (with covering letter) was sent out, yielding 11 replies from 26 posted. The enquiry was therefore extended to a further 30 offices, selected randomly, and 165 questionnaires issued. The aggregated response came to 65 – a 34 per cent response rate.

5. What will be the appropriate evaluation technique for you to use? ('the technique')
Questionnaire, distributed initially by post and – in the second tranche – through local training officers. A central consideration was that the workload of gathering and analysing data could be handled by one person, without drastically disrupting other work. The questionnaire is reproduced in Figure 20.1.

6. What will be the best time to carry out the evaluation? ('the timing')
The survey was restricted to those trained within the previous three months. It was felt that if this period was extended further back, respondents might have difficulty disentangling training-induced abilities from those learned in the workplace.

SUMMARY OF FINDINGS

The training aids were found to be used as intended, the extent of use varying with the subject matter rather than the format in which they were presented. Flow charts and algorithms scored no higher than summary notes or tables. A number of items continued to be regularly used as job aids after training.

On the basis of the data, the same methods would be employed for the new training package which itself should include an evaluation element from the start. In addition, those aids likely to have an extended life should be produced on card to increase durability.

It is worth noting that the questionnaire ran to five pages; Question 6 required tick responses to 36 items and Question 7 to 30 items. Although the design made answering comparatively easy, these questions are visually daunting and probably account for a significant element in the non-response level.

NEW ENTRANTS

1. When did you complete your new entrant training? Date

2. What job are you doing now?

   Activity option A ☐
   Activity option B ☐
   Activity option C ☐
   Other ☐   *(tick one box)*

   If you have ticked the 'Other' box, please state below the type of job you do.

3. At various stages in your training you were asked to look at job aids (contained in your Trainee's Handbook) and at handouts (given to you by your training officer). Please indicate the extent to which you referred to those job aids/handouts:

When instructed by the self-instruction books		When instructed by your training officer	
(tick one box)		*(tick one box)*	
Always	☐	Always	☐
Sometimes	☐	Sometimes	☐
Never	☐	Never	☐

4. During your training, when completing examples and exercises *set in the self-instruction books* did you use any of the following?

   The handouts provided by your training officer ☐
   The Technical Manual   ☐
   Neither of the above   ☐ *(Tick as many boxes as appropriate)*

5. During your training, when completing exercises or doing live work *set by your training officer*, did you use any of the following?

   The handouts provided by your training officer ☐
   The Technical Manual   ☐
   Neither of the above   ☐ *(Tick as many boxes as appropriate)*

6. In the table below, indicate how useful you found each of the job aids during your training.

   (Tick one column for each job aid)

Job aid no.	Job aid title	Not at all useful	Fairly useful	Extremely useful	No response
1.					
2.					
3.	Etc.				

Figure 20.1 New entrant questionnaire (continued overleaf)

CASE STUDIES

7. In the table below, indicate how useful you found each of the handouts during your training.

   (Tick one column for each handout)

Handout title	Not at all useful	Fairly useful	Extremely useful	No response
1.				
2.				
3. Etc.				

8. Now that you have completed your training do you continue to use any of the job aids/handouts to help you in your job?

   Yes/No *(delete whichever does not apply)*

9. If you answered 'yes' to Question 8, list below those which are still used and indicate how often you use each one.

   (Tick one column for each item)

Title of handout/job aid	At least once a day	At least once a week	At least once a month
1.			
2.			
3. Etc.			

10. For each of the job aids/handouts which you still use state below what it is that makes continued use necessary.

Figure 20.1 New entrant questionnaire (concluded)

21 Outdoor development for managers

A large retailing group required an evaluation of the organizational benefits of 'outdoor development' training undertaken by a group of its high-flyer younger managers.

A particular challenge in this project was the absence of specific objectives for the training. Of necessity, evaluation became a 'fishing expedition' to identify any and all outcomes – whether intentional or not – from the training activity. A further challenge is then to try to identify benefits to the organization that stem from the various outcomes of the training. Commitment to training with loosely defined aims requires a great deal of faith on the part of the buyer. For the evaluator, there is the frustration of knowing that identified outcomes, however beneficial, may not be replicated with the next group to undergo that kind of training and may, indeed, be accidental, not intentional results of the training.

EVALUATION – THE KEY QUESTIONS

1. For whom is the evaluation being undertaken? ('the client')

The direct client was the in-company trainer who managed the programme and, indirectly, that trainer's client group in management. The report was also made available to the external consultants who ran the courses but the evaluation was not conducted with them formally identified as a client.

2. Which particular training activity will provide the subject for the evaluation project? ('the course')

The pilot run of the outdoor development programme was made the subject of the evaluation, an issue for the company being the decision whether or not to extend the programme more widely in the future.

3. What is it about the training process that the client wants you to assess? ('the criterion of worth')

There was a twofold purpose to the evaluation: to review the benefits of the pilot programme; and to arrive at recommendations for the evaluation by the company of similar courses in the future.

4. Who is likely to have answers to your assessment questions? ('the subjects')

The 15 managers who took part in the project, 11 of whom were interviewed. Whereas the evaluator can use external observations (etc.) in cases where there are clear learning objectives, in a open-ended or undefined 'developmental' situation, only the participants themselves can engage in the introspective task of analysing the training experience and relating it to their work practices.

5. What will be the appropriate evaluation technique for you to use? ('the technique')

Interview: this allows an in-depth exploration of the respondent's experience and opinions; it has the flexibility to follow up on what may turn out to be quite divergent perceptions of what the training did or did not achieve. Interview also tends to encourage greater frankness than written methods of evaluation. Interviews were conducted at the various store locations in which the subjects worked. The interview schedule is shown in Figure 21.1.

6. What will be the best time to carry out the evaluation? ('the timing')

This was dictated by the timing of the client request although in fact it fell within the 'best practice' parameters for evaluation of this kind of training, where there often needs to be some interval for training experiences to translate into workplace activities. Interviews were carried out within three to four months of the pilot course.

SELECTIVE SUMMARY OF FINDINGS AND IMPLICATIONS

1. Expectations of the course

Participants possessed very selective and partially inaccurate information pre-course. There was a tendency to distance themselves from the course by their belief that they were excellent leaders already and their expectation that any learning would come from observing other people. Part of the success of the course was due precisely to overcoming this distancing factor, so that people learned by observing themselves.

2. Did the course meet – or differ from – expectations?

The conclusions were that the course differed greatly from expectations. Responses were very revealing about what made the course worthwhile – in particular the intellectual demands it placed upon analysis and planning and the interpersonal demands of working as an effective team. A clear distinction was drawn between this project and other outdoor courses where 'success' was measured in terms of physical competences such as climbing or canoeing.

```
Introduction: Time available
              Confidentiality
              Tape-recording

1.  Thinking back before the course, what did you expect to get out of it?

2.  Did the course meet — or differ from — your expectations?

    (Follow-up: in what ways?)

3.  Did the course achieve what it formally set out to do?

    (Prompt if necessary:
    'to re-examine your leadership skills'
    'to review methods of directing and building an effective team'
    'to develop ways of increasing your effectiveness with others at work')

4.  Was what the course achieved worthwhile?

5.  What do you do differently in your job as a result of the course?

    (Prompt for specifics)

6.  Have you any knowledge or experience of any other kind of leadership or team-building training?

    6.1  How does it compare with this course?

    6.2  How might this learning need be tackled in a better way?

7.  How do you feel about this interview as a way of evaluating your experiences?

    7.1  Would you find any other method preferable?

    (Prompt if necessary: questionnaire; performance-related assessment, etc.)

8.  Is there anything about the course that you would like to be different?

Conclusion: Thanks
```

Figure 21.1 Outdoor development interview schedule

3. Did the course achieve what it formally set out to do?

Several themes emerged in response to this question: leadership skills that the course highlighted (e.g. teamwork rather than the 'leading from the front' expert); communication skills that were developed; reflections upon the leadership style of the client company; and comments about leadership within peer groups as distinct from within formal hierarchies. There were many specific examples given of ways in which changed perceptions had been translated into different behaviour with store staff. The course was compared favourably with classroom-based teaching of leadership. The aim of 'increasing effectiveness with others' was not seen to be different from the leadership and teamwork objectives.

4. Was what the course achieved worthwhile?

All subjects answered 'yes' but responses were mainly 'goodwill' statements rather than attempts to analyse precisely what made it worthwhile. The next question was more informative.

5. What do you do differently in your job as a result of the course?

Responses were grouped in two areas – in-store management processes and in-store administrative measures. Examples were given of more efficient utilization of staff, gathering of constructive ideas from employees, and better planning leading to less fire-fighting. There must be some concern over the minority of respondents who described the course as a profound experience but did not see it having any influence on work behaviour.

6. Experience of any other kind of leadership or team-building training?

Comments emphasized how much more 'real' the outdoor course had been compared to classroom-based training events. The intensity of the experience evidently helped its retention in active memory. Furthermore, the experience exemplified in a very concrete way the skills and errors of leadership and teamwork, in a way that is rarely if ever achieved through classroom simulations.

7. Feelings about interview as an evaluation method

The interviews were well-received and seen as a valid way of extracting the subtlety and depths of the course experience. Most subjects expressed a preference for talking with an independent (external) evaluator. Their expectation was that this would produce a more objective and credible report, based upon more open and less political comments from subjects.

8. Is there anything about the course that you would like to be different?

The main themes to emerge were concerned with identifying other groups who might usefully attend the course and with debating the mix of grades that might be most fruitful. Although there are benefits from running the course with natural work teams, the likely problem is that the formal authority structure would override cooperative learning and teamwork.

GENERAL CONCLUSIONS

The study raises interesting points about evaluating 'developmental' activities, about the extent to which commercial benefits demonstrably follow from such activities, and about the extent to which an organization chooses to make use of evaluation data.

The external consultants expressed the view that the report was fair and constructive and felt that it put their programme in a positive light.

It may sometimes be possible to isolate the cost-benefit equation (e.g. where changes were instituted in a particular department and all else remains the same) but it is doubtful whether the attempt is worth the effort on a larger, store-based level. There are too many uncontrolled variables – marketing effort, state of the local economy, weather, etc. However, when a course leads to changes in job behaviours which contribute to the efficient running of the store, it is reasonable to attribute performance improvement to the training experience. Strict causality is not proven in the academic sense, but a reasonable balance of probabilities (in a quasi-legal sense) is proven.

In reviewing alternatives to interview, report-writing by course participants emerges as a method that is equally costly but more prone to political answers and to avoidance of controversy. Questionnaire is inherently unsuited to open-ended exploration of experience. Both end of course review and on-course video recording fail to address the question of whether the training makes any difference back in the job; the former is notoriously subject to distortions caused by end of course relief or euphoria. Two recommendations for future evaluation that did emerge from the project were a) a co-counselling self-evaluation by the participants themselves: this should provide satisfactory feedback on the amount of learning achieved by the course; it should also serve to reinforce the learning (and even to clarify its nature); and b) a periodic external scrutiny by an independent evaluator, with an emphasis on the applications made from the learning and on whether or not the most appropriate people were attending the programme.

22 The manager's role in training

A large central training unit in a high-technology manufacturing company wished to review the role played by managers in support of their training courses. An internal quality control function was established within the training department and the manager of the function worked closely with the evaluation consultant during all stages of the project. There was thus a significant training element built into the evaluation.

EVALUATION – THE KEY QUESTIONS

1. For whom is the evaluation being undertaken? ('the client')
The training department's internal quality control unit.

2. Which particular training activity will provide the subject for the evaluation project? ('the course')
There was an extensive range of courses (which particularly emphasized sales skills) making up the annual training programme of the department and encapsulated in an annual courses brochure. From this range, one course – negotiation skills – was selected as the vehicle for the research because it was well-established, involved assessment of skills rather than knowledge, possessed a clear organizational purpose, was believed to be a 'reasonably satisfactory' course, and offered a sizeable population from which the interview sample could be drawn.

3. What is it about the training process that the client wants you to assess? ('the criterion of worth')
There were four areas of interest:
   a) The extent to which managers prepared their staff for attendance at central courses.
   b) Whether managers were able to identify changes in work performance following training.

c) How much the managers knew about the aims and content of the courses for which they nominated their staff.
   d) The extent to which managers provided post-training reinforcement of learning.

4. Who is likely to have answers to your assessment questions? ('the subjects')
Managers in regional offices who were responsible for nominating members of their own staff to central courses. Within two regions of the company, a population of 23 managers was identified, of whom 9 were interviewed.

5. What will be the appropriate evaluation technique for you to use? ('the technique')
Interview was chosen for a number of reasons. It was inevitable that the kinds of question to be asked would require follow-up clarification. Also, as part of each interview, managers were shown a visual representation of the role of managers in training (similar to Figure 4.1, p. 45), as a basis for discussion within the interview. The purpose of the research was to explore managers' perceptions and opinions, for which there is no real substitute to the interview. The interview schedule is reproduced in Figure 22.1. All interviews were tape-recorded.

6. What will be the best time to carry out the evaluation? ('the timing')
This study offers a rare example of timing being irrelevant from an evaluation point of view. Although it was important to avoid certain particularly busy periods of the year, in order to obtain the cooperation of interviewees, the nature of the enquiry was not linked to a specific event at a certain date, but to activities that rolled on from year to year. Managers were selected for interview who had nominated someone to the negotiating skills course within a period 6 to 18 months prior to the interview. This allowed time for skills learned on the course to be used in the job and to be observed by the manager.

SELECTIVE SUMMARY OF FINDINGS AND IMPLICATIONS

Probably the most far-reaching conclusion of the research was that managers rarely had a better than tenuous grasp of the purpose and content of courses for which they were nominating their staff. (This is a finding reinforced by my research in a number of other companies.) The core of the problem was that the courses brochure was written by trainers, in 'trainer language'. Curiously, for a mainly sales-training unit, the descriptive emphasis was upon features of courses (e.g. 'use of role-play') rather than upon benefits (e.g. 'this course will enable you to . . .'). Training objectives need to relate to job tasks, rather than to course content.

Pre-training briefing was weak, partly because of the quality of information available to managers, and partly because managers had not seen such briefing as part of their role. Matching of individuals to courses needed to take account of identified performance shortfalls and job priorities. The implications were that trainers should provide managers with a short briefing document to structure the briefing session with

CASE STUDIES

> Introduction: Purpose
> Confidentiality
> Taping
> Off-record statements
> Confirm manager's connection to ex-participant
>
> 1. Thinking about training in general, what do you take account of when you decide to nominate someone for a particular course?
>
> 2. Can you recall what you anticipated would be the benefits to ... *(named participant)* in attending the negotiating course?
>
> 3. Have you noticed any specific changes in the way he/she does the job, that you would attribute to the negotiation course?
>   If yes,
>   3.1 What impact, if any, have those changes had on the effectiveness of the area you manage?
>   3.2 Here is a list of formal objectives for that course: can you give examples of occasions when you have seen ... *(named participant)* use any of these skills?
>
> 4. Did you do anything before the course to prepare ... *(named participant)* for it?
>
> 5. Did you do anything after the course to help him/her make use of what had been learned?
>   5.1 Did you hold any form of de-briefing after the course?
>
> 6. Do you feel that it was worth the time and money for .. *(named participant)* to attend the negotiating skills course?
>   6.1 What are taken into account in making that judgement?
>
> 7. Here is a framework [Figure 4.1] showing off-job training as a two-part process. The left-hand side is the manager's sphere and the right-hand side the trainer's. Thinking about your own job as a manager, does this framework make sense to you?
>   If no,
>   7.1 What do you see as the difficulties?
>   If yes,
>   7.2 Are there any practical problems in implementing this?
>
> 8. Have you any other comment on the central training department's courses in general?

Figure 22.1 **Manager's interview schedule**

the participant. There should be a common structure running through the pre-training briefing document, the on-course action plan and the post-training debriefing. Managers should receive some training in the skills that would enable them to play an effective partnership role with trainers.

GENERAL CONCLUSIONS

The survey proved to be the catalyst for a major re-appraisal of the internal marketing of training. It also proved effective as an action learning vehicle for the quality control unit. An interesting spin-off benefit was the enhanced perceptions of the central training department that were created simply by the fact that they had taken the trouble to go out into the field and explore line managers' views in an undefensive way.

23 Six mini-cases

This chapter contains six brief reports illustrating different approaches to training evaluation.

PRACTICAL TESTING

This application of evaluation techniques concerned update training for maintenance technicians. In the existing situation, all operatives were required to undergo a periodic three-week programme of training to update them on technical changes in the equipment which they serviced.

The updating process was inflexible, expensive and regarded as boring by the operatives. Varying amounts of the training were found unnecessary, to an extent that varied from one individual to another, depending on how much of the necessary knowledge and skills had been acquired either in previous employment or through learning on the job.

Practical tests were developed using examples of the equipment that was the subject of the update training. Faults were deliberately introduced into the test boards and a marking scheme devised. All operatives scheduled for training were then tested on the boards for their diagnostic accuracy. At the same time, the update training itself was restructured into a modular format so that operatives needed only to complete those elements in which the pre-testing showed them to be deficient. Time spent in update training was cut by over one-third and recorded satisfaction amongst participants increased.

REACTIONNAIRE

The training activity evaluated was a short course for shop sales staff. The aim of the course was to increase knowledge of marketing and selling and to improve selling skills. The evaluation used sessional reactionnaires and was conducted by the trainer who developed the course.

At the end of each session within the first two pilot runs of the course, the participants were asked to complete a short reactionnaire. This asked them to rate that session on a seven-point scale applied to four areas of interest: the extent that the session provided new information; their perception of the relevance of the session to their jobs; the amount that they felt they had learned; and the appropriateness of the time allocated to the sessional topics. This information was supplemented by end-of-day written comments.

Clearly, the data are vulnerable to all the distortions that can arise from self-reporting plus the problem of making judgements of 'relevance' before participants have any opportunity to try out new ideas in the shops. The use of unanchored scales simply adds to the subjectivity of the data and the uncertainty with which the data can be interpreted.

The ratings were in fact used to make a number of adjustments to the content of subsequent courses; however, the in-company conclusion that the ratings showed that course objectives had been met, is not justified. The study shows (just) the value of sessional ratings rather than complete course ratings when 'de-bugging' a new course.

More significant data would have been obtained by pre/post testing to measure learning gain, coupled with a follow-up based upon interview or action plan review in order to assess transfer of learning into work behaviour.

QUESTIONNAIRE

An industrial relations course for middle-level managers had been running for a number of years. An evaluation questionnaire was drafted and administered postally to the three most recent course groups. The response rate was just over 50 per cent.

The responses were interesting for the negative data they elicited: in particular, less than one-quarter of the total population mailed was able to identify at least one example of using the course learning. Furthermore, within this group, the examples quoted by respondents showed a very tenuous connection to the course objectives. Indeed, the examples had little to do with industrial relations but rather described more general interpersonal skills.

The use that people make of course material is a much more reliable indication that real needs are being met than is the level of 'yes' answers that may be obtained from a question such as: 'Is industrial relations training needed?' Further enquiry showed that the managers attending this course did not have any significant role in industrial relations and that the course was a 'nice to know' rather than a 'need to know' activity. Such evaluation data is useful to the organization because it enables training resources to be redirected to areas of greatest need.

CASE STUDIES

TEST RELIABILITY

The context was that of training apprentices in technical subjects, preparatory to City and Guilds examinations. Over a number of years a substantial test bank of questions had been compiled by the trainers and a sample of these questions was used each year for 'mock' examinations.

Data were available on the mock results and the actual results of examinations. As part of a workshop on evaluation methods, the lead trainers carried out a review of the effectiveness of test bank questions as accurate predictors of the trainees' City and Guilds examination performance, applying the index of discrimination measure.

Approximately 20 per cent of questions in the test bank were found to discriminate poorly between good and bad trainees and consequently had no predictive value when used for the mock examinations. These questions were eliminated from the test bank.

COST-BENEFIT ANALYSIS

The evaluation was designed by the in-company trainer in parallel with the trainer's new course for clerical staff who made inputs of customer-billing data to a computerized invoicing system. It offers an illustration of the application of CBA to training but also provides a cautionary example of careful evaluation methodology being undermined by faulty needs analysis.

The presenting problem was clear enough: a level of rejection of incorrectly completed input documents (6.8 per cent) that compared badly with similar systems in other organizations. The training need had then been specified as a requirement for clerical training and a decision was taken to undertake a cost-benefit analysis of the project.

The costs of developing and delivering the training were calculated and a number of expected, quantifiable benefits were identified, for example reduced duplication of clerical work, better utilization of computer time and reduced supervisory time correcting errors. There was a target maximum error rate of 3 per cent.

The value of potential savings was calculated at £2 700 per month and this substantially exceeded the one-off cost of £1 750 to produce the training. Error rates had been established already and were monitored for several months following the training, using computer-compiled performance records. This analysis unfortunately showed no statistically significant change in the level of input failures. The training had no identifiable effects and the anticipated benefits were not realized.

Review of the whole training and evaluation project, including some (previously omitted) observation of work practices, led to a revised definition of the training need: the emphasis switched to two other factors – supervisors' responsibility for quality control of input documents and the design of the documents themselves.

CRITICAL INCIDENT DIARY

A sample of supervisors was interviewed in a large organization. All the interviewed supervisors were encouraged to describe incidents which they perceived to have influenced the way they carried out supervision. Details of each incident were obtained by using standardized probing questions and were then analysed for patterns of recurring content.

The content of incidents was compared to formal training objectives. Applications of learning were found in about 6 per cent of critical incidents, a significant negative result which suggested that the training had little relevance to or impact on work tasks.

Supervisor behaviour within critical incidents was found to fall into one of two patterns – showing dependence on other people taking the lead, or being more proactive and self-directed about initiating action. The proactive supervisors were found to be those who had received substantially more training. (In other respects the total sample was quite homogeneous.)

A second pattern of differences in the content of incidents emerged. This was between supervisors who more frequently described negative incidents and ideas of what should be avoided, and those who reported positive incidents, and concepts about particular ways of doing things which had worked successfully.

Index

absorption costing 218–9
acceptability of learning methods 146
action plan review
   analyzing obstacles and resources 139
   and evaluation 140–2
   construction of formal action plan 138
   follow-up interview schedule 142
   in reactionnaires 150, 156
   overview 31
   personal action planning form 141
   personal action targets 138
   prioritizing 139
   tracking learning gains 138
   using the technique 137–42
Akeroyd, M. 252
analysing evaluation data *see* data analysis
analytical item *see* practical tests
appraisal systems 52
attitude change 31
   see also behavioural approach to learning objectives averages 111–2
'awareness' as learning objective 13, 39

behavioural approach to learning objectives 40–1
behaviour observation
   case study 271–4
   categories for observation 199, 206
   design of observation instruments 198–206
   frequency analysis 202–3
   introduction 195
   matrix format 199
   observation process 196–8
   observer training 206–10
      see also rating errors
   overview 32
   rating of observed behaviours 211–14
   reliability of observations 210–11
   time or unit sampling 196
   using behaviour observation data 214–216

when to use 195
   see also rating errors
binge, annual *see* appraisal systems
Birkbeck College xiii
bottom line penalties of lack of competence 7
Bramley, P. 36
break-even analysis 220–1

Cameron, K. 9–10
case studies
   summary matrix 264
   see also individual topics, by title
causality statements 117
chi-square test 113–6
City University xiii
comparing frequencies *see* statistics and evaluation
comparing groups *see* statistics and evaluation
completion items *see* written tests
compulsory training 19
conflict-handling 43
construct validity 257
content criterion referencing 246
content validity 256
control groups 237–40
corporate commitment to training 50–1
cost-benefit analysis
   case study 302
   cash flow budgets 225–8
   costable inputs of training 222–5
   cost benefit analysis 230–4
   cost benefit and cost effectiveness analysis 229
   cost effectiveness analysis 234–6
   cost identification matrix 225–6
   costing methods 218–222
   introduction 217–8
   overview 32
   performance indicators 231–2
   performance ratios 232–4
   priceable outputs of training 225–6
cost-effectiveness analysis

305

INDEX

overview 32
course content and reactionnaires 146
co-variation 116–7
criteria for choosing evaluation techniques
  acceptability to organization 72
  acceptability to subjects 71–2
  aptness for purpose 70
  evaluator skills 70–1
  resourcing 72
  secondary benefits 72
  use of multiple techniques 72
criteria of assessment
  appropriate choice 34
  criteria described 24, 26, 28
criterion- and norm-referencing 23–4, 171, 246
critical incident review
  case study 303
  choosing observers 120
  data analysis 124–6
  methods for collecting CI data 121–24
  overview 30
  timing of data collection 121
  using diary 123–24
  using group discussion 121
  using interview 121–22
  using performance appraisal interview 124–25
  using questionnaire 122–23
customer service – evaluation study 281–286

data analysis
  analysing responses to open questions 117–8
    consistency of data 267–8
    grounding of data 267
  as part of initial project design 72–5
  classifying responses 110
    categorizing responses to open questions 75, 117–18, 164
    coding frame 74
    data matrix 73–4, 110
    inter-coder reliability 74–5
  for reactionnaires 161–3
  frequency statements 110–16
    comparing frequencies 113–6
    types of data from interview and questionnaire 109–17
  frequency statements 110–16
    comparing frequencies 113–6
  illustrative insights 109
  statements of causality 117
  statements of co-variation 116–17
  see also behaviour observation, rating of observed behaviours
  behaviour observation, reliability of observations
  evaluation reports
  rating errors

statistics and evaluation
delivery of training 43–44
design of training content 42–3
dispersion 112–3
distance learning
  questionnaire, case study 287–90
  reactionnaire 152

essay and short answer items see written tests
euphoria at end of course 43, 160
evaluation
  academic analyses, difficulties due to 35
  and efficient training design 33
  and trainers' self-esteem 33
  as intervention strategy 34, 46–8, 49–50
  as track record of training success 34
  benefits from 33–4, 62–3
  Cameron, K. 21
  clients for 64–5
  contexts 26, 28
  defining the field 22, 24
  goal-free evaluation 41
  illuminative evaluation 42
  is it necessary? 57
  learning evaluation skills 50–52
  organizational framework for evaluation 46–8, 58, 65
  pilot implementation
    as part of planning the project 68
  politics of 59–60, 77
  project design and planning 60–72
  resources for 66
  scientific evaluation 22
  techniques and sample size 243–4
  timing of 70, 121
  validation 24
  vicious and benign circles 48–9
  within the training cycle 45–7
  without use of learning objectives 41–2
  worth 22, 24–6, 28
  see also criteria of assessment
    data analysis
    evaluation reports
    learning objectives
    resistance to evaluation
    statistics and evaluation
    starting evaluation
    techniques of evaluation
evaluation reports
  acting on findings 70
  reporting findings 118–119

face validity 256–7
facility values 258–9
frequency statements 110–16
  comparing frequencies 113–6

INDEX

gain ratios 166, 249–50
gatefever 160
guessing
   answers to multiple choice items 175
   answers to true/false questions 174
   guessing correction 252–3
      see also guessing

happy sheets 31, 143–4, 146
Harmon, P. 181
historical and standard costs 220
Honey-Mumford learning styles inventory 276, 279
housekeeping issues 146
how much evaluation is needed? 58–9
   cost criterion 59
   frequency criterion 59
   impact criterion 59
   importance criterion 58

ideas diary 5
illustrative insights in data analysis 109
index of discrimination 259–60
inter-rater reliability 210
interview
   action plan follow-up 140–2
   analysing responses to open questions 117–8
      consistency of data 267–8
      grounding of data 267
   applications 96
   case studies 265–70, 273, 275–80, 291–5, 296–9
   conducting the interview 106–109
   consistency 97
   drafting the interview schedule 97–106
   interviewing skills, development of 101–104
   listening skills 101, 103–104
   overview 30
   piloting the draft interview schedule 104–106
   sequencing the interview schedule 97–8
   silence 104
   tape recording 103–104
   time span 97
   see also letter of introduction
in-tray assessments *see* practical tests

job procedures training – evaluation study 275–80

Kelly, G. 128
Kipling, R. 101
Krijcie, R.V. et al 242

learning objectives 39–42, 67
   different levels of 181–2
   translated into training content 42
   used in reactionnaires 155
   see also data analysis
      letter of introduction
      question types

      personal objectives and expectations
letter of introduction 106
   for interviews 106
   for questionnaire 82, 91
   for reactionnaire 160, 161
listening skills
   observation checklist 200

manager/trainer collaboration *see* trainer/manager collaboration
manual dexterity test *see* practical tests
marginal costing 219–20
marketing approach 12, 37–9
marking schemes
   for essay items 171–2
matching items *see* written tests
mean and standard deviation 248–9
mean, arithmetic 111–2
median 111
'menu-bashing' 52
mission statements 10
mode 112
motivation and personality 16–17, 18
multiple choice items *see* written tests

neglect of evaluation 34–6
new entrant training – evaluation study 287–90

open questions
   see data analysis
      interview
opportunity cost 220–2
outdoor development – evaluation study 291–5

Pareto principle 221–2
Pearson correlation coefficient 254–6
percentile scores 246–8
personal constructs 128
personal development – evaluation study 265–70
   see also outdoor development – evaluation study
personal objectives and expectations
   personal objectives distinct from formal ones 41
   used in reactionnaires 146, 148, 155
population size and sampling 242–3
practical tests
   case study 300
   design 183–7
   in-tray assessments 192–3
   introduction 180
   levels of learning objective and 181–2
   manual dexterity item – example 193–4
   overview 32
   problem-solving/analytical item – examples 188–93
   procedure item – example 188
   process and product items 185–6
   recall/identification items – example 187

INDEX

see also statistics and evaluation
pre-course briefing and reactionnaires 146–7
predictive validity 257–8
preferred learning methods and reactionnaires 146
presentational issues and reactionnaires 146
presentation skills 43
priorities in training 39
problem-solving item *see* practical tests
procedure item *see* practical tests
process and product items *see* practical tests

quality control as benefit of evaluation 33
quartile deviation 112
questionnaire
  applications 78, 80
  case studies 287–90, 301
  compared to interview technique 78–80
  drafting questions 82–9
  instructions for completion 82–3
  interview as preliminary stage 83
  overview 27
  postal administration 90–1
  sequencing questionnaires 82–3
  strengths 79
  supervised administration 90
  weaknesses 80
  see also data analysis
    letter of introduction
    question types
question types
  double questions 84
  leading questions 84, 98
  loaded questions 84
  negative questions 84
  open and closed questions 83, 98–100
  reflective questions 100–101
  rhetorical questions 98
  see also data analysis
    letter of introduction
    question types
    Reactionnaires – question design
    Written tests – question design
predictive criterion referencing 246
purposive sampling 241

Rackham, N. et al 198, 211
random sampling 241
range 112
rating errors 212–14
  contrast error 213
  frame of reference error 213
  generosity error 213
  halo effect 212
  individual rating skill 213–4
  moderation error 213
raw scores 245–6

reactionnaire
  administration 159–60
  case study 300–01
  design 147–59
  end-of-event review 149–50, 153, 154, 155
  introduction 143–7
  limitations 145
  overview 31
  pre-course information 146–7, 148, 149
  question design 151–9
  resistance by trainees 144–5
  sessional feedback 148–9, 150, 151
  structure 147–50
  timing 159–160
  uses 145
  who should administer 160
  see also action plan review
    data analysis
    happy sheets
    learning objectives
    letter of introduction
    personal objectives and expectations
recall items *see* practical tests recall/identification items
  written tests recall items
recognition items *see* practical tests recall/identification items
  written tests recognition items
reliability 253–6
  case study of test reliability 302
  split-half method 254–6
repertory grid
  overview 30
  personal constructs 128
  repgrid form 130
  using the technique 129–36
reporting evaluation findings 118–9
resistance to evaluation
  by trainees 84, 144–5
  by trainers 48–9
risk analysis 222

sales skills
  observation checklists 201, 208–9
sampling
  concepts and sample size 240–4
  representativeness 109
  sampling reliability in behaviour observation 211
scientific method and evaluation 237
  see also control groups
    sampling
    statistical issues in testing
sessional feedback *see* Reactionnaires
Smith, M.E. 241
Solomon four-group design 240

INDEX

Spearman-Brown correction 255–6
split-half method *see* statistics and evaluation/reliability
standard deviation 112–3, 248–9
standard (Z) scores 249
starting evaluation 49–52, 58
  see also evaluation, as intervention strategy
  evaluation, how much is needed?
  evaluation, learning evaluation skills
  evaluation, organizational framework for
  evaluation, vicious and benign circles
statistics and evaluation
  averages 111–12
    arithmetic mean 111
    median 111
    mode 112
  chi-squared test 113–16
  coefficient of correlation 116–117, 254–6
  comparing frequencies 113–16, 250–2
  comparing groups
    gain ratios 249–50
    mean and standard deviation 248–9
    percentile scores 246–8
    see also comparing frequencies
  descriptive statistics – introduction 75,76
  dispersion 112–13
    quartile deviation 112
    range 112
    standard deviation 112–13
  frequency analysis 73–4, 110–16
  gain ratios 166, 249–50
  guessing correction 252–3
    see also guessing
  introduction 245
  item analysis 258–60
    facility values 258–9
    index of discrimination 259–60
  reliability 253–6
    case study of test reliability 302
    split-half method 254–6
  scoring tests
    criterion and norm referencing 23–4, 171, 246
    raw scores 245–6
    standard scores (Z-scores) 249
    see also guessing correction
  validity 256–8
    construct validity 257
    content validity 256
    face validity 256–7
    predictive validity 257–8
    see also data analysis
    sampling
strategy and training
  determining priorities 39
  organizational purposes 9
  see also marketing approach
tape-recording of interviews 103–104
TEAM xiii
techniques of evaluation
  choosing evaluation techniques 70–2
  choosing interview vs. questionnaire 78–80
  overview 26–33
  see also individual technique headings
    action plan review
    behaviour analysis
    cost-benefit analysis
    critical incident review
    interview
    practical test
    questionnaire
    reactionnaire
    repertory grid
    written test
test/retest reliability 210
trainee participation 43–4
  resistance to evaluation 84
trainer/manager collaboration
  benefits 38
  evaluation as intervention strategy 34
  evaluation case study 296–9
  getting it right 45
  setting training priorities 39
  what goes wrong 44
trainers' anxieties about evaluation 35–6
trainers' self-esteem and evaluation 33
training
  alternatives to training 37–8
  as part of employment package 16
  behavioural approach 13
  definition of 3
  design of training content 42–3
  developmental needs 37–8, 41
  diagnostics 13
  does training matter? 4
  efficient design as benefit of evaluation 33
  implementation (delivery) of training 43–4
  infrastructure 44
  systematic cycle 24
  to meet lack of competence 7
  true costs 6
  see also strategy and training
    training needs
    what is not a training need
training needs 12, 37–39
  enforced needs (compulsory training) 19
  see also marketing approach
    appraisal systems
    what is not a training need
training trainers – evaluation study 271–4

309

INDEX

true/false items – *see* written tests recognition items two-option...
type I and type II errors 243

validity *see* statistics and evaluation/ validity

what is not a training need 13–19
   cheque-book training 15–16
   country club training 16
   employment package 16
   fads 15
   have solution, will travel 15
   the MD says so 18–19
   rest and recreation 13
   solutionism 17–18
written tests
   case study 281–6
   construction 167–8
   introduction 166–7
   open and closed book tests 167
   overview 31–2
   question design 169
   recall/supply items 167
      completion items 172–4
      essay and short answer 170–2, 173
   recognition items 167
      matching items 177–9
      multiple choice items 175–7
      two-option alternative answer items 174–5
   true/false items *see* recognition items, two-option...
   types 167

Z-scores 249